Multi-stakeholder Processes for Governance and Sustainability

This book is dedicated to

WARREN 'CHIP' LINDNER
(1942–2000)

A dear friend and mentor, who contributed so much to sustainable development and focusing the struggle against HIV/Aids on those in the South

Multi-stakeholder Processes for Governance and Sustainability

Beyond Deadlock and Conflict

Minu Hemmati

with contributions from

Felix Dodds, Jasmin Enayati and Jan McHarry

Earthscan Publications Ltd
London • Sterling, VA

First published in the UK and USA in 2002 by
Earthscan Publications Ltd

ISBN: 1 85383 870 5 paperback
1 85383 869 1 hardback

Typesetting by JS Typesetting, Wellingborough, Northants
Printed and bound by Creative Print and Design, Ebbw Vale (Wales)
Cover design by Danny Gillespie

For a full list of publications please contact:

Earthscan Publications Ltd
120 Pentonville Road
London, N1 9JN, UK
Tel: +44 (0)20 7278 0433
Fax: +44 (0)20 7278 1142
Email: earthinfo@earthscan.co.uk
http://www.earthscan.co.uk

22883 Quicksilver Drive, Sterling, VA 20166–2012, USA

A catalogue record for this book is available from the British Library

Library of Congress Cataloging-in-Publication Data

Hemmati, Minu, 1963–.
    Multi-stakeholder processes for governance and sustainability : beyond
    deadlock and conflict / Minu Hemmati ; with contributions from Felix Dodds,
    Jasmin Enyati, and Jan McHarry.
        p. cm.
    Includes bibliographical references and index.
    ISBN 1-85383-869-1 (hardback) – ISBN 1-85383-870-5 (pbk.)
        1. Sustainable development–Decision making. 2. Sustainable development–
    International cooperation. 3. Sustainable development–Citizen participation.
    4. Intergovernmental cooperation. 5. Public-private sector cooperation. 6.
    Multiple criteria decision making. I. Title.

HC79.E5H456 2002
658.4'03–dc21

                                                                    2001007555

Earthscan is an editorially independent subsidiary of Kogan Page Ltd and
publishes in association with WWF-UK and the International Institute for
Environment and Development

This book is printed on elemental chlorine-free paper

Contents

List of Figures, Tables and Boxes

FIGURES

TABLES

BOXES

About the Authors

Felix Dodds

UNED Forum Executive Director, developing and managing projects for UNED, Felix represents UNED at UN events and helps to organize and facilitate the involvement of Major Groups in the UN system both domestically and internationally. He co-chaired the CSD NGO Steering Committee from 1997 to 2001 which coordinated the involvement of NGOs in the UN Commission on Sustainable Development. He has been NGO adviser to the UK Government at the UN Commission on Sustainable Development (1993–1996) and the European Commission (1997–1998). He has attended the UN Rio Summit, Habitat II, Earth Summit II, Beijing+5 and Copenhagen+5. He has published three books: *Into the Twenty-first Century: An Agenda for Political Realignment* (edited, 1988), *The Way Forward: Beyond Agenda 21* (edited, 1997) and *Earth Summit 2002: A New Deal* (edited, revised edition, 2001). Felix co-coordinated UNED's project on MSPs with Minu Hemmati and has written Chapter 4 of this book, putting MSPs in the context of the debate on global governance.

Jasmin Enayati

Jasmin holds an MSc in Social and Organizational Psychology from the London School of Economics and Political Science (LSE). She has been working as an independent consultant with UNED Forum on various projects since January 2000, such as the website on social development and Copenhagen+5 and the conference on 'Gender Perspectives for Earth Summit 2002'. Jasmin also edits UNED Forum's Newsletter *Connections*. She has contributed to the work on UNED Forum's project on MSPs as a project assistant and has produced the review of relevant scientific research (see Chapter 6).

Dr Minu Hemmati

A psychologist by profession, Minu's doctorate is in environmental and organizational psychology. She worked in research and teaching at the Department for Social Psychology and Women's Studies at the University of Saarbrücken, Germany, from 1992 to 1998. She has been working with UNED Forum as an independent project coordinator since 1998. Her projects focus on areas such as women/gender and sustainable development (tourism and consumption) as well as the participation and collaboration of various stakeholder groups. She has represented the Bahá'í International Community at the Habitat II Conference (Istanbul, 1996) and the Commission on Sustainable Development (CSD) meetings in 1997, as well as Earth Summit II and UNED Forum at all CSD meetings since 1998, and at Copenhagen+5 and Beijing+5. Minu co-coordinated the Women's Caucus to the UN Commission on Sustainable Development from 1999 to 2001. She co-coordinated UNED's project on MSPs with Felix Dodds.

Jan McHarry

Jan holds an MSc in Environmental Resource Planning, and is an independent writer and researcher specializing in sustainable development, waste and recycling issues. She works with national organizations and community groups and was involved in early work on Local Agenda 21 programmes and sustainability indicators for use at the community level. As a recycling specialist, Jan has been instrumental in the development of 'Buy Recycled' initiatives within the UK. She writes for a wide range of audiences, has over 25 years' practical involvement in environmental campaigning, including working as Information Officer for Friends of the Earth UK. She is a practising Buddhist with a particular interest in exploring the links between Buddhist ethics and environmental–social action. Jan has undertaken the major part of the research on the example processes studied for this publication.

Acknowledgements

This book has significantly benefited from many people's input. They helped us with their knowledge and ideas. They pointed us to useful references. They challenged our suggestions and argued the opposite, making us reconsider and differentiate. They took the time to be interviewed or fill in our questionnaire on MSP examples. They looked through draft documents and commented, providing guidance, question marks and amendments. This included many members of UNED Forum's International Advisory Board and Executive Committee, and many of those who have been involved in the example processes (see Appendix II). The work was also greatly helped by the 90 participants at a weekend workshop we held in New York in April 2001 where lively dialogues helped to sharpen our ideas.

Among all of them, one person was extremely helpful: Paul Hohnen, former Director of Greenpeace International and adviser to a range of international NGOs, organizations and corporations. He reviewed an earlier version of the text and provided a large number of invaluable contributions, comments, amendments and questions.

The book would by no means be the same without Paul and all the others. However, the authors take full responsibility for the contents of the book, including its shortcomings.

Second, our thanks go to those who supported UNED Forum's project on MSPs which led to this book: Novartis (Switzerland) provided the larger part of the financial resources and in-kind support by assigning Malou Lesquite to work with us on the project and the preparations for the workshop in New York. The Ford Foundation provided additional financial resources and supported a number of participants from developing countries in attending the workshop. BP Amoco plc hosted us at their conference facilities in New York, providing an environment which added to the enthusiasm and productivity of the event.

Minu Hemmati, Felix Dodds, Jasmin Enayati and Jan McHarry

Glossary, Acronyms and Abbreviations

ACCA	Association of Chartered Certified Accountants
APNCSD	Asia–Pacific National Councils for Sustainable Development
Bureau	Bureaus of UN Commissions or Secretariats are composed of a chair or two co-chairs and representatives of the five regional groupings of member states
BSAP	Biodiversity Strategy and Action Plan
CBD	Convention on Biological Diversity
CDW	Country Dialogue Workshop
CERES	Coalition for Environmentally Responsible Economies
CIEH	Chartered Institute of Environmental Health Officers
COP	Conference of Parties
CSD	UN Commission on Sustainable Development
CSD Intersessional	The official 22 sessions between meetings of the CSD
DAC	Development Assistance Committee
DAW	UN Division for the Advancement of Women
DESA	*see UNDESA*
DFID	UK Department for International Development
DPI	UN Department of Public Information
DSD	UN Division for Sustainable Development
DSTI	Directorate for Science, Technology and Industry
ECOSOC	UN Economic and Social Council
EEHC	European Environment and Health Committee
EU	European Union
FAO	UN Food and Agriculture Organization
FfD	Financing for Development (international conference 2002)
FLG	Forum Liaison Group
FSC	Forest Stewardship Council

G-77/China	The Group of 77 and China was the original group of the so-called non-aligned states. It is in effect the negotiating bloc of the developing countries and seeks to harmonize the negotiating positions of its over 140 members.
GA	UN General Assembly
GC	Global Compact
GEF	Global Environment Facility
GMI	Global Mining Initiative
GMO	genetically modified organism
GNP	gross national product
GPP	Global Public Policy
GRI	Global Reporting Initiative
HCHR	High Commission for Human Rights
High level segment	The ministerial-level part of the CSD meetings where most significant issues are decided
HIPC	Heavily Indebted Poor Countries
ICC	International Chamber of Commerce
ICFTU	International Confederation of Free Trade Unions
ICLEI	International Council of Local Environmental Initiatives
IFEH	International Federation of Environmental Health
IIED	International Institute for Environment and Development
ILO	International Labour Organization
IMF	International Monetary Fund
INSTRAW	International Research and Training Institute for the Advancement of Women
IPCC	Intergovernmental Panel on Climate Change
ISO	International Organization for Standardization
IUCN	International Union for the Conservation of Nature (now known as The World Conservation Union)
IULA	International Union of Local Authorities
LA21	Local Agenda 21
LASALA	Local Authorities Self-Assessment of Local Agenda 21
Major Groups	The term used in Agenda 21 to describe nine sectors of society fundamental to achieving sustainable development. The Major Groups are: Women, Children and Youth, Indigenous Peoples, Non-governmental Organizations, Local

	Authorities, Workers and Trade Unions, Business and Industry, Scientific and Technological Communities, and Farmers
MAP	Mediterranean Action Plan
MCSD	Mediterranean Commission on Sustainable Development
Member State	A nation that is a member of the UN
MISP	Multi-stakeholder Integrative Sustainability Planning
MMSD	Mining, Minerals and Sustainable Development
MOU	Memorandum of Understanding
MSC	Marine Stewardship Council
MSD	multi-stakeholder dialogue
MSP	multi-stakeholder process
NCSD	National Councils for Sustainable Development
NEPA	National Environmental Policy Act (US)
NGLS	Non-governmental Liaison Service
NGO	non-governmental organization
NGT	nominal group technique
NIS	Newly Independent States
NOAA	National Oceanic and Atmospheric Administration (US)
North	The current widely used term to describe developed, industrialized countries
NSSD	National Strategies for Sustainable Development
OECD	Organisation for Economic Co-operation and Development
OFP	Operational Focal Point
PA21	Philippine Agenda 21
PCB	programme coordinating board
PCSD	Philippine Council for Sustainable Development
PfA	Platform for Action
Plenary	A meeting of all participants where formal decisions are taken
PRSP	Poverty Reduction Strategy Paper
RC	Regional Coordinator
REC	Regional Environment Centre for Central and Eastern Europe
SAFS	Sustainable Agriculture and Food Systems
SC	Steering Committee
South	The current widely-used term to describe developing, non-industrialized countries
STAP	Scientific and Advisory Panel (Global Environment Facility)
TNC	transnational corporation

TOR	Terms of Reference
UKCAP	UK Coalition Against Poverty
UNAIDS	United Nations HIV/AIDS Programme (coordinating the activities of seven international agencies in the area of HIV/AIDS, including WHO, UNDP, UNESCO, UNFPA, UNDCP and the World Bank)
UNA-UK	United Nations Association, UK
UNCED	United Nations Conference on Environment and Development
UNCHS	United Nations Centre for Human Settlements
UNDCP	United Nations International Drug Control Programme
UNDESA	United Nations Department of Economic and Social Affairs
UNDP	United Nations Development Programme
UNDSD	United Nations Division for Sustainable Development
UNECE	United Nations Economic Commission for Europe
UNEP	United Nations Environment Programme
UNESCO	United Nations Educational, Scientific and Cultural Organization
UNFPA	United Nations Population Fund
UNGASS	United Nations General Assembly Special Session
UNICEF	United Nations (International) Children's (Emergency) Fund
UNIFEM	United Nations Development Fund for Women
UNU	United Nations University
WB	World Bank
WBCSD	World Business Council for Sustainable Development
WCD	World Commission on Dams
WEDO	Women's Environment and Development Organization
WEF	World Economic Forum
WFUNA	World Federation of United Nations Associates
WHO	World Health Organization
WIPO	World Intellectual Property Organization
WTO	World Trade Organization
WWF	World Wide Fund For Nature

A Call to Readers

Sustainable development is a process, and multi-stakeholder processes are one of the tools that can help us to achieve a more sustainable future. Increasing the utility of MSPs requires that we understand and evaluate how they have been used in the past, that we gain more experiences in more such processes, that we experiment with them:

> *Since the answers to fundamental and serious concerns are not at hand, there is no alternative but to keep on trying to find them.* (Brundtland, 1987, pix)

We very much want our readers to join us in this learning process. Please contact us at UNED Forum, c/o UNA-UK, 3 Whitehall Court, London SW1A 2EL, UK.

Regular updates on UNED Forum's work on MSPs can be found at: www.earthsummit2002.org/msp.

1

Introduction

Business as usual, government as usual, and perhaps even protest as usual are not giving us the progress needed to achieve sustainable development. Let's see if we can't work together to find better paths forward (Hohnen, 2001)

This book is about how people and organizations from very different backgrounds can work together in an increasingly complex political, social and economic environment.

The Earth Summit in Rio in 1992 alerted the world to a large number of pressing environmental and developmental problems and put sustainable development firmly on the agenda of the international community, many national and local governments and stakeholders. Many individuals, organizations and institutions have been responding to the challenge of sustainable development. Yet many still seem reluctant to take the need for change seriously, and even more have not even learned how they can get involved and contribute.

We have a long and difficult way to go if we want to live up to the values and principles of sustainable development and make them a reality. Taking one step beyond the stalemates which we face in many areas, we will need to learn how to listen to each other, to integrate our views and interests and to come to practical solutions which respect our diversity.

'Traditional processes of coordination need to be supplemented by a series of practical arrangements which provide for more active, cooperative management . . . both within the United Nations system and extending to other involved intergovernmental and non-governmental organizations' (Annan, 2000a). This holds true not only at the international level and not only in relation to official (inter)governmental decision-making and practice, but also at regional, national and local levels, and between the various 'players', forces and powers.

This book puts forward a framework for designing multi-stakeholder processes (MSPs), aiming to contribute to the advancement of such mechanisms as will produce practical solutions. MSPs seem a promising path, both around (inter)governmental processes and independent of them. We are witnessing a beginning of and a search for new partnerships. We need to become more clear about the nature of such processes, what principles should govern them and how to design and manage them effectively. We need common yet flexible guidelines and to learn from experience.

BOX 1.1 STAKEHOLDERS

Stakeholders are those who have an interest in a particular decision, either as individuals or representatives of a group. This includes people who influence a decision, or can influence it, as well as those affected by it.[1]

The term multi-stakeholder processes describes *processes which aim to bring together all major stakeholders* in a new form of communication, decision-finding (and possibly decision-making) on a particular issue. They are also based on recognition of the importance of achieving equity and accountability in communication between stakeholders, involving equitable representation of three or more stakeholder groups and their views. They are based on democratic principles of transparency and participation, and aim to develop partnerships and strengthened networks among stakeholders. MSPs cover a wide spectrum of structures and levels of engagement. They can comprise dialogues on policy or grow to include consensus-building, decision-making and implementation of practical solutions. The exact nature of any such process will depend on the issues, its objectives, participants, scope and time lines, among other factors.

Hence, MSPs come in many shapes. Each situation, issue or problem prompts the need for participants to design a process specifically suited to their abilities, circumstances and needs. However, there are a number of common aspects: values and ideologies underlying the concept of MSPs, questions and issues which need to be addressed when designing an MSP and the stages of such a process. Our suggestions form a *common yet flexible framework* which we offer for consideration to those who design, monitor and evaluate MSPs.

MSPs are not a universal tool or a panacea for all kinds of issues, problems and situations. They are akin to a new species in the ecosystem of decision-finding and governance structures and processes. They are suitable for those situations where dialogue is possible and where listening, reconciling interests and integrating views into joint solution strategies seems appropriate and within reach.

MSPs have emerged because there is a perceived need for a more inclusive, effective method for addressing the urgent sustainability issues of our time. A lack of inclusiveness has resulted in many good decisions for which there is no broad constituency, thus making implementation difficult. Because MSPs are new, they are still evolving. Because they are people-centred, people need to take ownership and responsibility for them, using and refining them to serve their own purposes and the larger purposes of the global community of which they are apart.

BOX 1.2 SUSTAINABLE DEVELOPMENT

Develop: bring to maturity; elaborate; improve value or change use of; evolve; bring forth, bring out; grow to a more mature state
Development: stage of growth or advancement
Sustain: keep, hold up; endure; keep alive; confirm; nourish; encourage; stand
Sustainable development '. . . is development which meets the needs of the present without compromising the ability of future generations to meet their own needs' (The World Commission on Environment and Development, *Our Common Future*, 1987)
'The right to development must be fulfilled so as to equitably meet developmental and environmental needs of present and future generations' (United Nations, *Rio Declaration on Environment and Development*, 1992)

Among the key aspects of Agenda 21 are those chapters dealing with the role of Major Groups (women, youth, Indigenous Peoples, non-governmental organizations (NGOs), business and industry, workers and trade unions, the science and technology industry, farmers and local authorities).[2] Agenda 21 is the first United Nations (UN) document to address extensively the role of different stakeholders in the implementation of a global agreement. In each of its chapters Agenda 21 refers to the roles that stakeholder groups have to take in order to put the blueprint into practice. Stakeholder involvement is being described as absolutely crucial for sustainable development.

Reflecting upon the practical implications, there are numerous ways to design stakeholder involvement. These range from governments consulting stakeholders to creating multi-stakeholder dialogues and partnerships as part of official decision-making and implementation.

WHERE WE ARE

*One of the major achievements of the UN system both
at Rio and beyond has been the integration of global
partnership principles into the international policy
process.* (Murphy and Coleman, 2000, p210)

Internationally, the most advanced multi-stakeholder discussions have
been taking place at the UN Commission on Sustainable Development
(CSD) where there are well-prepared multi-stakeholder dialogues each
year on different topics. They have also initiated ongoing MSPs.
Although the approach at the CSD is still evolving, it has become a
model of multi-stakeholder engagement within the UN system on
sustainable development issues. For the process towards Earth Summit
2002, the UN General Assembly has decided to conduct stakeholder
dialogues, panels and round-tables at all preparatory meetings, both
regional and international, and at the Summit itself.

MSPs have also generated considerable interest in other fora, around
intergovernmental bodies and at national and local levels. For example,
in 1996, the International Council for Local Environmental Initiatives
(ICLEI, 1997) counted 1812 Local Agenda 21 initiatives in 64 countries.[3]
The World Commission on Dams, in November 2000, launched its
report after two years of research, hearings, debate and dialogue. With
the Global Compact initiative, the UN Secretary-General has embarked
on developing a new approach to partnerships between the UN and
stakeholders, and discussions about this process have been as prominent as they have been controversial. The Organisation for Economic
Co-operation and Development (OECD) as well as individual companies
have undertaken activities and organized events providing platforms
for multi-stakeholder dialogues on contentious issues in the area of
biotechnology and healthcare. Debates on stakeholder involvement
around the UN, the United Nations Environment Programme (UNEP),
the World Bank (WB), the International Monetary Fund (IMF) and the
World Trade Organization (WTO), among others abound in recent years,
also as part of efforts towards institutional reform. For example, Poverty
Reduction Strategy Papers (PRSPs) are becoming increasingly important
at the national level for debt relief initiatives and concessionary lending
by the WB and the IMF, while PRSP stakeholder participation mechanisms are being critically debated.

Studies such as the ones conducted by Wolfgang Reinicke and
Francis Deng et al (Reinicke and Deng, 2000) on Global Public Policy
partnerships (GPPs) have made a significant contribution to the analysis
of the role and potential of multi-sectoral networks, identifying them
as 'institutional innovation in global governance' (Reinicke, 2000). They

have also highlighted many of the key challenges and organizational implications.

So far, however, it looks as if stakeholder dialogues, ways of feeding them into decision-making and concrete follow-up are mostly being organized and prepared on a rather ad hoc basis. There is vast experience with participation at community levels and increasing experience at national and global levels. Yet studying and comparing the different approaches and distilling some common but flexible guidelines from a stakeholder perspective is lagging behind. Governments and inter-governmental bodies, industry, NGOs, local governments and other stakeholders are trying out various approaches. Thus many different set-ups come under the same flag. Furthermore, the relationship between stakeholder participation and decision-making remains unclear in many cases.

The UN-Secretary General asserts this view:

> *Major Group's participation in sustainable develop-ment continues to face numerous challenges. Among them are geographical imbalances in participation, particularly at the international level, growing depend-ence on mainstream major groups as intermediaries, the need for further work on setting accountable and transparent participation mechanisms, lack of mean-ingful participation in decision-making processes, and lack of reliable funding for major groups.*

And:

> *One of the many challenges ... is to find ways of enhancing meaningful and practical involvement of major groups in sustainable development governance structures at various levels, both national and inter-national. Another is generating new participatory mechanisms aimed at implementation of national, regional and international programmes of action.*
> (UN Secretary-General's Report, 14 March 2001, paras 19 and 29)

However, it is not only the lack of funding for NGOs, or the unwilling-ness or inability of governments to develop a consistent approach to stakeholder involvement that is making progress difficult. We want to highlight two more reasons.

First, there is an unwillingness to engage on the part of many people and organizations and on all sides, albeit for different reasons. Many businesses simply don't see why stakeholders, and not only shareholders, should have a say in their policies. They claim that while operating within government regulations, those 'outside' their companies should not be able to tell them what to do or not to do. And some simply don't want to have to interact with NGOs, grassroots organizations or women's groups. Governments and intergovernmental bodies may feel threatened by the growing influence of stakeholders, viewed as unelected powers with insufficient transparency and undeterminable legitimacy. Among NGOs, there is a widening split between those who seek to engage with other stakeholders and those who define their role outside the conference rooms. The latter question the seriousness of governments and, in particular, industry who are seen to engage in stakeholder dialogues solely for the purpose of 'greenwash'. Protests in Seattle, Prague, London, Cologne and elsewhere have articulated these concerns, with an underlying criticism of the free market system and the enormous increase of corporate power. Naomi Klein (2000) in her best-selling book *No Logo* has collected and analysed these concerns and the movement in which they are expressed by a large and diverse number of people around the globe.[4] In a similar vein, Noreena Heertz (2001) describes the 'silent takeover' of power by corporations. She asserts that her book shows that 'protest by the consumer public is fast becoming the only way of effecting policy and controlling the excesses of corporate activity' (p3).

Second, many of us live in what Deborah Tannen (1998) has so eloquently described as *'the argument culture'*. Scrutinizing public political and mass media discourse, Tannen unfolds the widespread automatic tendency towards adversarial forms of communication, confrontational exchange, use of military metaphors, aggressively pitching one side against the other and forever thinking in dualisms: 'There are always two sides to a coin.' The author unfolds the roots of these patterns as based in the Western, Anglo-Saxon culture, and diagnoses an increasing spread of the argument culture via its global expression in Western-dominated media. Outlining the enormous impact of language and ritualized forms of interaction, she voices concerns about the consequences for democracy, quoting the philosopher John Dewey: 'Democracy begins with conversation' (p27).

ONE STEP BEYOND

Many issues today cannot be addressed or resolved by a single set of governmental or other decision-makers but require cooperation between many different actors and stakeholders. Such issues will be incapable of successful resolution unless all parties are fully involved

in working out the solutions, their implementation and
the monitoring of results. (Rukato and Osborn, 2001, p1)

In other words, where possible and appropriate, we should aim to take one step beyond our current practice of communication, policy-making and implementation.

Tannen (1998) suggests a move from debate to dialogue – because 'smashing heads does not open minds' (p28).[5] Dialogue – as opposed to fighting, debate and discussion – is an essential part of MSPs, if not the most crucial one, and most of the suggestions we offer on how to design such processes aim to create a situation where dialogue can take place in a group of people of diverse backgrounds, expertise, interests, views, needs and concerns. Learning to engage in dialogue means to move from hearing to listening. It means taking one step beyond fighting, beyond adversarial, conflictual interaction.

Dialogue is the foundation for finding consensus solutions which integrate diverse views and generate the necessary commitment to implementation. It can form the basis to take us one step beyond talking towards common action.

That does not mean that MSPs will be all calm, quiet and orderly. Kader Asmal (2000), who chaired the World Commission on Dams, has summed up his experiences with this extraordinary process:

> *A parting warning: doing so* [conducting an MSP] *is never a neat, organized, tidy concerto. More often, the process becomes a messy, loose-knit, exasperating, sprawling cacophony. Like pluralist democracy, it is the absolute worst form of consensus-building except for all the others.*

The multi-stakeholder approach takes one step beyond traditional concepts and hierarchies of power (money and enforcement). It asserts that influence and the right to be heard should be based on the value of each stakeholder's unique perspective and expertise.

MSPs also take one step beyond the current democratic paradigm. They are a logical development to where elections (every few years) and traditional lobbying (giving unfair and unhelpful advantage to those well resourced) will not generate the best solutions or practical implementation of policies.

AN ECLECTIC APPROACH

Sustainable development is a mixed concept, comprising values (such as environmental protection and equity) and strategies (such as healthy economic growth, stakeholder involvement and global perspective). We can address it within different frameworks or discourses. For example, we can argue on the basis of a value-based approach, pointing to the ethical and/or moral need for equity, justice, self-determination and democracy. This discourse will lead to suggesting mechanisms to improve transparency, to enable meaningful participation and to create equal access to information, fair communication and consensus-building, on the grounds that such political realities would further the realization of said values.

Many people assert that a set of shared values is indispensable for human survival, and this has been reflected by the international community on many occasions.[6] A number of existing international agreements, such as the Universal Declaration of Human Rights or the Rio Principles represent a shared set of values.

But we can also use a more pragmatic approach.[7] Based on scientific and empirical analysis, we can look at what has been proven to work to address certain problems and/or how we can combine various tools in an effective manner. This discourse will lead to suggesting strategies for bringing a multitude of perspectives into decision-making; listening to each other; and facilitating meetings. Arguing for a multi-stakeholder approach in this manner will lead to suggesting strategies which increase creative thinking, commitment to implementation and multiplying effects in order to address problems such as resource depletion and human and environmental security.

Including various discourses appeals to different kinds of people and is therefore strategically important. Some people want to relate to shared values and a common normative vision; others need statistics that prove that one approach will yield success with greater likelihood than another. But that is not the main reason for trying to do that. The main reason is rather that behaviour – and behavioural changes – are grounded in many factors such as: our beliefs, attitudes and emotions; the information we have; positive rewards (monetary or social); behavioural options; and social pressures. In other words, if we want to achieve sustainable development we need to identify the appropriate values and ideological concepts as much as to increase our knowledge on behaviour, interaction, and factors and relationships in the economic, social and political context. Hence, proposing tools for sustainable development, such as MSPs, should be based on considering basic values and ideologies (as a set of criteria) as much as practical experiences and empirical knowledge of how such processes can work in various contexts.[8] We hope that the way we have looked at MSPs in this book – be it called 'eclectic' or 'holistic' – will help to move the multi-stakeholder approach forward.

It is interesting to see how much the different discourses converge in terms of practical recommendations. The appeal of multi-stakeholder approaches seems to be that practising strategies that are designed to fulfil certain values are very much the same as those emerging as conclusions from scientific research on group diversity and effectiveness. For example, normative calls that we should 'respect our fellow human beings as much as ourselves' actually converge with scientific findings that active listening and equal speaking time help to create fair interaction; they lead to very much the same suggestions on how to design MSPs.

Nothing New?

Many of our suggestions for designing MSPs are not new, and neither is the MSP approach. What we are trying to do is to ground them in values, experience and science, and to generate a more conscious and comprehensive dialogue about them. Even if most of our suggestions were indeed common sense, it seems that we have a problem practising common sense.

Problems do not go away just because we look away. Necessities don't disappear just because we become cynical. Haven't love (for each other and for our environment) and justice been preached for ages? Don't we know how painful war, poverty, disease, injustice and oppression are and how they destroy us and our societies? Don't we know that we need to listen to each other rather than fight in order to come to lasting, sustainable solutions? Haven't we learned that without pooling our resources of expertise and power we will not be able to tackle the complex and urgent problems we are facing?

Well – yes. But life is a journey of learning and unlearning. What we understand in our minds, we won't necessarily put into practice. Have we really proven that we cannot do better? Whether humankind can indeed learn and change as a collective remains an open question. It will help if we try to do so together and consciously.

The Book

In Part I, we present a number of building-blocks as a basis for the suggested framework and guide. As outlined above, we have tapped into various discourses to develop our suggestions on designing MSPs: faith/belief systems, traditional and cultural values, philosophical, theoretical and empirical-scientific and pragmatic approaches.

In the past few years, terms such as '(multi-)stakeholder dialogue', 'stakeholder forum', 'stakeholder consultation', 'discussion' and 'process' have been used by various actors. Meanings of these terms overlap

and refer to a variety of settings and modes of stakeholder communication. Chapter 2 clarifies the various terms that refer to MSPs and
outlines the definitions that we use. It also addresses different kinds of
MSPs, varying with regard to the issues they address, their objectives,
scope and their time lines. They range from informing processes to
monitoring mechanisms and implementation processes, which include
consensus-building, decision-making and joint action. MSPs can be
conducted at local, national or international levels, with some processes
involving activities at several levels. They can involve different numbers
of stakeholder groups and thus vary in diversity, with increased diversity
posing specific challenges as well as opportunities. Finally, there are
those which are linked to official decision-making and those which
operate independently.

MSPs are an important tool for sustainable development. Their
objectives are to promote better decisions by means of wider input; to
integrate diverse viewpoints; to bring together the principal actors; to
create trust through honouring each participant for contributing a
necessary component of the bigger picture; to create mutual benefits
(win–win rather than win–lose situations); to develop shared power
with a partnership approach; to reduce the waste of time and other
scare resources that are associated with processes that generate recommendations lacking broad support; to create commitment through
participants identifying with the outcome and thus increasing the
likelihood of successful implementation. They are designed to put people
at the centre of decision-finding, decision-making and implementation.

MSPs relate to the ongoing debate on global governance and global
governance reform (see Chapter 3). We discuss some of the history of
and the increase in stakeholder involvement with the UN and the impact
of recent UN reform packages. Mechanisms of stakeholder involvement
developed by the CSD receive particular attention as they are the most
interesting political space for Major Groups within the UN and in the
area of sustainable development. The United Nations HIV/AIDS Programme (UNAIDS) offers another innovative example. The chapter
concludes with a discussion of the supplementary and complementary
role of stakeholder involvement vis-à-vis the roles and responsibilities
of governments, and a call for clear norms and standards. MSPs are
meant to give voices, not votes, to stakeholders, and our suggestions
aim to make these voices heard and used most effectively.

As with any problem-solving or governance approach, there are
certain value bases or ideological fundaments underlining the promotion of MSPs. These include fundamental concepts such as sustainable
development; good governance; democracy; participation; equity and
justice; unity in diversity; leadership; credibility and public opinion.
Other important concepts and strategies can be derived from these,
such as (economic) success; learning; partnerships; transparency; access

to information; inclusiveness; legitimacy; accountability; informed consent; responsibility, and appropriate ground rules for stakeholder communication. Chapter 4 outlines these concepts as they relate to MSPs. The suggestions for MSP design attempt to identify strategies and mechanisms that allow these values and concepts to be put into practice.

Scientific research that is relevant to the practical design of MSPs can be found particularly in social and organizational psychology. Chapter 5 reviews findings on decision-making processes in groups of high diversity. Among the conclusions are: MSPs and their participants need to take a learning approach to operate within a transparent, agreed and yet flexible framework. Aspects of group composition need to be considered carefully. Trust-building and overcoming stereotypical perceptions are among the first important steps. Formal group procedures are an important tool to successful communication and decision-making. Allowing the space for group members to reflect on the process they are engaged in is equally important (meta-communication).

Related to an increased interest in public participation and to the implementation of Agenda 21, numerous examples of MSPs have been conducted over the last few decades. Not surprisingly, since the 1990s there has been a significant increase of such processes within the area of environment and sustainable development. Chapter 6 looks at a number of examples, many around official decision-making processes at the international, national or local levels, and some independent initiatives. The examples vary with regard to, among other things, the issues they address, their size and scale, the way they have been designed and their linkage into official decision-making. We have conducted literature research and interviews with people who have been or are involved in these processes. The goal was not to evaluate but to obtain a descriptive analysis of the respective MSPs and to collect practical approaches, problems encountered and creative ideas on how to deal with them. The wealth of experiences provides valuable insights and examples of creative solutions to common problems of MSPs which we have used as a key resource for our suggestions.

On the basis of the findings of Part I, Part II goes on to draw conclusions. Chapter 7 presents a detailed framework for designing MSPs, going through the sequence of possible steps in the lifespan of such a process. We identify five stages – context; framing; inputs; dialogue/meetings; and outputs – and an additional sixth category of aspects which need to be addressed throughout the process. The strategies and mechanisms we are suggesting are based on a careful analysis of the values that are realized through them as well as empirical evidence that they are likely to work. In other words, all our suggestions are based on conclusions drawn from more than one approach.

Finally, we have summarized our conclusions in a set of principles and a checklist to design MSPs (see Chapter 8).

No 'one-size-fits-all' framework exists for all kinds of MSPs and the suggestions made here are not intended to pretend that there is one. Rather, they should be taken as an open-ended checklist of aspects which need to be addressed when designing, carrying out and evaluating MSPs.

In order to promote and validate the MSP approach further, there will be more steps to take than designing such processes. In an attempt to look ahead, Chapter 9 reflects on the overall conclusions from the book.

Part I

Building-blocks

2

Terms, Variety and Goals

CLARIFICATION OF TERMS

Certain terms that are related to communication and decision-making are used throughout this book. The meanings we give to them here are similar to those in general use, but we use some terms in a more differentiated manner. For example, we believe that it is very important to distinguish between dialogue, discussion and debate. These terms are often used interchangeably. For the MSP approach, however, engaging in dialogue for the purpose of understanding between stakeholders is essential, whereas discussion and debate refer to clarifying differences and arguing who is right or wrong.

To help clarify the meanings we intend, Box 2.1 lists some key terms and some of the meanings generally associated with them.

All of the above-mentioned terms refer to mechanisms and modes of stakeholder communication. To clarify the concept of MSPs and our classification of different types of MSPs, we will use the following definitions of these terms:

Communication. Our primary use of this term is on the exchange of views (opinions) among stakeholders in an MSP. It includes the expression of views in combination with the understanding of views to the point that there is mutual understanding. 'Meta-communication' is a useful tool for successful communication.

Consensus-building. In a consensus-building communication process, participants state their views and explore their views with one another in dialogue in order to develop mutual understanding. Then, based on mutual understanding, they seek to come to a consensus on future common action. 'A consensus process is one in which all those who have a stake in the outcome aim to reach agreements on actions and

BOX 2.1 TERMS USED TO DESCRIBE MULTI-STAKEHOLDER AND SIMILAR PROCESSES

Communication: an act of transmitting; exchange of information or opinions (*Merriam-Webster's Pocket Dictionary*)

Conflict: 'The perceived incompatibility of goals between two or more parties' (Smith and Mackie, 1995, Glossary)[1]

Consensus: general agreement; unanimity; the judgement arrived at by most of those concerned; group solidarity in sentiment and belief (*Merriam-Webster's Collegiate Dictionary and Thesaurus*)

Consult: to have regard to; consider; to ask the advice or opinion of <*consult* a doctor>; to refer to <*consult* a dictionary>; to consult an individual; to deliberate together; confer; to serve as a consultant. *Synonyms:* confer, advise, collogue, confab, confabulate, huddle, parley, powwow, treat. *Related words:* cogitate, counsel, deliberate; consider, examine, review (*Merriam-Webster's Collegiate Dictionary and Thesaurus*)

Consultation: council, conference; the act of consulting or conferring

Debate: to discuss or examine a question by presenting and considering arguments on both sides; to take part in a debate (*Merriam-Webster's Pocket Dictionary*)

Dialogue: a conversation between two or more persons; an exchange of ideas and opinions; a discussion between representatives of parties to a conflict that is aimed at resolution (*Merriam-Webster's Collegiate Dictionary and Thesaurus*)

Discussion: consideration of a question in open and usually informal debate; a formal treatment of a topic in speech or writing (*Merriam-Webster's Collegiate Dictionary and Thesaurus*)

Forum: the marketplace or public place of an ancient Roman city forming the centre of judicial and public business; a public meeting place for open discussion; a medium (as a newspaper) of open discussion or expression of ideas; a judicial body or assembly; court; a public meeting or lecture involving audience discussion; a programme (as on radio or television) involving discussion of a problem usually by several authorities (*Merriam-Webster's Collegiate Dictionary and Thesaurus*)

Meta-communication: [from Greek 'meta' = higher] communication about communication; exchanging information, views, opinions about the way we communicate in a given situation and structure. An important tool in communication processes, particularly in groups of high diversity of language, culture and background

Process: progress, advance; something going on; proceeding; a natural phenomenon marked by gradual changes that lead toward a particular result <the process of growth>; a natural continuing activity or function <such life processes as breathing>; a series of actions or operations conducing to an end; the series of actions, operations or motions involved in the accomplishment of an end <the process of making sugar from sugarcane>. *Synonyms:* procedure, proceeding. *Related Words:* fashion, manner, method, mode, modus, system, technique, way, wise; routine; operation (*Merriam-Webster's Collegiate Dictionary and Thesaurus*)

Statement: *Synonyms:* expression, utterance, vent, voice. *Related words:* outgiving; articulation, presentation, presentment, verbalization, vocalization (*Merriam-Webster's Collegiate Dictionary and Thesaurus*)

Understand: to grasp the meaning of; comprehend; to have a sympathetic attitude. Understanding: knowledge and ability to apply judgment; ability to comprehend and judge (*Merriam-Webster's Pocket Dictionary*)

outcomes that resolve or advance issues related to environmental, social, and economic sustainability. In a consensus process, participants work together to design a process that maximizes their ability to resolve their differences. Although they may not agree with all aspects of the agreement, consensus is reached if all participants are willing to live with 'the whole package' (Canadian Round Tables, 1993, p6). In other words, they can 'accept' the decision, even if they are not in complete agreement, and, more importantly, they are willing to do their part in implementing the decision. Consensus-building 'brings together different parties with the aim of finding mutually satisfactory solutions to which all are committed. It is based on 'win–win' outcomes rather than on traditional 'win–lose' outcomes' (The Environment Council).

Consultation. The term has been used to refer to a communication situation where an institution, such as a government body, calls for stakeholders to share their views with the institution (similar to hearings). The link of this input into decision-making is loose or remains unclear in many cases. The term is therefore too loaded with reference to a situation which does not represent our concept of MSPs (multi-party decision-finding).

Debate. The term refers to stakeholders stating their views, both arguing 'their case'. Debates imply a party-political approach and are usually 'won', meaning that they don't lead to an integration of views.

Dialogue. In a dialogue of stakeholders, representatives not only state their views but listen to each other's views for the purpose of developing mutual understanding, including each other's value-base, interests, goals and concerns. Dialogue requires the willing participation of all participants; even one person whose primary orientation is towards getting her or his way can destroy the dialogue.

Discussion. The term can be used to describe a frank exchange of views, followed by mutual exploration of the benefits and shortcomings of those views. More than 'dialogue', the term 'discussion' recognizes the differences between views and people and is less focused on mutual understanding in order to open possibilities to consensus-building.

Global public policy (GPP) networks. A term used by Reinicke et al (2000) in their work with the World Bank Global Public Policy Program. GPP networks are described as multisectoral collaborative alliances, often involving governments, international organizations, companies and NGOs. They 'take advantage of technological innovation and political liberalization'; 'pull diverse groups and resources together'; 'address issues that no single group can resolve by itself'; and, by doing so, rely on 'the strength of weak ties' (ibid).

Hearing. The term refers to processes where governments or intergovernmental bodies invite stakeholders to state their views on a particular issue. Listening to stakeholders is meant to provide the decision-making bodies with information that they otherwise might not have. Hearings may or may not allow for questions and answers and discussion following presentations.

New social partnerships. A term used primarily in Europe, for example by the Copenhagen Centre: 'People and organizations from some combination of public, business and civil constituencies who engage in voluntary, mutually beneficial, innovative relationships to address common societal aims through combining their resources and competencies' (Nelson and Zadek, 2001, p14). Similar to MSPs (but in more of a 'business-type language'), new social partnerships are characterized by societal aims, innovation, multi-constituency, voluntary participation, mutual benefit and shared investment, and what is described as the 'alchemical effect of partnerships'.

Stakeholder forum. This is a rather broad term and can refer to various settings where views are stated and discussed. Forum-type events tend to make use of various forms of interaction (plenary presentations, break-out groups, panel discussions, and so on) and allow a lot of space for informal exchange.

Statements. Stakeholder statements are communications through which stakeholder groups make public their views on a certain issue, in oral or written form. Statements do not necessarily lead to anything further – such as a discussion of views or consensus-building. (Statements, hearings and consultation tend not to be *multi*-stakeholder processes as they usually involve each stakeholder group separately rather than bringing them together.)

Understanding, to understand. Stakeholder statements are true communication only if they are understood by those to whom they are directed. And by 'understanding' we mean comprehending another person's views (without regard to one's own and specifically without regard to 'agreement').

Win–win, win–lose and all–win. These terms refer to the attitudes that people have towards others when seeking to resolve conflicts, and to the results of conflict resolution. 'Win–win' means that people care about others as well as themselves. They seek to resolve conflicts so that others and themselves 'win' – so, in the case of multiple stakeholders, they seek an 'all–win' resolution. And when all stakeholders achieve what is important to them, those results can be described as 'all–win'. When people care only about themselves and their views, their attitudes are 'win–lose'. They will tend to 'debate' in order to determine who is 'right or wrong'. When right and wrong cannot be determined, – or no one can win the 'fight', people end up with a 'lose–lose' situation where no one achieves what is important to them.

Multi-stakeholder processes. We use the term to describe processes which:

- aim to bring together all major stakeholders in a new form of communication, decision-finding (and possibly decision-making) structure on a particular issue;
- are based on recognition of the importance of achieving equity and accountability in communication between stakeholders;
- involve equitable representation of three or more stakeholder groups and their views;
- are based on democratic principles of transparency and participation; and
- aim to develop partnerships and strengthened networks between and among stakeholders.

MSPs cover a wide spectrum of structures and levels of engagement. They can comprise dialogues or grow into processes that encompass consensus-building, decision-making and implementation.

A VARIETY OF PROCESSES

MSPs vary with regard to the issues they address, their objectives, participants, scope, time lines and degree of linkage into official decision-making. These characteristics are described below. They do not form the basis of distinct categories and some processes will evolve over time.

Issues

The examples we have looked at range from the development of a regional environmental convention, to the implementation of a global plan of action on gender equity, global, national and local development policies, to water, large dams, energy, tourism, sustainable agriculture, environmental health, biotechnology, paper, mining, the decommissioning of an oil platform, corporate conduct, environmental reporting, and so on.

So it seems that MSPs can be used to address all kinds of issues. However, when there is too much conflict to allow dialogue, or when issues are too broad and abstract to allow concrete outcomes, MSPs would not be an appropriate tool.

Objectives

MSPs can be designed to inform decision-making of governments or intergovernmental bodies, businesses, trade unions and NGOs, among others. Such processes sometimes take the form of dialogues, often held as a single event, with more or less extensive preparations. In dialogues, there is no need to come to a consensus. Compared to separate hearings with stakeholders, the advantage of a multi-stakeholder dialogue is that it challenges stakeholders to debate the pros and cons of their analysis and suggestions in more detail. A dialogue will comprise questions and answers between the groups which will deepen the information provided to decision-makers. It will also offer insights into some practical consequences of decisions – possible partnerships as much as likely opposition. Multi-stakeholder dialogues held for the purpose of obtaining information should be held, of course, *before* decision-making processes commence, otherwise they will become 'fig-leaf' or token exercises. Stakeholders increasingly oppose processes which they perceive as merely 'rubber-stamping' decisions that have already been taken. Most of the examples we have looked at are informing processes. Others seem to begin with developing information, such as the corporate guidelines being developed in the Global Reporting Initiative (GRI), but can/will develop into implementation or monitoring mechanisms.

MSPs can also be used to conduct monitoring: decision-making bodies can establish an ongoing process of dialogue with stakeholders to obtain information on the effects of the implementation of their decisions (or lack thereof). This can be developed into accountability mechanisms, initiated by stakeholders independently. Such monitoring and evaluation of decision-making bodies is particularly powerful when it takes the form of an MSP.

At the local level, participatory monitoring and evaluation has been developed over more than 20 years. Instead of externally controlled data-seeking evaluations, participatory monitoring and evaluation recognize the processes for gathering, analysing and using information which are locally relevant or stakeholder-based (Estrella, 2000). At the international level, SocialWatch is an excellent example of an advanced monitoring process.[2] SocialWatch regularly updates its research on progress made towards implementing the agreements of the Copenhagen Social Summit and the Fourth World Conference on Women. However, this is being conducted by an NGO cooperating with other NGOs and with women's organizations; it is not a multi-stakeholder effort integrating very different viewpoints. To monitor labelling schemes, stakeholders can work together to set standards independently from governments (for example the Forest Stewardship Council (FSC); the Marine Stewardship Council (MSC)).

MSPs can also be used to further the implementation of existing agreements and policies. The international community has increasingly included recommendations in their resolutions and agreements which address not only governments and intergovernmental bodies, but also a range of stakeholders such as business, trade unions, local authorities and NGOs.

At the community level, Local Agenda 21 processes can include not only participatory planning mechanisms but also components of joint implementation. At the international level, UNED Forum's planned Implementation Conference around the 2002 summit is another example. The conference plans to gather key stakeholders to work out what roles stakeholders at the local, national and international levels will take in implementing the agreements, and to devise implementation tools and plans.

Participants

MSPs can involve different numbers of stakeholder groups and different degrees of diversity. Some processes work on the basis of the nine Major

Groups in Agenda 21. Others use customized definitions of relevant stakeholder groups, depending on the issues at hand. Some use a trisectoral approach of governments, business and civil society as stakeholders.[3]

For example, Local Agenda 21 processes ideally involve all Major Groups as of Agenda 21, but including the elderly, faith communities and teachers might be desirable. Stakeholder Dialogues at the Commission on Sustainable Development have involved four or five stakeholder groups (plus governments). The Ministerial Dialogues in Bergen, Norway (in September 2000) involved four stakeholder groups during the preparations (local authorities, business, trade unions and NGOs), with women providing input into the NGO paper, and six stakeholder groups at the dialogues themselves (local authorities, business, trade unions, NGOs, women and Indigenous Peoples), plus governments.

Scope

MSPs can be conducted at different levels: local, national or international, or a mix of those. For example, the World Commission on Dams (WCD), a global process, conducted regional hearings and commissioned studies into single dam projects. Including involvement at several levels can be a very useful option, and feedback loops between different levels (eg local, national, regional and international) can be an important part of the strategy. This can work to build on local and national experiences to inform dialogue or decision-making at the regional or international level, or it can serve to allow the practical implications of global agreements being worked out at the local level.

Time lines

MSPs can range from single, one-off events to processes going on over several years. This will depend on the issues, the objectives, the participants, the resources available and possibly the willingness of an official body to engage with stakeholders in a sustained fashion. For example, the UN Global Compact is an open-ended process, the WCD conducted its process over a period of two years, whereas CSD Stakeholder Dialogues continue for two days after several months of preparations.

Linkage to official decision-making

Principally, we can distinguish between those processes which are linked to official decision-making and those which are developed by stakeholders at their own initiative, operating independently.

Most processes which are linked to official decision-making are purely informing. At the moment, it seems that different bodies and organizations, for example at the international level, are experimenting with different structures and mechanisms. Given this variety, it is indeed sometimes difficult for stakeholders to understand what is expected of them, what they are being invited to do and how reliable that role will be. In the past, stakeholders have tended to put forward separately their respective ideas on participation in official decision-making processes. It can be expected that they will begin to develop common positions on desirable procedures and take them forward together.

Examples for independent MSPs, designed by a group of stakeholders, are the Global Reporting Initiative (GRI) or the WCD. Such processes often operate on the basis of long-negotiated, detailed parameters, an effort that pays off in terms of credibility, legitimacy and quality of outputs. Multiple funding sources are an important component of securing independence. Consequently, these very elaborate examples have over the last few years attracted a lot of attention.

THE GOALS

MSPs are an important tool for sustainable development. They aim to create space where such communication can take place that will help (maybe not immediately but in the future) to bring about agreement so that concrete action can bring about change.

MSPs aim to bring together all relevant stakeholders in order to:

- promote better decisions by means of wider input; integrate diverse viewpoints;
- bring into the process those who have important expertise pertaining to the issues at hand;
- allow for groups un- or under-represented in formal governance structures to have their say in policy-making;
- create trust through honouring each participant's contribution as a necessary component of the bigger picture;
- create mutual benefits (win–win rather than win–lose solutions);
- develop shared power with a partnership approach;

- create commitment by enabling participants to identify with the outcome and to value it, thus increasing the likelihood of successful implementation;
- put issues of concern to stakeholders on to the political agenda; and
- allow for clear and shared definitions of responsibilities in the implementation of change.

In a real sense, they are designed to put people at the centre of decision-finding, decision-making and implementation.

MSPs are a new species in the complex biodiversity of governance and decision-finding structures. However, they are not fully evolved or defined. The task of improving their role and effectiveness falls to all such processes. In this regard, it is essential to experiment with MSPs for all to learn how to carry them out successfully.

MSPs serve to build trust and can provide a basis for dealing with other complicated issues in the future. MSPs should be used to:

- look into alternative measures to develop viable frameworks of participation at all levels;
- increase the impact of un- or under-represented groups and protect their interests;
- identify stakeholders' roles in policy-making and implementation;
- identify viable strategies of implementation of existing agreements (and MSP outcomes in line with these agreements);
- develop indicators of good and bad practice;
- create monitoring and evaluation mechanisms and collective review procedures;
- enhance learning from the MSP experience;
- create and implement effective techniques for increasing commitment (when possible) and overcoming impediments to compliance (when necessary); and
- create and carry out joint action plans.

By holding the potential to reach goals that would be unattainable if each participating sector worked alone, MSPs also provide a foundation for broader change. Finally, successful MSPs also help to build larger coalitions and thus create political power and advantage.

For different stakeholder groups, MSPs hold different potential: for those under-represented they offer an entry point into the political process; for governments, they offer much needed expertise and engagement in the refining of broad policies and their implementation; for NGOs, they provide new opportunities for campaigning (towards all participants; see Hohnen, 2000a); while for the academic community, they offer opportunities to contribute up-to-date findings to the political process.

For those wielding considerable (unelected) power (such as industry and NGOs), MSPs offer opportunities to increase transparency, accountability and in the long run acceptance of their often contentiously debated activities – particularly as, or if, they change through such processes. Engaging in MSPs is the logical next step for corporations adopting a wider perspective which they need to do in increasingly globalizing markets. The fierce debate around the WTO, the Bretton Woods Institutions and the World Intellectual Property Organization (WIPO), for example, has brought inequalities and injustice to the attention of a wider public, and the already considerable pressure on Northern governments and on trans-national corporations (TNCs) to address these injustices are likely to increase. The virtual vacuum of international regulation, monitoring and enforcement will not remain as large a 'playing-field' as it is at the moment.

MSPs are not the mechanism of choice for all situations or problems, not even for all those that need stakeholder participation. An essential prerequisite is the presence of at least one common goal, or at least a reasonable probability that one such goal will emerge as a result of the process. If the goal is not shared by everybody who should be involved, other mechanisms such as bilateral interaction, traditional lobbying and campaigning will be more appropriate.

MSPs are not a panacea for any kind of problem, contentious issue, conflicts of interest, and so on. They are a tool or catalyst which will be applicable in some situations and not in others. Being guided by agreed principles of governance and experimenting with various forms of MSPs will help us to learn when and how best to use that tool.

3

The Context: Multi-stakeholder Processes and Global Governance

By Felix Dodds

> *Governance is the sum of the many ways individuals and institutions, public and private, manage their common affairs.* (Commission on Global Governance, 1995, p2)

The United Nations was originally set up when 50 countries met in San Francisco in June 1945. By February 2001, membership of the UN had expanded to 189 countries.

Since 1945 not only are there many more countries but there has been an enormous increase in the number of intergovernmental fora. There are now more than 1000 international institutions that have been set up, with highly diverse and often overlapping mandates. Many commentators have argued that some form of streamlining is well overdue to improve efficiency, to focus, and to reduce duplication and confusion. If you add to this situation the growth and influence of the 'non-governmental sector',[1] then it can easily be seen how much more complicated the intergovernmental process has become in the past 55 years. It has caused considerable fragmentation in the agenda and one of the key words that people are using in the preparation for 2002 is *integration* – integration at all levels, which the UK Government calls 'joined-up government thinking', not to mention intergovernmental or NGO joined-up thinking.

The UN was originally set up recognizing the supremacy of the nation state; it now needs to factor in the impact of globalization on the intergovernmental system. In the last ten years, there has been an increased role of other players such as multinational corporations, NGOs, women, local government, trade unions and others. At the same time, there has been a move towards some lower levels of government, closer to the people where many of these groups have direct experience of the impacts of globalization.

One of the most interesting and challenging areas of work that many stakeholders are involved in is the development of new governance processes at local, national and international levels. There are many reasons that have contributed to this, including the changing role of the nation state, globalization, the information age and the recognition that stakeholders play an increasing role in implementing what has been agreed at international level. As UN Secretary General Kofi Annan said in a speech to the World Economic Forum (1999):

> *The United Nations once dealt only with governments. By now we know that peace and prosperity cannot be achieved without partners involving governments, international organizations, the business community and civil society. In today's world, we depend on each other.*

At international level, the debate on global governance and the role of stakeholders has developed initially in an unstructured way. The Commission on Global Governance outlined that:

> *Global governance, once viewed primarily as concerned with intergovernmental relationships, now involves not only governments and intergovernmental institutions but also NGOs, citizens' movements, transnational corporations, academia, and the mass media. The emergence of a global civil society, with many movements reinforcing a sense of human security, reflects a large increase in the capacity and will of people to take control of their own lives.* (1995, p335)

The Commission did recognize that global governance now required the active involvement of stakeholders but it did not offer a real vision of how this might happen at the UN level. During the same time period, we had seen an enormous increase in the number of NGOs that are accredited to the UN and active in the UN Conference processes. In 1946, there were only four NGOs accredited; by 1992, this had grown to 928 and by the end of 2000 to over 1900. Table 4.1 reviews the

Table 4.1 *Number of ECOSOC Recognized NGOs Before and After Each Review of Consultative Status*

Year	Category A or I or General Status	Category B or II or Special Status	Register or Roster	Total
1946	4	0	0	4
1949	9	77	4	90
1950	9	78	110	197
1968	12	143	222	377
1969	16	116	245	377
1992	41	354	533	928
1996	80	500	646	1226
1998	103	745	671	1519

Source: Willetts, 1999, p250

number of the UN's Economic and Socal Council (ECOSOC) recognized NGOs before and after each Review of Consultative Status.

The rules that governed NGOs' involvement within the ECOSOC were based on the previous review, held in 1968 when only 377 had accreditation. These have since been revised. In July 1996 the ECOSOC adopted a resolution dealing with the new consultative relationship of NGOs with the UN. It was hoped that this would extend beyond ECOSOC to the General Assembly but as yet has not happened.

Some of the larger global networks such as the International Chamber of Commerce (ICC), the International Confederation of Free Trade Unions (ICFTU), World Federalists Movement, the World Federation of United Nations Associations (WFUNA) and the like have had offices in New York since the beginning of the UN.

This all changed with the enormous influx of new international, national and local NGOs and community-based organizations that occurred during the 1990s, kicked off by the 1992 Rio Earth Summit and followed up by the conferences on Human Rights, Population, Social Development, Women, Human Settlements and the Food Summit. Together, they set out the standards by which the UN, governments and now stakeholders operate in most of the key areas that affect our lives. They also brought a new generation of organizations and individuals into the UN who saw it as a vehicle to highlight their concerns and a place to put pressure on their governments as well as other governments.

Through nine chapters in Agenda 21, the Rio Conference formally introduced into the agenda the concept of Major Groups or key stakeholders in society. It recognized the need to engage these 'stakeholders' in the development, implementation and monitoring of the global agreements. Agenda 21 sets it out in the Preamble:

Agenda 21 addresses the pressing problems of today and also aims at preparing the world for the challenges of the next century. It reflects a global consensus and political commitment at the highest level on development and environment cooperation. Its successful implementation is first and foremost the responsibility of Governments. National strategies, plans, policies and processes are crucial in achieving this. International cooperation should support and supplement such national efforts. In this context, the United Nations system has a key role to play.

Other international, regional and sub regional organizations are also called upon to contribute to this effort. The broadest public participation and the active involvement of the non governmental organizations and other groups should also be encouraged. (Earth Summit '92, 1992, p47)

Through the 1990s, the reform packages that have had an impact on the UN and global governance have nearly all been accompanied by an increase in the role and responsibilities of stakeholders.

IMPACT OF UN REFORM PACKAGES

The UN Track One and Track Two Reports of the UN Secretary General addressed an increased role for stakeholders in the UN's work. Track 2 (Section 215) recognized

that our common work will be the more successful if it is supported by all concerned actors of the international community, including non-governmental organizations, multilateral financial institutions, regional organizations and all actors of civil society. We will welcome and facilitate such support, as appropriate.

The UNEP Task Force on Environment and Human Settlements (1998) called for:

- a coordinated UNEP Governing Council with structured meetings of major groups;
- enhanced major group participation in UNEP governing council meetings at the same level as the CSD;

- exploration of ways of engaging the private sector; and
- identification of the special needs of Southern NGOs.

And the UN Secretary General's Millennium Report (2000, p13) stated:

> *Better governance means greater participation, coupled with accountability. Therefore, the international public domain – including the United Nations – must be opened up further to the participation of the many actors whose contributions are essential to managing the path of globalization. Depending on the issues at hand, this may include civil society organizations, the private sector, parliamentarians, local authorities, scientific associations, educational institutions and many others.*

Some organizations have been promoting the idea of adding a People's Assembly to the United Nations. Prima facie, this would not necessarily require a Charter Amendment since the General Assembly has the power under Article 22 of the UN Charter to create auxiliary bodies to itself. Such a body would, of course, only have advisory power. One of the questions raised against this idea is the legitimacy of such a body. NGOs are not in many cases democratically constituted, and what about trade unions, industry associations, youth organizations, women's organizations, local government associations and other stakeholders? Another key concern is that the Assembly might be too Northern and that the costs involved in participating would make it very difficult for NGOs from the South to take part. This would then just mirror the problems of the UN where the Northern governments are well resourced and those from developing countries are not.

Just as the People's Assembly can be created under Article 22, so can the other interesting idea that of creating a UN Parliamentary Assembly. Again this would be only advisory, but it would have the strength of being built on the idea of electing our representatives to the world body that is creating the norms and standards by which we live our lives. We have an example of what this might look like with the European Parliament. As with the European Parliament, it could be done in a gradual way, first perhaps with sitting parliamentarians from the national parliaments, but then building up to directly elected representatives over a period of time. The advantages are clearer than with a People's Assembly of NGOs as the representatives would actually have a mandate from being elected. They would enable the discussion to move away from just a narrow national perspective to a global perspective. Also, governments could be held accountable to what could be seen as the 'voice of the people'. The Global Governance Commission does warn:

> *When the time comes we believe that the starting with an assembly of parliamentarians as a constituent assembly for a more popular body is the right approach. But care would need to be taken to ensure that the assembly of parliamentarians is the starting point of a journey and does not become the terminal station.* (1995, p258)

There are some difficulties, though, and that includes what can be done with countries that are not democracies.

On the issue of size and composition, Dieter Heinrich (1995, p99) says:

> *The ideal would be representation by population, but this would be impractical in the beginning, especially if it meant giving a 20 per cent of the assembly to the world's largest non-democracy.*

These ideas for a more formal increase in the role of particular stakeholders have occurred at the same time as the UN Commission on Sustainable Development has been exploring a different approach. Globalization has had a negative impact on the role of national parliaments and parliamentarians and a World Assembly of Parliamentarians might redress this if it had some powers. Unfortunately, governments are unlikely to give up any power to such a body.

THE ROLE OF THE CSD IN EVOLVING CHANGE

In creating the mandate for the UN CSD, governments recognized the important role that Major Groups would have in the realization of Agenda 21. There is no question that the CSD gives the Major Groups the greatest involvement in the work of any UN Commission. The CSD's mandate is to:

- monitor progress on the implementation of Agenda 21 and activities related to the integration of environmental and developmental goals by governments, NGOs, and other UN bodies;
- monitor progress towards the target of 0.7 per cent gross national product (GNP) from developed countries for Overseas Development Aid;

- review the adequacy of financing and the transfer of technologies as outlined in Agenda 21;
- receive and analyse relevant information from competent NGOs in the context of Agenda 21 implementation;
- enhance dialogue with NGOs, the independent sector and other entities outside the UN system, within the UN framework; and
- provide recommendations to the General Assembly through ECOSOC.

The CSD, created in 1993, is to date the most interesting political space within the United Nations for Major Groups to experiment with individual and joint advocacy, and with multi-stakeholder engagement. One indicator of the success of this has been the increase in their involvement. In 1993, around 200–300 Major Groups' representatives attended; by 2000, this had increased to between 700 and 800. The 'political' leadership shown by the Chairs of the CSD had some impact on this. The CSD is the only functioning Commission of ECOSOC to have a government minister as the chair. It also has between 40 and 60 ministers attending and has ministers or ex-ministers as the chair. The CSD has 53 states as members elected for three-year terms of office. Some of the creative activities relating to the development of political space at the CSD have included:

1993   Stakeholders being admitted to informal and 'informal informal' meetings and then invited to speak
1994   Stakeholders being able to ask their government questions in front of their peer group (other governments) as they present their national reports
1994   The establishment of the CSD NGO Steering Committee to facilitate NGO involvement in the CSD
1995   The introduction of 'Day on a Major Group'
1997   The introduction of the Dialogue Sessions, as a series of five half-day Major Group presentations;
1997   Presentations of ten Major Groups: representatives for the first time addressed the UN General Assembly at the review of UNCED ('Rio+5'). (NGOs have no right of access to the General Assembly)
1997   At the 19th UN General Assembly Special Session on Rio, negotiating committees operated on the basis of the norms from the UN Commission on Sustainable Development – a first in the UN
1998   The Dialogues developed as an interactive two-day discussion among governments and certain stakeholder groups on a specific topic (industry)

1998   The setting up of the first multi-stakeholder process to follow
       up a CSD decision (on voluntary agreements and initiatives of
       industry)

1999   The Dialogues' outcomes (on tourism) were given higher status:
       they are put on the negotiating table by the CSD chair, together
       with the ministerial discussion and the CSD intersessional
       document for governments to draw on

1999   The Dialogues on tourism set up a second multi-stakeholder
       process to follow up the CSD decision

2000   The Dialogues on agriculture set up a process under the Food
       and Agriculture Organization (FAO) to continue to develop new
       governance approaches in that agency to take forward issues
       raised in the CSD

2000   The UN General Assembly agreed to multi-stakeholder processes
       to be an integral part of the Earth Summit 2002 process,
       including multi-stakeholder Dialogues or Panels at Regional
       PrepComs, PrepComm 1, 2 and at the Summit itself

2001   PrepCom 1 for Earth Summit 2002 opened up the formal section
       of the meeting with presentations by each of the nine Major
       Groups

The CSD has pioneered a greater involvement of Major Groups in the
sessions of the Commission. None of the sessions are now closed; even
the small working groups are held open for Major Group representatives
to attend and in many cases to speak. However, this approach is an ad
hoc one and is at the discretion of the chair of the CSD. While the
formal ECOSOC rules do not allow for this to happen, the 'tradition'
of the active involvement of Major Groups has led to it being allowed.

The increased involvement of Major Groups in the implementation
of the UN Conference agreements has seen an increased involvement
in the framing of the agreements. Perhaps the Habitat II Conference
in Istanbul expanded the involvement to where the norm should be.
At that Conference and its preparatory meetings, NGOs and local
governments were allowed to submit proposals for textual amendments.
To do this, they were required to organize themselves into a negotiating
block for the Habitat II Conference. The UN then published the
consolidated NGO amendments as an official UN document (A/Conf.
165/INF/8). This was the first time that this had happened at a UN
Conference.

Habitat II had another first and that was Committee 2. In Committee 2 in Istanbul there was a series of half-day dialogues between
stakeholder groups. The reality, however, was that as the negotiations
were going on in Committee 1, the level of participation was low and
the input into the negotiations was close to zero.

At UNED's suggestion, the idea of the Dialogues was taken up by the CSD NGO Steering Committee who wrote to the Under Secretary General Nitin Desai in August 1996, requesting his support for the introduction of Dialogues at the CSD in 1997. The General Assembly agreed in November 1996, and asked each of the Major Groups to prepare for half a day dialogue sessions on the role they had taken in implementing Agenda 21.

It is interesting to note that the five-year review for Habitat II in June 2001 saw none of the practices adopted in Istanbul survive.

At present, none of the other UN Functioning Commissions operate such a model similar to the CSD, but some interesting approaches are evolving in the area of UN bodies (see Chapter 8). It might be noted at this point that practice varies widely in other international forums as regards NGO access and rights. In some forums and treaty negotiations, such as the London Convention, NGOs were given the right to make amendments to proposed text from the floor. In other cases, they were obliged to do this through friendly countries or by means of written submissions. The practice seems to vary according to the discretion of the chair. Increasingly, governments appear to be taking the line that NGOs or other stakeholders may comment and suggest but cannot 'negotiate', meaning intervene from the floor on draft text.

Since many of the Major Groups serve as the 'delivery system' for implementing Agenda 21 and the other global agreements, it has become increasingly clear that they must be more involved in more formal (multi-stakeholder) debates and consultations. If this does not happen, governments lack the 'reality checks' that NGOs and other stakeholders can bring to the table, and the commitment they can bring to implementation. [2]

Stakeholders know they are not elected and are not asking for a seat at the table to vote on agreements. What they want is the opportunity to present their ideas and expertise. Governments, as (in most cases) the elected representatives of the population, should make the final decisions on global regimes. However, those decisions will be better informed, more rooted in reality and more likely to be implemented on the ground if all the relevant stakeholders have been involved in the discussions. This also applied to decision-making at local and national levels. Governments, national or local, should make more informed decision-making by involving stakeholders. They may also find more of the policies actioned if they involve stakeholders. The challenge for the next ten years is how we move from good policies to good action.

UNAIDS

UNAIDS offers another example of the increasing involvement of stakeholders in global governance. The programme coordinating board (PCB) of UNAIDS coordinates the activities of seven international agencies in the area of HIV/AIDS – the World Health Organization (WHO); the United Nations Development Programme (UNDP); the UN Educational, Scientific and Cultural Organization (UNESCO); the UN (International) Children's (Emergency) Fund (UNICEF); the UN Population Fund (UNFPA); the World Bank and UNDCP (United Nations International Drug Control Programme). The PCB is a tripartite body including representatives of the donor and recipient countries and of the NGO sector, with ten full and alternate NGO members on it. Dennis Altman explains:

> *This is the first time a United Nations body has included representatives of affected communities on its governing board. The move was opposed by some governments, notably China (but also the Netherlands), for fear of the precedent it might set for other international agencies.* (Altman, 1999, p20)

One of the problems faced is who selects those ten NGO representatives to go on the Board. To quote Dennis Altman again:

> *The choice of the ten full and alternate NGO members of the PCB were made by the three official NGO observers at the WHO Global Program on AIDS Management Committee. While they made huge efforts to consult significant networks across the world there has been some discontent with the process and the actual choice of NGO delegates, though no one has proposed an alternative way of doing it.* (p22)

Although UNAIDS offers an interesting model for the involvement of NGOs, there are still questions about its legitimacy by those it seeks to represent.

The Future

The emerging diplomacy for NGOs is different from what it is for governments. The role of diplomacy for governments is based on their national interest (although there are particular exceptions to this, the

Scandinavian countries coming to mind), while other stakeholders and advocacy groups can often take a broader view. This is particularly true in the area of the environment and development where global commons issues (such as climate change) or issues of global significance (such as loss of ancient forests or trade policy) demand an approach both global and local in perspective:

> *We are seeing the emergence of a new, much less formal structure of global governance, where governments and partners in civil society, private sector and others are forming functional coalitions across geographical borders and traditional political lines to move public policy in ways that meet the aspirations of a global citizenry. These coalitions use the convening power and the consensus building, standard setting and implementation roles of the United Nations, the Bretton Woods Institutions and international organizations, but their key strength is that they are bigger than any of us and give new expression to the UN Charter's 'We the people.* (Mark Malloch Brown, 1999, piii)

It is worth remembering that the first international body to recognize the role of relevant stakeholders was the International Labour Organization (ILO) which in 1919 set a model for tripartite representation from governments, employers and unions. The ILO has a Governing Body which has 28 member governments, 14 members who represent workers and 14 who represent employers. Also, the ILO has 168 member states; each national delegation has four members, two government representatives, one worker's delegate and one employer's delegate.

Some organizations such as European Partners for the Environment promote the idea of tripartition within the sustainable development area. They suggest that the three parties should be governments, industry and civil society.[3] Agenda 21's approach is that it does not adequately enable an issue to be addressed if every other stakeholder is to be part of civil society. How can you put together NGOs, women, trade unions, scientists and local government, to mention a few, in one grouping? The essence of Agenda 21, although it identifies nine Major Groups, is that it is promoting the idea of bringing together all relevant stakeholders who need to address a particular issue. One problem with Agenda 21 is that it only identifies nine. There are others that should be considered – such as education community, older people, the media. Unfortunately, the addition of other stakeholders has been fought over the past eight years. The reason put forward is that we cannot 'renegotiate Agenda 21'. A more flexible approach is required as we move towards a clearer focus on implementing Agenda 21 and the other international agreements.

On issues such as health and safety at work a tripartite approach is probably the right approach. In fact, the Agenda 21 chapter on trade unions (Chapter 29) does recommend: 'to establish (within the workplace) bipartite and tripartite mechanisms on safety, health and sustainable development'.

We are witnessing the recognition that, in a highly complex, globalizing and interdependent world, governments no longer have the power and ability to forge and fully implement all the various agreements that they conclude. Society is made up of interacting forces – some economic, some institutional, some stakeholder-based, some citizen-based. This recognition can be liberating but at the same time it can be very daunting. If you take away the belief that governments might know best, then it can become a very insecure and thus a more frightening world for some. The multi-stakeholder processes can make this process less frightening and can also contribute to a higher likelihood that agreements will be implemented as the stakeholders themselves have been involved in the creation of the agreements. This approach also offers the opportunity to hold stakeholder groups accountable.

What we need in this increasingly globalized world are agreed norms and standards by which we can operate. This will require a clearer definition of the role and responsibility of governments, as well as of stakeholders, and an agreement on the modes of interaction.

In this context, MSPs offer significant attractions for those concerned with the improvement of global governance. As Reinicke (2000) has observed:

- Networks are multisectoral collaborative alliances, often involving governments, international organizations, companies and NGOs.
- Networks take advantage of technological innovation and political liberalization.
- Networks pull diverse groups and resources together.
- Networks address issues that no single group can resolve by itself.
- By doing so, networks rely on 'the strength of weak ties'.

As a final note, it is useful to recall that MSPs are yet to be seen uniformly favourably by all stakeholders in all forums. On the one side, many governments (or arms of government) are not persuaded that their approach to decision-making is wanting. Major Groups regularly encounter official objections from nation states to their meaningful inclusion in some forums.

On the other hand, some NGOs have reservations about the potential of MSPs to erode further the role of governments in decision-making. There are also long-term conflicts with industry on certain issues. While recognizing the greater access they themselves might be afforded to important policy discussions, they argue that if MSPs increase the role of industry, or promote the role of non-binding voluntary agreements for the business sector, or lead to a reduction in the use of legally binding regulations, MSPs are inappropriate. What is required, they argue, is more – not less – government and better implementation of existing commitments. Smaller NGOs, particularly from Southern countries, argue that they do not have the time, experience or resources to engage in MSPs, or express concern that their voices will not be heard.

Some stakeholders do question the issue of involvement in MSPs from a resource level. The question for them is priority: will their involvement in the MSP impact on the work they are doing on the ground? The more there is an obvious link between the local and the global the more interest they would have.

These are all important issues and will need to be taken into account as stakeholders develop frameworks for specific MSPs. It is not our contention that MSPs should be a substitute for existing governance processes based on democratic governments, but rather they should be a supplementary and complementary process to improve the quality of issue-finding, decision-finding and, where appropriate, decision-making and implementation.

MSPs create opportunities for stakeholders to contribute constructively to not only the improvement of global decisions but also to national and local decisions. MSPs can also become a driver for better implementation of the decisions, particularly at the national and local levels.

4

The Concepts: Key Values and Ideologies of MSPs

As with any other problem-solving or governance approach, there are certain ideological fundaments or value bases underlining the promotion of multi-stakeholder processes. The list of values and ideological concepts discussed below is not meant to be exhaustive or distinct. These concepts are being mentioned in debates on public participation and various mechanisms of stakeholder involvement, and in the wider debate on governance and governance reform. Many of them are also discussed in Agenda 21 and other international agreements, and are closely linked with the overarching concept of sustainable development.

All of these concepts are being interpreted slightly differently in different cultures. What we are trying to do is to outline their key aspects as they relate to MSPs.

Particularly with regard to the ethical-normative bases of MSPs, we have to keep in mind that the values that people subscribe to only influence their actual behaviour to a rather limited extent. This finding is well-established in psychology and other disciplines, and one which we can easily recognize in our own lives. To put values into practice, desirable behaviour needs to be reinforced by rewards, education, regulation, social images and desirable identities, and by providing information and appropriate options: 'If we are to expect people to act morally and to cooperate, then we surely have to provide them with processes for participation that are both fair and competent' (Renn et al, 1995, p366).

We have structured the list of values and ideological concepts using a two-tiered approach: fundamental (first-tier) concepts are discussed first, followed by a set of second-tier concepts which can be derived from the first set.[1]

FUNDAMENTAL VALUES

Sustainable development

First and foremost it is the concept of sustainable development itself which provides the ideological underpinning of multi-stakeholder processes. Having been put forward by the Brundtland Commission (1987) and embraced by the international community in the Rio Declaration and Agenda 21 (1992), it is based on the fundamental values of respect for nature, respect for an all-encompassing interdependence of people and the planet, and of inter- and intragenerational justice.

Basic societal processes related to sustainability are economic and social processes, and those of governance and political participation, such as 'participation in, and the responsiveness of, decision making processes, but also the capability of institutions to accommodate changing conditions' (Becker et al, 1997, p19).

Sustainable development requires a process of dialogue and ultimately consensus-building of all stakeholders as partners who together define the problems, design possible solutions, collaborate to implement them, and monitor and evaluate the outcome. Through such activities, stakeholders can build relationships and knowledge which will enable them to develop sustainable solutions to new challenges.

In fact, the multi-stakeholder approach reflects some of the most frequently and fervently discussed issues in discussions on governance, democracy, equity and justice of recent years – transparency, accountability, corporate social responsibility, solidarity, good governance, economic justice, gender equity, and so on.

Good governance

BOX 4.1 GOVERNANCE

Exercise of authority; direction; control manner or system of government or regulation. (*Websters Dictionary*, 1992, p420)

'Governance is the sum of the many ways individuals and institutions, public and private, manage their common affairs.' (Commission on Global Governance, 1995, p2)[2]

Good governance is a core concept and includes many of the other aspects discussed here or that relate closely to them. It comprises the rule of law, predictable administration, legitimate power and responsible regulation. It is indispensable for building peaceful, prosperous and democratic societies. Good governance demands the consent and participation of the governed. Here, the full and lasting involvement of all citizens in the future of their nations is key (see Annan, 1997). Good governance creates an enabling, non-distorting policy environment for all actors of civil society.

Participants at an international UNDP workshop in 1996 identified the following core characteristics of good governance systems (UNDP, 1996; see Bernstein, 2000):

- Participation, which implies that all stakeholders have a voice in influencing decision-making. Participation is the foundation of legitimacy in all democratic systems.

- Transparency, which implies that the procedures and methods of decision-making should be open and transparent so that effective participation is possible. Transparency is based on the free flow of information so that processes, institutions and information are directly accessible to those concerned with them.

- Accountability of decision-makers to the public and to key stakeholders; checks and balances as they exist in national governance systems are mostly lacking at the level of global governance.

- Effectiveness and efficiency in carrying out key functions.

- Responsiveness to the need of all stakeholders.

- Grounded in the rule of law, which implies that legal frameworks guiding decision-making must be fair and enforced impartially.

- Gender equity, which implies that all institutions and organizations of governance have responsibilities for ensuring gender equality and the full participation of women in decision-making.

As a new governance tool, MSPs should be developed further and defined through experimentation, particularly as regards their linkage with (inter)governmental decision-making processes and in the design of their implementation. MSPs have the potential for enhancing people's ability to govern themselves.

Democracy

BOX 4.2 DEMOCRACY

A theory of government which, in its purest form, holds that the state should be controlled by all the people, each sharing equally in privileges, duties, and responsibilities and each participating in person in the government, as in the city-states of ancient Greece. In practice, control is vested in elective officers as representatives who may be upheld or removed by the people. A government so conducted; a state so governed; the mass of the people. Political, legal, or social equality. (*Websters Dictionary*, 1992, p261)

Etymology: Middle French *democratie,* from Late Latin *democratia,* from Greek *demokratia*: government by the people; *especially*: rule of the majority: a government in which the supreme power is vested in the people and exercised by them directly or indirectly through a system of representation usually involving periodically held free elections: a political unit that has a democratic government: the common people especially when constituting the source of political authority: the absence of hereditary or arbitrary class distinctions or privileges. (*Merriam-Webster's Collegiate Dictionary and Thesaurus*)[3]

UN Secretary General Kofi Annan (2000) had this to say about democracy:

> *We need to understand that there is much more to democracy than simply which candidate or party has majority support... Yes, democracy implies majority rule. But that does not mean that minorities should be excluded from any say in decisions. Minority views should never be silenced. The minority must always be free to state its case, so that people can hear both sides before deciding who is right.*

In this context, MSPs represent an advanced mechanism of participation and indeed one step further in the development of democracy. Democracy ensures that the people express their agreement with their government; free and democratic elections provide alternatives for people to choose from. However, elections only allow people to choose between different versions of broad policies being promoted by one or the other candidate or party. They do not allow for citizens to influence day-to-day decision-making on the precise strategies chosen to implement such broad policies. For that to happen, there is a need for effective participatory mechanisms.

People First, a trust promoted by Development Alternatives, India, state in their 'Earth Charter Initiative' that in

> *a democracy, all power flows from the people who are the sovereign power. Democracy can therefore be truly defined as how the common people would like to be governed, not how some people, including elected representatives, think they should be governed.*

They outline a Gandhi-inspired vision of local empowerment of grassroots democracy, effective transparency laws over the right to information, the right to be consulted through public hearings and to participate in planning and other key issues, and the power to decide through referendum. Mirroring the 1992 Earth Summit outcome, People First suggest that councils should consist of representatives of the disadvantaged communities, religions, women, trade unions, farmers, industry, professionals and NGOs, among others.[4]

MSPs and multi-stakeholder institutions, such as the National Councils on Sustainable Development (NCSDs) (see Chapter 8), are (or could be) the logical next step for implementing Agenda 21 at national level. Based on the concept of the 'Independent Sector', Agenda 21 identifies key stakeholder groups, the so-called Major Groups, acknowledging that they need to be involved in developing solutions and implementing them. The NCSDs do vary in their make-up and independence from government. The Earth Council has worked extensively with National Councils to draw up guidelines on the development of NCSDs. To some, this might be understood in a narrow sense, where governments consult Major Groups and invite them to hearings. In the true sense of participatory democracy, however, MSPs would go further than hearings or consultations. It would mean that governments (or other facilitating or decision-making bodies) gather all stakeholders for consultations, dialogue and/or consensus-building and/or for ongoing implementation, monitoring and evaluation processes.

Participation

BOX 4.3 PARTICIPATION

Participate: to take part or have a share in common with others; partake. Participatory: based on or involving participation, especially active, voluntary participation in a political system. (*Webster's Dictionary*, 1992, p708)

The act of participating: the state of being related to a larger whole. (*Merriam-Webster's Collegiate Dictionary and Thesaurus*)

Public participation can be defined as 'forums for exchange that are organised for the purpose of facilitating communication between government, citizens, stakeholders and interest groups, and businesses regarding a specific decision or problem'. (Renn et al, 1995, p2)[5]

> *[A] distinction needs to be made between democracy and participation ... Democracy entitles them [the people] to choose leaders with broad policies most acceptable to them. Participation in public affairs enables them to influence the details of policy-legislation, and to continuously monitor their implementation.* (Mohiddin, 1998)

An important prerequisite for meaningful participation is capacity, such as information and knowledge, time and resources. Ultimately, the overarching vision is as follows:

> *[a] world, in which every person – regardless of citizenship, country of residence, wealth, or education – has access to the information and the decision-making processes necessary to participate meaningfully in the management of the natural environment that affects them. This greater and informed public access produces more effective, legitimate, and just decisions on projects and policies. It ensures sustainable development by acting as an antidote to ignorance, greed and corruption and building social capital.* (World Resources Institute, 2000)

In many cases, this will primarily mean to mainstream civil society access to information and participation since the private sector typically already has access and is well represented.

Participation works on the basic assumption that all views of stakeholders are being subjective and therefore limited.[6] MSPs take advantage of stakeholder participation, as bringing in the wealth of subjective perspectives, knowledge and experience increases the likelihood of better decisions.

Stakeholder involvement and collaboration beyond 'hearings' are revolutionary in the sense that we have not acted or interacted that way before. They are not revolutionary, however, in the traditional sense as aiming to replace one party (or group/class/person) with another one. It is part of a significant development in democracy aimed at replacing one power with many and creating a situation where decisions taken are informed and owned by all relevant stakeholders.

Thus, participation serves two major objectives: increasing the quality of decisions and generating necessary commitment.

Box 4.4 Commitment

Commitment: the combined forces that hold the partners together in an enduring relationship.

Norm of social commitment: the shared view that people are required to honour their agreements and obligations. (Smith and Mackie, 1995, Glossary)

To commit: to pledge or assign to some particular course or use. (*Merriam-Webster's Pocket Dictionary*)

Many of the decisions to be taken along the path to sustainable development will imply significant changes in many people's lives. Such decisions can only be effective if they receive general support among the people. Participation creates ownership. By taking part in the initial communications and, ultimately, the decision-making process itself, people are much more likely to take ownership of the decisions that emerge. Without stakeholder participation, commitment to solutions will be low and implementation will not work. Participation often seems to be very difficult, time-consuming and expensive. However, the cost of failing to engage stakeholders can be orders of magnitude greater.

Participation is also not only a citizen's right. It also involves duties and responsibilities. For all stakeholder groups in MSPs, requirements such as representativeness, democratic structures, transparency and accountability are required. They are key elements of a stakeholder's legitimacy (see below).

An important question concerns the appropriate measurement of the effectiveness of participatory mechanisms in sustainable development. It will be important to develop monitoring and evaluation mechanisms for MSPs. This needs to be done in collaboration with practitioners and academic researchers. Case studies of individual MSPs have been published and more are under way. These also provide comparative analysis and general conclusions (for example Montreal International Forum, 1999; Reinicke et al, 2000). Local Agenda 21 processes have been surveyed and analysed (for example ICLEI, 1997; Church, 1997). Work by Wiener and Rihm (2000) specifically focuses on short-term indicators of the impacts of LA21 (an important component as it helps officials to justify expenses for participation). Estrella (2000), for example, provides work on participatory monitoring and evaluation. Renn et al (1995) have based their development of indicators of fairness and competence in citizen participation on a comprehensive theoretical analysis of such participation. It will be necessary to develop shared sets of indicators and standardized tools for evaluation in order to further develop MSPs and to promote those features and components which have indeed proven to work.

Equity and justice

Box 4.5 Equity

Fairness or impartiality; justness. Something that is fair or equitable. (Law) A justice administered between litigants which is based on natural reason or ethical judgment. That field of jurisprudence superseding the legal remedies of statute law and common law when these are considered inadequate or inflexible for the purposes of justice to the parties concerned. (*Webster's Dictionary*, 1992, p330)

Justice according to natural law or right; *specifically*: freedom from bias or favouritism. *Related Words*: equitableness, justness. *Contrasted Words*: bias, discrimination, partiality, unfairness. (*Merriam-Webster's Collegiate Dictionary and Thesaurus*)

Norm of equity: the shared view that demands that the rewards obtained by the partners in a relationship should be proportional to their inputs. (Smith and Mackie, 1995, Glossary)

BOX 4.6 JUSTICE

Etymology: Middle English, from Old English and Old French; Old English *justice,* from Old French *justice,* from Latin *justitia,* from *justus.* The maintenance or administration of what is just especially by the impartial adjustment of conflicting claims or the assignment of merited rewards or punishments: the administration of law; *especially*: the establishment or determination of rights according to the rules of law or equity: the quality of being just, impartial, or fair: the principle or ideal of just dealing or right action: conformity to this principle or ideal: righteousness: the quality of conforming to law: conformity to truth, fact, or reason: correctness. The action, practice, or obligation of awarding each his just due. *Synonym:* equity. *Related Words*: evenness, fairness, impartiality. *Contrasted Words*: foul play, inequity, unjustness; bias, leaning, one-sidedness, partiality. (*Merriam-Webster's Collegiate Dictionary and Thesaurus*)[7]

Equity can be understood as fairness, the standard by which each person and group is able to maximize the development of their latent capacities. Equity differs from absolute equality in that it does not dictate that all be treated in exactly the same way. While everyone has individual talents and abilities, the full development of these capacities may require different approaches. Access and opportunity need to be fairly distributed so that this development might take place. Equity and justice are intertwined conditions of a functioning society. Equity is the standard by which policy and resource commitment decisions should be made. Justice is the vehicle through which equity is applied, its practical expression. It is only through the exercise of justice that trust will be established among diverse peoples, cultures and institutions.

'A consensus process provides an opportunity for participants to work together as equals to realize acceptable actions or outcomes without imposing the views or authority of one group over another' (Canadian Round Tables, 1993, p6). This can represent an enormous challenge since many MSPs bring together stakeholders of very different perspectives and power – such as local or indigenous communities and transnational corporations (see Hemmati, 2000d). To do justice to the various points of view and interests, participants need to treat each other as equals. They need to work out which interests are most important or if they are equally important, and if, ultimately, all interests can be met. This requires tolerance, mutual respect, the willingness to find consensus and a strong sense of justice. It is equity in practice.

Unity in diversity

BOX 4.7 UNITY

The state, property, or product of being united, physically, socially, or morally; oneness. Union, as of constituent parts or elements: national unity. Agreement of parts: harmonious adjustment of constituent elements; sameness of character: the unity of two writings. The fact of something being a whole that is more than or different from its parts or their sum. Singleness of purpose or action. A state of general good feeling; mutual understanding; concord: brethren dwelling together in unity. (*Webster's Dictionary*, 1992, 1057)

The quality or state of not being multiple: a condition of harmony: continuity without deviation or change (as in purpose or action): a totality of related parts: an entity that is a complex or systematic whole. The condition of being or consisting of one <*unity* – the idea conveyed by whatever we visualize as one thing>. *Synonyms*: individuality, oneness, singleness, singularity, singularness. *Related Words*: identity, selfsameness, soleness, uniqueness, uniquity. *Antonyms*: multiplicity. *Synonyms*: harmony, concord, rapport. *Related Words*: agreement, identity, oneness, union; solidarity; conformance, congruity. (*Merriam-Webster's Collegiate Dictionary and Thesaurus*)

BOX 4.8 DIVERSITY

The state of being diverse; dissimilitude. Variety: a diversity of interests. (*Webster's Dictionary*, 1992, p286)

Diverse: Differing essentially; distinct. Capable of various forms; multiform. (*Webster's Dictionary*, 1992, p286)

Synonyms: variety, diverseness, multeity, multifariousness, multiformity, multiplicity, variousness. *Related Words*: difference, dissimilarity, distinction, divergence, divergency, unlikeness. *Antonyms*: uniformity; identity. (*Merriam-Webster's Collegiate Thesaurus*)

Unity or consensus are concepts associated with multi-stakeholder processes which include decision-making and implementation. In a dialogue, a frank exchange of views and learning about each other's interests, motivations and opinions is sufficient. In a dialogue, ambiguity, disagreements and mutually exclusive positions can be simply recorded as they are. Once we want to move into common action, however, we need to find consensus about the appropriate path of action. While we do not have to agree on each and every point (unanimity), we do need to come to a point where everybody can live with the 'whole package' (agreement, compromise). In an MSP, consensus and unity stand in contrast to uniformity – the concept is rather unity in diversity. The MSP approach cherishes the diversity of expertise, talents, interests, variegated experiences, cultures and viewpoints among stakeholders and individuals inasmuch as they contribute to a creative process of finding innovative solutions. The immense wealth of diversity is vital to sustainable development; and diversity of views is an important component of high-quality decision-making. Maintaining and celebrating diversity are indeed among the major reasons to embark on designing MSPs, and the integration of diverse views is the major challenge.

Diversity often implies conflict of values, goals and interests which can lead to highly conflictual debates, anger, frustration, mistrust and hostility. When attempting dialogue in a conflict situation, the experience might be negative and discourage people from further interaction. In some cases, it will therefore be advisable to work at first with the different groups separately before bringing them all together.

The fact that emerges strongly from the scientific research on group dynamics and from studying a number of MSP examples, is that groups who come together in MSPs tend to build a group culture and identity, including a certain degree of loyalty and commitment to the group.[8] This is indeed a useful effect as it helps people to listen and come to agreements. However, once people have developed a common group identity within the MSP, they might agree more quickly and compromise before they have exhausted all points of discussion. Thus the group might lose some of the benefits of its initial diversity. The challenge for all participants, but especially for NGOs (and, one might add, for United Nations bodies), is to strike a balance between a serious commitment to a process and its success (which implies commitment to mutual learning and openness to change) and keeping their own identity.

Leadership

BOX 4.9 LEADERSHIP

The office or position of a leader; guidance. (*Webster's Dictionary*, 1992, p556)

Leadership: a process in which group members are permitted to influence and motivate others to help attain group goals. (Smith and Mackie, 1995, Glossary)

The office or position of a leader: capacity to lead: the act or an instance of leading. (*Merriam-Webster's Collegiate Dictionary*)

Leader: one who leads or conducts; a guide; a commander. That which leads, or occupies a chief place, as the foremost horse of a team. (*Webster's Dictionary*, 1992, p556)

Lead, to: to go with or ahead of so as to show the way; guide. To draw along; guide by or as by pulling: to lead a person by the hand. To serve as a direction or route for: the path led them to the valley. To cause to go in a certain course of direction, as wire, water, etc. To direct the affairs or actions of. To influence or control the opinions, thoughts, actions of; induce. To begin or open: to lead a discussion. To act as guide; conduct. To have leadership or command; be in control. (*Webster's Dictionary*, 1992, p556)

'Collaborative leadership: a style of leadership where leaders view their roles primarily as convincing, catalyzing, and facilitating the work of others. Collaborative leadership focuses on bringing citizens together and helping them build trust and the skills for collaboration.' (Markowitz, 2000, p161)

> *The world has for so long been run by those who have usurped the power to run it, and in the manner that is to their best advantage, we frequently forget that they have no more right to do so than anyone else.* (Khosla, 1999)

Autocratic, paternalistic, manipulative and 'know-it-all' modes of leadership, which are found in all parts of the world, tend to disempower those whom they are supposed to serve. They exercise control by over-centralizing decision-making, thereby coercing others into agreement.

Those who exercise authority have a great responsibility to be worthy of public trust. Leaders – including those in government, politics, business, religion, education, the media, the arts and community organizations – must be willing and indeed seeking to be held accountable for the manner in which they exercise their authority. Trustworthiness is the foundation for all leadership.

Visionary, empowering and collaborative leadership will be necessary to inspire those in power, stakeholders and individuals to overcome their preoccupation with narrow-minded interests and to recognize that the security and well-being of all at local and national levels depend on global security and require sustained commitments to long-term ecological and human security.

One of the difficulties in thinking about leadership is that our usual perception is that leadership is what leaders do – leaders lead and followers follow. However, the emergence of 'servant' or 'collaborative leadership' has contributed to a shift in orientation – namely, an orientation to leaders as *serving* the needs of 'followers' so that the followers are in fact the leaders. And visionary leadership tends to shift our concept of leadership away from leaders and towards shared purpose and vision (images of success in serving a purpose). When purpose and vision are clearly understood and people honestly care about them, then people can lead themselves and work together to bring *their* vision into reality.

Within the framework of sustainable development, leadership no longer means 'to issue orders' or 'to be in control'. Rather, it will express itself in service to and empowerment of others and to the community as a whole. It will foster collective decision-making and collective action and will be motivated by a commitment to justice and to the well-being of all humanity. MSPs represent a model where new forms of leadership can be explored and developed. Among those new forms are ones in which leaders are servants.

Credibility and public opinion

Finally, there is a related issue in support of MSPs. This is the need for governance processes to engage those partners who – although not elected – enjoy wide public support, trust and credibility. For many years, public opinion polls around the world have suggested that several leading advocacy organizations enjoy higher public esteem that corporations or even governments. Generally speaking, such polls indicate that the public tends to give greater credence to information provided by organizations like Greenpeace and Amnesty International than media or official sources.

These results tend to reinforce the MSP approach for at least two reasons. First, as noted above, to ensure that groups which have good information and creative ideas about how to move ahead are brought to the table in a framework that is outcome-driven. Second, to give those sectors which suffer (rightly or wrongly) from a lower public opinion an opportunity to define, defend and develop their perspectives in a policy forum where they can engage directly and methodically on areas of difference.

If public opinion polls are any guide, the MSP concept is likely to prove an appealing approach to the resolution of the many outstanding sustainability issues.[9]

DERIVED CONCEPTS AND STRATEGIES

(Economic) success

Increasingly, there is recognition of the need for businesses to win a 'licence to operate' in the public domain. Against the background of continuing low public opinion poll ratings, it is not enough that businesses produce goods, services and a profit. They also need to act as responsible citizens. They need to show not only that they do 'no harm', but that they 'do good'. Within this framework, many commentators believe that without the agreement of stakeholders to business policies and practices, businesses will not be sustainable. In short, businesses need to engage with their stakeholders to ensure their businesses' success.[10]

More progressive sectors of business now acknowledge that business practice itself was a major contributor to environmental and social problems in the past. Business associations lobbying against tougher workplace and environmental standards and poor performance on the ground in many cases prompted the rise of advocacy organizations seeking safer factories, cleaner production processes and less waste.

For some, this is today more obvious than for others. Corporate share values nowadays significantly depend on 'soft factors' such as social performance, environmental responsibility and management personality. Good practice achieved through pressure on large corporations (for example via media attention) can lead to appropriate regulation and self-regulation. Thus it can lead to to increased compliance also by small and medium-sized businesses whose performance is less controlled and controllable by civil society stakeholders.

Successful solutions are those which create mutual benefits: win–win situations rather than win–lose situations. Corporations have been vocally advertising the virtually infinite possibilities of creating win–win business options. It is for them, in partnership with their stakeholders, to deliver the creativity required to develop these options.

Learning

Life-long learning is a common characteristic of all human beings and a main initiating factor of change. MSPs will only work if all participants are willing to learn from each other. In a successful MSP, everybody will learn and therefore, to some degree, change.

MSPs themselves also need to take a learning approach. This emerges very strongly from the review of scientific literature as well as from studying the examples.[11] Social and organizational psychology indicates that processes and mechanisms, modes of leadership and facilitation, and the means of communication have to be flexible. MSPs need to strike a balance between an agreed, foreseeable agenda and process on the one hand, and the ability to respond flexibly to changing situations on the other.

Renn et al (1995, p7) claim that 'it should be possible to move away from a subject-centred view of participation to shared values and interests'. Developing new values and acting upon them is a learning process triggered by sincere dialogue: speaking openly and honestly, and listening rather than hearing.

Learning is related to self-reflection, role-taking and change of perspective, and to the ability to embrace change. The courage to venture into 'unknown territory' is essential within a dialogue or consensus-building process, not only to make it a true group process but also an individual adventure into new, 'unexplored space'. In that space, we will find ideas and solutions which could not have emerged without the process of interaction.

Embracing change and moving out of our comfort zones is not easy. Human values, thinking and behaviour are very resistant to change. We don't necessarily have a problem embracing new ideas but breaking old habits is very difficult. Our habits of thinking and behaviour form a large part of our identity, ourselves. Particularly in Western cultures, where individual identity is closely associated with autonomy, self-control and self-consistency, the experience of undergoing change through social interaction can be rather disquieting.

Therefore, even when change is strongly and wholeheartedly perceived as beneficial, it tends to elicit fear (of the unknown, of peers' reactions, and so on) – hence security and encouragement from a trustworthy source can be essential.[12]

PARTNERSHIP, COLLABORATION AND SOLIDARITY

BOX 4.10 PARTNERSHIP AND COLLABORATION

The state of being a partner: participation. A legal relation existing between two or more persons contractually associated as joint principals in a business: the persons joined together in a partnership: a relationship resembling a legal partnership and usually involving close cooperation between parties having specified and joint rights and responsibilities. *Synonyms*: association, affiliation, alliance, cahoots, combination, conjunction, connection, hook-up, tie-up, togetherness. *Related words*: consocation, fellowship. (*Merriam-Webster's Collegiate Dictionary and Thesaurus*)

Collaboration: to work jointly with others or together especially in an intellectual endeavour: to cooperate with an agency or instrumentality with which one is not immediately connected. *Etymology:* Late Latin *collaboratus,* past participle of *collaborare* to labor together. (*Merriam-Webster's Collegiate Dictionary and Thesaurus*)

BOX 4.11 SOLIDARITY

Unity (as of a group or class) that produces or is based on community of interests, objectives, and standards. (*Merriam-Webster's Collegiate Dictionary and Thesaurus*)

A feeling of unity (as in interests, standards, and responsibilities) that binds members of a group together <*solidarity* among union members is essential in negotiations>. *Synonyms*: cohesion, solidarism, togetherness. *Related Words*: cohesiveness; oneness, singleness, undividedness; integrity, solidity, union, unity; esprit, esprit de corps; firmness, fixity. *Contrasted Words*: separation; discord, dissension, schism; confusion, disorder, disorganization. *Antonym*: division. (*Merriam-Webster's Collegiate Thesaurus*)

Individual pursuit of self-interest coupled with the possibility of using a 'free-ride' position has been a main cause for environmental degradation. By contrast, sustainable development requires stakeholders – all of whom are polluters in some form – to build partnerships based on a sense of solidarity, collaboration and trust. Participatory approaches such as MSPs should be designed 'to catalyse people into adopting an attitude that is oriented to cooperation rather than pursuit of individual interests' (Renn et al, 1995, p365) and forge new partnerships, even of unlikely partners.

What does a partnership approach mean? Is 'stakeholder dialogue', for example around (inter)governmental decision-making, forging partnerships and leading to common action? Or is it entertainment for officials – perhaps some kind of 'cathartic entertainment' or ritualistic show-event? Are the stakeholders merely like jesters at medieval court, the only ones able to speak of higher values and essential goals, of love and justice, vis-à-vis a 'real world' of power and capital?[13] Invited to relieve the ones in power, articulating some 'higher thoughts', and enabling decision-makers to assert they have listened to the voices of ideals, visions, even religion? So that negotiators then may return to the conference room to make a decision, oblivious to what they have heard?

This does happen, and purely informing processes around official decision-making seem to be particularly susceptible to it. It can leave stakeholders frustrated and less inclined to contribute next time. Stakeholders' criticism of this kind of process does not mean that stakeholder participation should (always) be part of decision-making. However, for participation to develop into partnerships, official bodies need to make clear to stakeholders – and themselves – what they embark on, what stakeholders are invited and expected to do, and how reliable that role will be.

Partnerships need to be based on trust, equality, reciprocity, mutual accountability and mutual benefit. There are fundamental differences between sharing versus personalizing control and benefits; between listening versus imposing relationships; and between creating a shared vision versus winning and losing in a 'business relationship'. All parties face the challenge of understanding the needs and concerns of the others and of cultural and behavioural change in order to create successful partnerships. 'Common objectives or shared interests are obviously the most powerful motives for forming a partnership; but they are not sufficient in themselves. There are other factors which are necessary for both creation and sustainable operation of a partnership. These are trust, respect, ownership and equality. Without trust between people partnership is impossible' (Mohiddin 1998). Trust is promoted when:[14]

- there is a high likelihood that participants will meet again in a similar setting;
- interaction takes place face-to-face in regular meetings over a reasonable period of time and people have a chance to get to know each other;
- participants are able to secure independent expert advice;
- participants are free to question the sincerity of the involved parties;
- stakeholders are involved early on in the decision-making process;
- all available information is made freely accessible to all involved;

- the process of selecting options based on preferences is logical and transparent;
- the decision-making body seriously considers or endorses the outcome of the participation process; and
- stakeholders are given some control of the format of the discourse (agenda, rules, moderation, and decision-making procedure).

For some stakeholders, the issue of collaboration versus co-option has emerged within the context of increasing involvement in dialogues and MSPs at various levels. This is a serious issue, particularly for NGOs whose ability to play their role effectively is largely dependent on their independence. When NGOs participate in MSPs of any kind, they are exposed to the influence of other participants whose political and economic powers might be used to divide or dilute the positions taken by the advocacy community.

We would argue, on the basis that nobody holds the ultimate truth or key to the single best solution, that the attractions and advantages of mutual learning need to be an explicit part of the motivation of people entering an MSP.

Furthermore, in some cases where NGOs are invited to join an MSP, there is reason to suspect that the invitation is extended to ensure a higher degree of legitimization for the process which might not be coupled with the willingness to take NGOs' contributions fully into account. In these cases, such suspicions should be carefully examined and exposed as a lack of seriousness about dialogue and the idea of change.

In this context, Paul Hohnen (2000a, p9) has asserted:

> *To the extent that multi-stakeholder engagement processes sharpen the capacity to define, refine and integrate diverse viewpoints, and bring together the principal actors, they are to be encouraged. Where they tend to ignore, dilute, distort, or otherwise weaken independent viewpoints, they are to be discouraged.*

Transparency

BOX 4.12 TRANSPARENCY

The quality or state of being transparent: something transparent; *especially:* a picture (as on film) viewed by light shining through it or by projection. (*Merriam-Webster's Collegiate Dictionary and Thesaurus*)

MSPs require transparent communication channels. People need to be able to know who is talking to whom, when and about what. Lobbying and bargaining behind the scenes can undermine trust which leads to weakened commitment. On the other hand, decentralized, flexible, and spontaneous communication opportunities are desirable, as informal modes of communication are suitable to build trust and discover commonalities. There is a need to strike a balance between those benefits and the need for transparency.

The procedures and methods of decision-making should be open and transparent so that effective participation is possible. Transparency is based on the free flow of information so that processes, institutions and information are directly accessible to those interested in them.

In the same vein, MSPs need to be as transparent as possible towards the outside. Lack of disclosure of information of any of the aspects, decisions or steps related to an MSP will decrease its credibility and, consequently, its effectiveness. Obscure or unclear structures and processes create an open door to the abuse of processes or accusations of abuse. It is in the interest of an inclusive process to enable participants and non-participants to comment, question and input. MSPs can be designed to include individuals as representatives of stakeholder groups or in their individual capacity.[15]

At every step of an MSP, crucial decisions need to be taken regarding what information should be available to the public, or at least to the core constituencies involved.

Access to information and informed consent

Box 4.13 THE RIO DECLARATION, 1992: PRINCIPLE 10

'Environmental issues are best handled with the participation of all concerned citizens, at the relevant level. At the national level, each individual shall have appropriate access to information concerning the environment that is held by public authorities, including information on hazardous materials and activities in their communities, and the opportunity to participate in decision-making processes. States shall facilitate and encourage public awareness and participation by making information widely available. Effective access to judicial and administrative proceedings, including redress and remedy, shall be provided.'

Disclosure and access to information are a key element of accountability. For MSPs to work, equal access to information for all involved is absolutely essential. Some examples show that there are difficulties providing equal access to information, and in some cases non-participating stakeholders and/or the general public have not been sufficiently informed.

MSPs rely on information-sharing. The principal and most cost-effective strategy is for participants to bring their own information into the process. Developing a common information base is a priority task at the beginning of each MSP and needs to be maintained throughout the process. A common information base does not need to be in one place, but all information needs to be accessible to everyone.

Access to information enables participants to be fully competent partners. As the competence of all involved is an essential fundament of success, it is in the interest of all to allow free and equitable access to information. Financial inequalities need to be levelled to allow for the effective participation of all groups (for example computer equipment and communication budgets).

While disclosure of all relevant information is crucial, there is also a need to consider carefully the means and channels of information dissemination that are being used. For example, some processes we studied have used the Internet for a large proportion or even all of their communication, relying on websites and email. There are numerous and significant advantages of internet-based information dissemination and communication. These include speed, low costs and the ability to interconnect a theoretically unlimited number of people and stakeholder groups. However, in global processes, involving countries and regions with limited internet connectivity, and disadvantaged social and linguistic groups (ethnic minorities,[16] women, the poor), there are huge gaps in access. The digital divide runs alongside traditional divides: between South and North, between women and men, between poor and rich, ethnic minorities and majorities, and so on (UNDP, 1999; UNED Forum, 2000).

Closely linked to access to information is the requirement that those who agree to something must understand its implications and consequences. Any MSP needs to ensure that individuals and the stakeholders they represent fully understand all information exchanged and all decisions they may be asked to make.

This may require making information and suggestions available in the appropriate language. Translations into other languages or translations into non-jargon (non-UNese!) are examples. It seems that this can be a major challenge for some MSPs where stakeholders experienced in such processes need to work with others who are new to them. Scientific research indicates the value-added of such mixed groups, but achieving that requires finding a common language.

This concept also requires everybody involved to ask for explanations in case something is not understood. An open and equitable atmosphere helps people to ask what they might perceive as 'stupid questions'. The general rule should be that 'we're all here to learn'.

Inclusiveness

Box 4.14 Inclusive

Synonyms: all-around, comprehensive, general, global, overall, sweeping; encyclopaedic, comprehensive. (*Merriam-Webster's Collegiate Dictionary and Thesaurus*)

MSPs try to bring the main interest groups into the process of dialogue and/or decision-making and implementation, especially those who are usually left out, such as minority stakeholders, poor people, 'uneducated' people, rural people.[17] In some processes, the public is represented by individuals from organizations who have relevant expertise. In others, it is both logistically possible and more appropriate for the individuals involved to attend meetings in person.

As a general rule, MSPs should be inclusive and not exclusive. 'Exclusion breeds resistance' (Asmal, 2000). Inclusiveness is generally beneficial as it allows all views to be represented and increases the legitimacy and credibility of a process. In structuring an MSP, the question is more 'Have we integrated all the major viewpoints regarding the issue?', rather than 'Do we have all the important players?'. As history has amply demonstrated, major shifts (take universal suffrage) were initially catalysed by a small number of people with a clear vision of how society might be improved.

However, there are also limits to the breadth of inclusiveness. If processes employ selection criteria for participation, these need to be agreed by all those involved. To avoid any suggestion of 'self-selection', the criteria and the reasons for adopting them should be made public, and participants need to be prepared to discuss, defend and change them if necessary.

Size, too, is a functional constraint. If a group is too large there is a risk that it will not be able to hold effective plenary discussions. As a general rule, however, caution should be exercised where exclusion may be involved, and processes need to be developed to deal creatively with the challenge.[18]

Legitimacy

BOX 4.15 LEGITIMACY

The quality or state of being legitimate.

Legitimate: lawfully begotten; *specifically:* born in wedlock: having full filial rights and obligations by birth <a *legitimate* child>: being exactly as purposed: neither spurious nor false: accordant with law or with established legal forms and requirements <a *legitimate* government>: conforming to recognized principles or accepted rules and standards. *Synonym*: lawful, innocent, legal, licit, true, rightful. *Related Words*: cogent, sound, valid; acknowledged, recognized; customary, usual; natural, normal, regular, typical. *Antonym*: illegitimate, arbitrary. (*Merriam-Webster's Collegiate Dictionary and Thesaurus*)

'*Legitimacy* is generally understood as the right to be and to do something in society – a sense that an organization is lawful, admissible and justified in its chosen course of action.' (Edwards 2000, p20)[19]

MSPs need to be perceived as legitimate in order for the process and its outcomes to be accepted by all concerned. Legitimacy is an important resource, especially in largely communication-oriented systems like MSPs. Actors, processes and issues which do not fulfil basic requirements and are not perceived as legitimate will either be ineffective in the long run or at least be vulnerable to undermining by opponents (Neuberger, 1995b).

The fact that MSPs may also create larger coalitions and thus more influence makes the question of their legitimacy all the more important. MSPs and their individual participants need to reflect upon the question of their legitimate role within the governance system, be it at the local, national or international levels. The following are among the preconditions of legitimacy:

- The design of the MSP has been agreed in a democratic, transparent and equitable manner, including the identification of stakeholder groups and participants, the framing of agenda and work plan.[20]
- The majority of those concerned – within and without the process – perceive the process as legitimate; minority views regarding legitimacy are being addressed by the process.
- Participating stakeholders are perceived as having legitimacy.
- The process addresses the question of its own legitimacy and the legitimacy of its participants.

The issue of civil society engagement is both a very important and a difficult point which needs to be addressed within the global governance debate in general and in MSPs in particular. The legitimacy of NGOs, for example, has been raised as a critical point by various actors, in a more or less constructive way (see detailed discussions by Edwards, 1999, 2000). Some of the criticism – for example with regard to democratic decision-making within NGOs or the question of who they effectively represent – can be raised equally with regard to other stakeholder groups such as business associations or trade union federations. For the purpose of the discussion here, we want to underline again that the legitimacy of a process depends on the democratic, transparent and equitable structures that the process as well as its participants operate.

MSPs are meant effectively to give 'a voice, not a vote' (Edwards, 2000, p29), or rather, voices, not votes. This principle, 'structured to give every interest in civil society a fair and equal hearing – is crucial to resolving the tensions that have emerged over NGOs and their role' (ibid). For this principle to be an acceptable guiding line, certain conditions have to be met. Options include certification and self-regulation, and increased equity between various civil society actors (Edwards, 2000). Certification could certainly be a way forward; yet the question of who should govern or control a certifying body remains unsolved. In many cases, NGOs have been developing mechanisms of self-governance to ensure democratic, transparent and truly participatory processes as a basis of their mandate. Some networks have been organizing themselves within frameworks of agreed rules and procedures. Increasing equity will be very important – between different stakeholders, such as business and NGOs, between stakeholder representatives from developing and developed countries, between women and men, rich and poor, ethnic majorities and minorities and Indigenous Peoples, and so on. In international processes, equitable regional representation is particularly important; NGO participation from developing countries needs to increase much more and it needs more predictable, reliable support.

It is also worth noting that a large number of developments which aim to increase the legitimacy of processes has been coming from the NGO community. For example, within the CSD process, the NGO community's preparations (dialogue background papers, selection of participants) are widely considered to be the most transparent. NGO Issue Caucuses' around the CSD also employ measures of additional inclusiveness by taking on input from Major Groups caucuses. The same applied to the preparations for the Bergen Ministerial Dialogues. It is also NGOs who usually have the least problems with publishing their views and (self-)criticism regarding a process.

The legitimacy and credibility of processes and participants also depend on the competence and expertise of the actors involved. Equitable access to information and capacity-building, where necessary, should be provided to ensure competence on all sides.

The involvement of high-level representatives from stakeholder groups also adds legitimacy as these people both represent larger groups and have the authority to implement any outcomes.

The legitimacy of a process also needs to be evaluated in the context of the goals it seeks to achieve. If it is an informing process, where an organization wants to learn about the views of particular stakeholders, the choice of issues and relevant stakeholders and setting the agenda might not, by themselves, raise the question of the legitimacy of the process. If an MSP aims to arrive at decisions on further action, however, the question of who identifies the participants, sets the agenda and so on, becomes crucial to its legitimacy.

Accountability

BOX 4.16 ACCOUNTABILITY

The quality or state of being accountable; *especially:* an obligation or willingness to accept responsibility or to account for one's actions *accountable. Synonyms:* responsible, amenable, answerable, liable. *Contrasted Words:* absolute, arbitrary, autocratic; imperious, magisterial, masterful. (*Merriam-Webster's Collegiate Dictionary and Thesaurus*)

'Accountability simply means that individuals and institutions are answerable for their actions and the consequences that follow them. Democratic accountability means that decision-makers must be answerable to the public, "we the people". Without it, decisions lack legitimacy. Accountability may take many forms, from merely "taking into account", so that those affected by decisions are consulted or considered, to independent inspection, external monitoring, public reporting, judicial review and elections.' (Alexander, 2000)

Titus Alexander (2000) describes accountable decision-making as follows:

> *Accountable decision-making tends to be better, because it takes a wider range of views and experiences into account. Accountable decisions are more likely to be consistent and rule-governed, rather than arbitrary,*

since they are open to challenge and set precedents. Accountability also means that mistakes are reduced, because decision-makers think harder before acting, and when mistakes occur, they are more likely to be spotted and rectified. Public accountability also contributes to greater social stability, since it is easier to identify grievances, correct mistakes or remove officials without massive social upheavals, as occurs in unaccountable political systems.

Box 4.17 Measuring Accountability and Transparency

Charter 99 and the OneWorldTrust, UK, are leading a campaign for greater democratic accountability in international decision-making, arguing that the issues of democracy and accountability at the global level have been neglected. As more and more decisions are taken on the international stage the pressure is increasing to find ways of ensuring that decision-makers are accountable to 'we the peoples'. The new project, the *Charter 99 Global Accountability Index*, addresses these concerns, identifying the key criteria for an international organization to be open, democratic and accountable. Like UNDP's Human Development Index, the new index aims to rank organizations according to the degree they fulfil this criteria. The index is likely to become an important advocacy tool for promoting global democracy. By highlighting good practice, the index will provide clear and practical reform proposals for institutions lacking democratic accountability.

More information about the Global Accountability Index campaign can be found at http://www.charter99.org/, from info@charter99.org or by writing to Charter 99, c/o 18 Northumberland Avenue, London, WC2N 5BJ, UK.

In the context of MSPs, accountability means to employ transparent, democratic mechanisms of engagement, position-finding, decision-making, implementation, monitoring and evaluation. Accountability of all participants towards all is one primary goal of designing and conducting MSPs based on agreements by all stakeholders participating.

Towards non-participating stakeholders and the general public, accountability needs to be ensured by making the process transparent and understandable for everybody. In addition, all those who initiate, facilitate and participate in an MSP should be prepared to engage in open dialogue about it with those seeking to comment or inquire.

Responsibility

BOX 4.18 RESPONSIBILITY

The quality or state of being responsible: moral, legal, or mental account-ability: reliability, trustworthiness: something for which one is responsible: burden.

Responsible: liable to be called on to answer: liable to be called to account as the primary cause, motive, or agent: being the cause or explanation: liable to legal review or in case of fault to penalties: able to answer for one's conduct and obligations: trustworthy: able to choose for oneself between right and wrong: marked by or involving responsibility or accountability: politically answerable; *especially:* required to submit to the electorate if defeated by the legislature – used especially of the British cabinet. *Synonyms*: responsible, answerable, accountable, amenable, liable. (*Merriam-Webster's Collegiate Dictionary and Thesaurus*)

Social Responsibility: 'An organisation's obligation to maximise its positive impact and minimise its negative impact on society.' (The Copenhagen Centre)

'The social responsibility of a the private sector (also referred to as corporate social responsibility) concerns the relationships of a company not just with its clients, suppliers and employees, but also with other groups, and with the needs, values and goals of the society in which it operates . . . social responsibility go beyond compliance with the law, beyond philanthropy, and, one could add, beyond public relations. Corporate social responsibility therefore requires dialogue between companies and their stakeholders.' (UN Secretary General, 2000, A/AC. 253/21, p2)

Stakeholder involvement and meaningful participation are the means to ensure more responsible decisions and actions. MSPs create the space to bring all concerns into the process of planning and decision-making. Relevant information, particularly about possible impacts of decisions, is made available to decision-makers, enabling them to act responsibly, ie to take into account the concerns and effects which might otherwise be not known to them. This can range from realizing that more information needs to be provided to stakeholders, to changing policies, or to overthrowing decisions due to new information.

Within the framework of sustainability, responsible action means to take into account the effects of one's actions with regard to the environment, and economic and social development. It requires active investigation into solutions which will ensure environmental protection, enable healthy and sustained economic growth and increase social equity. Hence, it requires the inclusion in the decision-making process of those who might be affected economically and socially, and those who work to ensure environmental protection, otherwise the necessary expertise will not be available. This cannot be delivered by 'experts' alone. In fact, 'a genuinely democratic society is one in which both experts and nonexperts alike contribute to the understandings . . . that are eventually settled on' (Sampson, 1993, p187).

Industry's role and responsibility is increasingly being addressed, particularly with a view to corporate responsibility, as some businesses explicitly recognize the need to contribute to the good of the communities in which they operate. In many cases, industry's participation in dialogue processes needs to increase and to be based on long-term commitments to work with advocates and those affected by their activities.

Governments' responsibilities include providing an enabling and protective legal and administrative framework for meaningful negotiation of stakeholder agreements, such as between owners of land and natural resources and those seeking access for business purposes. Governments also have responsibilities to support full and equal participation of under-represented groups.

The responsibility for an MSP outcome lies with all those involved – the more equitably the process has been conducted, the more equitably will responsibility be spread.

Ground rules for stakeholder communication

Box 4.19 Communication

An act or instance of transmitting: information communicated: a verbal or written message: a process by which information is exchanged between individuals through a common system of symbols, signs, or behaviour *also* exchange of information or opinions: personal rapport: (plural) a system (as of telephones) for communicating: a technique for expressing ideas effectively (as in speech). *Synonyms*: message, directive, word, contact, commerce, converse, communion, intercommunication, intercourse. Interchange of thoughts or opinions through shared symbols. *Related Words*: exchange, interchange; conversing, discussing, talking; conversation, discussion, talk; advice, intelligence, news, tidings. (*Merriam-Webster's Collegiate Dictionary and Thesaurus*)[21]

Stakeholder participation and cooperation are forms of social interaction. MSPs aim to create space for such interaction that will allow people to *dialogue*. This is not an easy task and for many reasons. Therefore, it seems all the more important to consider carefully which modalities of communication and interaction are desirable for multi-stakeholder processes and to suggest some ground rules.

Many MSPs gather people who often would not even talk to each other, but would begin – and end – with arguing.[22] Sustainable development requires dialogue and forging collaboration and partnership wherever possible. Many of the decisions we face in the years ahead demand that we find ways to listen to opposing points of view, find ways to accommodate deeply held and differing values and satisfy opposing interests. Traditional systems of governance and decision-making tend to repeat the pattern of domination that has characterized most societies throughout history: men have dominated women; one ethnic group has dominated another; the rich have dominated the poor; and nations have dominated nations. Conventional communication and decision-making mechanisms in what Deborah Tannen (1998) has labelled our 'argument culture' tend to exclude rather than include diverse interests, focusing on two opposite sides rather than a multitudes of views. They are not designed to cope well with the complexity of sustainability issues.

In contrast, MSPs bring together stakeholders of very different cultures. Corporations, for example, follow the principles of profit-orientation and the protection of intellectual property, efficiency and speed, while many NGOs promote the principles of equity, sharing, participation and the protection of vulnerable groups, and do not see market mechanisms as the fundamental basis of societies and their development. MSPs need to employ ground rules of communication that allow clarification of cultural differences, differences in the understanding of values and information, and help to integrate them in relation to a particular issue.

Another major issue is the challenge of dealing with *power gaps* between stakeholder groups. They clearly exist and need to be dealt with, including through the appropriate modes of communication. Minorities are at a specific disadvantage.[23] Research on group dynamics has shown that minorities are less listened to and are more often interrupted; that minority members tend to speak less and that their contributions are taken less seriously. Powerful stakeholders and their representatives often find it difficult to 'take a back seat'. Particularly in traditional international fora governments, donor agencies and business representatives show difficulty in listening to other stakeholders such as NGOs, women's groups and Indigenous Peoples.[24] For the sake of equity, fairness and justice, but also for the sake of allowing real ownership of the process to develop on all sides, it is essential that everyone involved should be given genuine access and employ equitable modes of communication. Ensuring this is also an important part of the role of facilitator of an MSP, and dialogue aimed at mutual understanding is one of the best modes of communication.

But how do we communicate best when we present our views, dialogue, or consensus-build? How do we deal with power gaps between different stakeholder groups? What practical mechanisms, attitudes and individual behaviour are required to ensure the potential benefits of stakeholder communication?

There are a great number of sources for guidance on the conduct of successful dialogue and consensus-building, including social scientific research (see Chapter 6); philosophical models; standards of qualitative research methodology, and models used by faith communities, to name but a few. They provide a basis for practical conclusions about the appropriate size of consulting groups, and successful ways of chairing, facilitating and structuring meetings. They also address aspects of individual attitude and behaviour which promote dialogue and successful consensus-building. Below, we summarize a few of the most interesting examples. The choice is subjective, but has been guided by their close relevance to the needs of the MSP approach.

First, Jürgen Habermas (eg 1984, 1989), a German philosopher and dominant figure in the tradition of critical theory, developed a framework called the 'ideal speech situation'.[25] It is an attempt to describe the presuppositions that discourse participants must hold before *communication without coercion* can prosper. Habermas defines four conditions of discourse:

1   All potential participants of a discourse must have the same chance to employ communicative speech acts.[26] Everybody needs to have the same chance to speak.
2   All discourse participants must have the same chance to interpret, claim or assert, recommend, explain, and put forth justifications; and contest, justify, or refute any validity claim.[27] Everybody needs to be free to challenge whether what has been said can be verified.
3   The only speakers permitted in the discourse are those who have the same chance to employ representative speech acts: everybody needs to have the same chance to contribute to the issue at hand.
4   The only speakers permitted in the discourse are those who have the same chance to employ regulatory speech acts: everybody needs to have the same chance to contribute to the process of communication.

These conditions can be thought of as 'rules for discourse'. Participants abiding by these rules will produce an agreement (or at least understanding) based on rational arguments, as opposed to one created through manipulation and coercion. Habermas' normative theory outlines an unconstrained model of discourse, where values and norms can be discussed and agreed upon, free of coercion.

Dietz (2001) has used Habermas' approach to define the criteria of 'better decisions', considering 'a good decision as one that:

1 makes full use of available information about the facts of the situation and about people's values;
2 allows all those affected by a decision to have a say;
3 takes account of the strengths of individual and group information and decision-making; and
4 provides individuals and society with a chance to learn from the decisions'.[28]

Second, standards of qualitative research methodology are a useful resource when trying to design a situation of productive dialogue (eg Sommer, 1987). Developed through empirical research experiences in psychology and sociology, they are designed to create a communication situation where researchers will be able most successfully to obtain data from research participants (interviewees). Some general, practical rules have been established:

• The researcher enters into the dialogue/interview with a respectful, non-judgemental attitude.
• Interviewees/participants are presented with rather open questions.
• Interviewees/participants are allowed to impact the agenda/questionnaire and to decline answering questions.
• Interviewers react flexibly to the information given, leaving defining the course of the interview to the interaction of those involved rather than prescribing a set agenda.
• Every finding is fed back to research participants, including for further comments; finalizing a research outcome depends on agreement from all involved.

Third, there are models used by faith communities, eg the Bahá'í model of 'consultation'.[29] Individual development involves investigating the 'truth' for oneself.[30] Continual reflection, based on experience in applying this truth, is critical to the process of individual (spiritual) development. For collective investigation of the truth and group decision-making, consultation, which draws on the strength of the group and fosters unity of purpose and action, is indispensable. Consultation plays a major role in Bahá'í communities because it is seen as the only way to get all relevant expertise to the table, to come to consensus about future action and to create the commitment to implement solutions. The basic assumption is that no member of a community has some kind of exclusive access to the 'truth' (see note 30), and that everybody's subjective views and knowledge have to be integrated in order to achieve the best results. Bahá'í communities and elected assemblies conduct consultations on the basis of detailed rules – for example the rule of honesty; openness and not holding back any views; group ownership of any ideas; striving for consensus if possible and voting if there is no consensus.[31]

BOX 4.20 CONSENSUS-BUILDING?

One commentator contributed an example illustrating how inappropriately some people deal with consensus-building. A person, supposedly funding and running a consensus process, was heard to reply when asked how the process was going, 'We've nearly convinced them, the bastards.'

Seeking consensus 'requires that individuals not hold fast to personal opinions simply in order to have their views prevail. Instead, they must approach matters with a genuine desire to determine the right course of action. If consensus cannot be achieved, the majority vote of a quorum prevails, and the decision is equally valid and binding' (US Bahá'í Community).

With regard to openness, Bahá'ís assert that the clashing of diverse views will spark off the best ideas whereas holding back one's views is counterproductive. People are encouraged to air their opinions even if an individual is the only one with an opposing view.

Interestingly, this coincides with the kind of advice that the acclaimed management expert Peter Drucker (1967) offers the decision-making executive:

> *... disagreement alone can provide alternatives to a decision ... There is always a high possibility that a decision will prove wrong – either because it was wrong to begin with or because a change in circumstances makes it wrong. If one has thought through alternatives during the decision-making process, one has something to fall back on, something that has already been thought through.* (p153)

> *Above all, disagreement is needed to stimulate the imagination. One does not, to be sure, need imagination to find the right answer to a problem. But then*

> *this is of value only in mathematics. In all matters of*
> *true uncertainty . . . one needs creative solutions which*
> *create a new situation. And this means that one needs*
> *imagination – a new and different way of perceiving*
> *and understanding.* (p155)

There are, of course, many more guidelines being employed by faith communities which we are unable to outline here. They all stress the importance of a moral attitude and prioritizing of the common good over self-interest. They promote love and respect for the human being, no matter if they be friend or foe, and maintain that mutual trust and respect depend on a basic attitude of tolerance.

The bases for ground rules of stakeholder communication outlined above are meant to be just that: fundaments or ideals. We do not believe that an 'ideal speech situation' or indeed perfect selflessness and devotion to a community can be achieved. Nor can any researcher be completely open and non-suggestive. The concepts are rather meant as ideal rules which, if adopted as objectives by participants, help to create a situation which is more likely to generate successful dialogue and consensus.

Some aspects of the different normative systems outlined above are contradictory as regards the practical recommendations that emerge from them. For example, one of the main reasons for using Habermas' theory as a basis for developing criteria of appropriate modes of stakeholder communication, is its fundamental link to the concept of *individual autonomy*:

> *In the tradition of critical theory . . . individuals ought*
> *to be free of all forms of domination. Once they are*
> *free, people are able to enter into social relations that*
> *encourage personal development as well as social and*
> *cultural reproduction. The key is critical self-reflection.*
> *Habermas promotes introspection among free and*
> *autonomous beings so that they will think about the*
> *type of society that they want, before committing to new*
> *relations.* (Renn et al, 1995, p9)

However, some have argued that this concept is specific to the Western, Anglo-Saxon cultural context and there is indeed empirical evidence supporting this view (eg Triandis, 1989, 1995; see discussion in Chapter 6). Different cultures have different understandings of identity and priorities for the individual. For example, in more collectivistic cultures, we will not begin by looking at self-reflection, individual societal ideals and their impact on the individual choices people make as regards their social relations. Rather, we will start by looking at what the collective tradition and culture identifies as benefiting the collective and where it should be going. That will include shared norms of behaviour for the individual who is expected to make the best possible contribution to the collective and its goals, effectively placing the priorities of the collective above those of the individual.

The notion of individual versus collectivistic cultures affects, for example, the second condition that Habermas puts forward: that everybody should be able to address the question of other participants' claim to validity. In societies with strong collectivistic norms, such open questioning of individuals may not be appropriate. The condition also contradicts other normative systems' rules of not openly questioning the honesty of dialogue partners as this is seen as undermining the building of trust within the group. Accordingly, in our conclusions towards practical guidelines to designing MSPs (Chapter 8), we have suggested different options. Choices will depend on the respective cultural contexts and individual participants. Quite specific answers to these questions will have to be found in each process, through dialogue and experimentation.

BOX 4.21 'PARTING THE WATERS' IN THE DEBATE OVER DAMS

'Starting on December 10, 1998, two hundred pro- and anti-dam forces from Pakistan, India, Bangladesh and Nepal converged upon our first meeting in Colombo, with a real potential to explode. Instead, we sat the protagonists opposite each other and asked them to explain to the Commission, in words of one syllable, their opposing perceptions. First, that dams, if done right, are critical tools for governments to use. Second, that over-centralised planning can devastate nature, cut off water that had been the lifeblood of villages for generations, and flood religious and cultural sites and homes with minimal concern for those affected. To be sure, there were heated moments. Government officials spoke passionately of growing populations, increasing demands for food, power and drinking water, national development goals and their responsibility to the people. Affected peoples responded equally passionately of their villages destroyed, resettlement in inadequate sites and the impersonal nature of the State when faced with real people living real lives with little food security and real livelihood risks. For three full days they talked. We listened. We absorbed a clash of perspectives. And we built on common ground, noting and respecting divergences. We made progress if only due to the fact that people felt they finally had the chance to put their case in a neutral arena, and that the Commission had listened to all sides. No crackdowns. No arrests.

But perhaps that was just beginner's luck.

In São Paolo, Brazil, on August 11, 1999 we had no sooner banged the gavel than word came that our meeting would quickly be overrun by nearly a thousand people who had been displaced by dams in Brazil. They had not been invited, but were moments away. Should we contact the police? Disband? Instead, we welcomed most of them inside, while the rest queued peacefully, sat listening to the debate and departed as quietly as they had come, their points made, listened to, and documented.

In Cairo, December 8, 1999 we had to grapple with the delicate Middle Eastern politics of trans-boundary waters between Turkey and Syria, Jordan and Israel, and even protests from people directly affected by dams financed in large part by South Africa where I was Minister for water affairs. Again, we left unscathed, having brought both sides closer together.'

(Kader Asmal, Chair of the World Commission on Dams, 2000)

5

The Research: Effective Communication and Decision-making in Diverse Groups

By Jasmin Enayati[1]

INTRODUCTION

The purpose of this chapter is to review relevant bodies of scientific research. It is particularly the areas of social and organizational psychology that provide information on how to design multi-stakeholder processes. Studying the findings on effective decision-making processes in groups of high diversity gives our suggestions theoretical and empirical basis.

We will start by looking at some basic findings of social and organizational psychology. Although we have included reviewing some 'popular' management literature, most research in this area is conducted in isolated laboratory settings as a means of controlling the multiple conditions of 'real life' social processes. This enables conclusions about a single phenomenon or factor but can impede more general conclusions. That is why we have mostly used sources which assemble the knowledge gained in large numbers of experiments and studies.

It is particularly noteworthy that, while there is an extensive body of research in the area of social psychology[2] into group processes, group dynamics, communication and decision-making within groups, there is hardly any research (yet) into the specifics of multi-stakeholder processes. Intergroup cooperation and conflict in realistic settings has been addressed by organizational psychology, however, with a clear focus on team-based, often hierarchical structures within corporations.

These function under conditions which are in many ways different from those in multi-stakeholder processes, where representatives from different sectors of society aim to discuss or collaborate on a certain issue for a certain period in time. Therefore, some of the research findings reported here can be transferred only to a certain extent.

Clarifying the impact of diversity on communication patterns and decision-making processes will lead us to examining the impact of various methods for achieving consensus. We will explore different forms of diversity, such as gender and ethnicity in more detail and look at the consequences of these and other differences, such as status and power, on effective decision-making and implementation. The chapter will conclude by looking at the role of leadership, mediation and interactive conflict resolution as a means of assisting diverse groups in achieving their full potential.

The intention is to make the information obtained in existing research accessible, relevant and applicable to multi-stakeholder processes. The suggested analytical framework for multi-stakeholder processes has been checked against these findings.

OVERVIEW OF FINDINGS

Diversity and its impact on decision-making

The increasing popularity of group-based decision-making reflects a widely shared belief that group decision-making offers the potential to achieve outcomes that could not be achieved by individuals working in isolation. Diverse perspectives allegedly are beneficial to decision-making processes. Members with diverse perspectives are supposed to:

- provide the group with a comprehensive view of possible issues on the agenda, including both opportunities and threats; and
- alternative interpretations of the information gathered and creative courses of action and solutions that integrate the diverse perspectives (Triandis et al, 1965).

Diverse groups offer immense potential for increased quality of group performance and innovative decision-making (Jackson, 1996; Seibold, 1999; Phillips and Wood, 1984; Pavitt, 1993). The direct involvement in the decision-making process is likely to lead to a change of norms and to individual commitment. However, benefits from decision-making groups are not automatic.

Stereotyping

When analysing the potential problems that can emerge through diversity in decision-making groups from a social psychological perspective, *stereotyping* is of particular importance. A social stereotype is 'a set of beliefs about the personal attributes of a group of people' (Ashmore and DelBoca 1986, p16). Such sets of beliefs are being 'activated' (that is start influencing perception in a given situation) through identifying the group membership of a person. In other words, once we identify a person as a woman, for example, our stereotypical beliefs about women in general will influence our perception and judgement towards that person.

It is important to note that stereotyping is not some 'bad habit'; it is inherent in our cognitive processes. It makes our perception quicker and more economic; we simply cannot meet everybody as a completely 'new person', a blank sheet. Nor are stereotypes necessarily completely wrong. Having our perceptions and expectations shaped through stereotyping can indeed have positive social effects. For example, when we meet an elderly person, we might take into account that they cannot walk very quickly and, somewhat 'automatically', walk at a slower pace. For many elderly people, this might be annoying as they do not have a problem keeping up, but for others, it will be a friendly gesture.

Once stereotypical beliefs come into play in the cognitive process, they affect people's perception, attitude and behaviour. The impact of stereotyping can increase in difficult decision-making processes when strong emotions like anxiety, irritation or anger arise and overshadow our judgement (Mackie and Hamilton, 1993). However, contact with members of the stereotyped group might be the first step in overcoming stereotyping if it happens repeatedly and with more than one – typical – group member (Pettigrew, 1989). In many cases, the best strategy in order to overcome prejudice has proved to engage both groups in a common activity – working together, particularly if the activity is successful, can significantly contribute to reducing prejudice and improve relations between different groups (Sherif and Sherif, 1953; Smith and Mackie 2000).[3]

As discussed, stereotyping does not necessarily imply negative evaluation but often it does, and then it implies social prejudice (negative attitudes) and discrimination (negative behaviour): a person is judged negatively merely because they belong to a certain social group. Impacts on behaviour can include avoidance, exclusion, fear and aggression. It is important to note that being discriminated against can elicit 'counter-discrimination' and hence further increase distance between social groups (Hemmati et al, 1999).

Overcoming stereotyping and prejudice is therefore an important component of successful processes with groups of high diversity.

Group composition

The composition of diverse groups has implications for:

- problem-solving and decision-making processes;
- the development of status hierarchies;
- patterns of participation and communication;
- the development of cohesiveness; and
- the group's ability to perform and implement decisions (Jackson, 1996).

In practice, diverse decision-making teams have often not achieved their potential. The interaction problems associated with diversity often lead to lower performance than if the group had fewer resources. The need for the integration of diversity is great (Maznevski, 1994).

Diverse groups are designed to differ with regard to various characteristics, such as the demographic composition of the group, for example gender, age and ethnicity; educational and occupational background; knowledge and area of expertise; attitudes and values; as well as status and power – or, in the case of multi-stakeholder processes, they differ with regard to a mix of those characteristics. An additional facet to diversity in groups is specified by Belbin (1993). Based on training experience with management teams, he distinguishes nine functional team roles that contribute to the effective performance of decision-making teams: plant, resource investigator, coordinator, shaper, monitor evaluator, team worker, implementer, specialist, completer and perfectionist. Optimal group composition is given when all roles are represented, leading to a high degree of compatibility within the team (for a further discussion see Beck et al, 1999).

In the context of groups consisting of representatives from various stakeholder groups, Belbin's approach cannot easily provide us with pragmatic recommendations. However, his categories of team roles make a strong point about the significance of diversity in appreciating personal and functional differences. Differences provide a space to build on each other's strengths and can be a means to reduce competition and enable cooperation.

There is, it should be said, some ambiguity about the importance of group composition. Group composition can be seen as an important determinant of the performance of a group. However, group composition is also merely a determinant of the resources available to a group.

Studies on task- or expertise-based status have received little empirical attention. An interesting phenomenon observed within groups composed of experts and relative novices is the 'assembly bonus effect' which occurs when both experts and non-experts perform better within the team context than they would alone (Shaw, 1981). One explanation for this effect is that experts learn during interactions with non-experts because of a need to clarify assumptions they automatically make when dealing with issues in their domain of expertise. Findings such as these suggest that performance is enhanced when both experts and novices are represented in one problem-solving group (Jackson, 1996).

The implications of diversity are far-reaching in the way that members of a group process information, make decisions and implement them. No single theory explains the complex relationship between the different dimensions of diversity and its possible consequences on effective performance of the group, such as communication patterns within a group, communication across group boundaries, cohesiveness, and so on. A variety of perspectives have guided the studies, including Social Identity Theory (Tajfel and Turner, 1979; Turner et al, 1987)[4] and research on management composition (Hambrick, 1994).

The following section describes some of the consequences of diversity in more detail.

Communication and decision-making in groups

Communication is an essential process in the development of group culture. The type of communication structure determines leadership, roles and the status hierarchy within the group; group morale and cohesiveness; and it limits or enhances productivity (Hare, 1992).

The balance between task-focused and socio-emotional communication is crucial if a group is to be effective. Different types of communication are needed for different tasks. If a group's task is relatively simple, a centralized communication network in which interaction between members is limited, tends to increase effectiveness. Complex problem-solving is facilitated by decentralized communication networks (Shaw, 1981). As recommended by Wheelan (1994, p33), the choice of a communication network might be more effective if strategies of decision-making were outlined in advance and if urges to stabilize the structure too early were resisted, as there is considerable resistance to change once these structures are established. Awareness of these issues is usually low and it is one of the tasks of the group leader or facilitator to bring them to the group's attention. It is notable that a decentralized communication network does not exclude the existence of a group leader (see discussion below).

Communication standards, and thus performance, are raised if the group has clear, performance-oriented goals; an appropriate task strategy; and a clear set of rules; fairly high tolerance for intermember conflicts and explicit communication feedback to ensure that information is understood (Maznewski, 1994, p532).

SOCIAL INFLUENCE

Decision-making is not simply rational information-gathering (Jackson, 1996). For example, information held by only one member of the group is often ignored. Research on social influence and conformity indicates the value of having on a team at least two people who agree on an answer. The well-known social influence studies are the classic experiments by Salomon Asch, who asked people in a group to judge line length after hearing the erroneous judgements of several other people. This research revealed that when a person's private judgement was unlike the judgements expressed by others, they soon abandoned their own judgement, even when their answer was verifiably correct. However, in the presence of just one other person who agreed with them, people persevered in the face of opposition (Asch, 1951, 1956).

Also, just as an individual is likely to lack confidence, the team may lack confidence that, in an ambiguous situation, a deviant opinion could be correct. This is particularly true if the individual with the correct answer is of relatively low status. Such evidence suggests that for diverse groups to fulfil their potential, group members should have overlapping areas of expertise, instead of a sole expert for each relevant knowledge domain (Jackson, 1996).

As demonstrated by a substantial body of research (Seibold, 1999), applying formal procedures might control the potential problems of 'free' group discussions. Formal procedures offer various models to decrease social influence which can undermine the value of contributions from low status members, as described above, and facilitate effective group discussions (see the discussion of various procedures).

CONFORMITY PRESSURE

If individual members of a group initially have opposing views on an issue and the number of supporters on both sides are (more or less) evenly split, the communication process usually results in compromise (Wetherall, 1987). Through processes of social influence, the position reflected in the final decision becomes more moderate, an effect called 'depolarization'. Divergence between a final decision and member views is generated. This process can reduce the motivation of individual members to participate up to their capacity in group decision-making, thus reducing the chances that decisions will reflect their views (Latane et al, 1979).

A consensus cannot be trusted if it arises from reliance on others' positions without careful consideration of contamination by shared biases,[5] based on the belief that we can better trust a consensus because multiple individuals have reached the same conclusion, particularly if these individuals differ significantly in a relevant variable. Public conformity, defined as people behaving consistently with norms they do not privately accept as correct, can potentially undermine true consensus. Such a consensus only offers the illusion of unanimity.

A series of experiments claiming the exact opposite to research findings on conformity had a big impact on the field of group dynamics.

GROUP POLARIZATION

When a majority of the group initially leans towards one position, their consensus tends to influence others in the group that hold a more moderate position. Both their positions and arguments make a polarization of group positions more likely, leading to a more extreme position. The consensus makes the majority arguments more persuasive: they are more numerous, receive more space for discussion and are usually presented in a more compelling fashion, as members of the majority use a less cautious style of advocacy. Thus, majority viewpoints are reinforced and advocates of the minority viewpoint are won over. Group interaction moves the group's average position in the direction favoured by the majority initially or to an even more extreme position. Group polarization towards a more extreme pole can be the consequence (Moscovici and Zavalloni, 1969).

An additional explanation is based on Festinger's social comparison theory (1954) which proposes that polarization is caused by group members competing with one another to endorse the socially most desirable viewpoints. Agreeing with a consensus (or going even beyond that) fulfils people's desire for holding the 'correct' views.

Almost all the studies in which polarization has been found were conducted in laboratory settings with ad hoc groups in which the outcome was almost always hypothetical. In naturalistic settings the polarization effect is less consistent. An explanation for these discrepancies might be that more permanent bodies establish norms about the communication structure which might inhibit polarization (Brown, 2000).

Consensus-building

Making a decision by establishing consensus rather than some voting procedure typically increases the effectiveness of decisions – that is, decisions that have a high potential to be implemented in due course. Effective groups have a sound commitment to a clear goal and a combination of members' personalities, skills and roles, their morale and appropriate experience (McGrath, 1984).

Productivity of the group is increased if group members have a communication network that allows for maximum communication. Leavitt (1972) (see Hare, 1982, p33) emphasized that 'if the group's problem require that every member carry out of the group a desire to act positively on the group's decision, then it is imperative that every one accept, both consciously and unconsciously, the decision reached by the group'.

Dialogue practitioner Hare (1982) has produced a set of guidelines for the consensus method, based on Quaker and Gandhian principles and results from laboratory experiments that have demonstrated the advantages of consensus over majority votes:

1   Participants are urged to seek a solution that incorporates all viewpoints.
2   Participants must argue on a logical basis, giving their own opinion while seeking out differences.
3   Participants are asked to address the group as a whole, while showing concern for each point of view, rather than confronting and criticizing individuals.
4   A group coordinator is useful to help formulate consensus.
5   It is essential not to press for agreement, but to hold more meetings if necessary and to share responsibility in the group for the implementation of the consensus (Hare, 1982).

Effective leadership (see below) can also be crucial for achieving consensus. Maier (1970) suggests a list of nine principles for the discussion leader to take into account:

1   Success in problem-solving requires that effort be directed toward overcoming surmountable obstacles.
2   Available facts should be used even when they are inadequate.
3   The starting point of a problem is richest in solution possibilities.
4   Problem-mindedness should be increased while solution-mindedness is delayed.
5   Disagreement can either lead to hard feelings or to innovation, depending on the discussion leadership.

6   The 'idea-getting' process should be separated from the 'idea-evaluation' process because the latter inhibits the former.
7   Choice-situations should be turned into problem-situations (a choice between two alternatives directs the energy towards making a choice and thus detracts from the search for additional/innovative alternatives).
8   Problem situations should be turned into choice situations. (Problem situations tend to block behaviour – the discovery of the first possibility tends to terminate the search for alternative and often better and innovative solutions. Decision-making requires both choice behaviour and problem-solving behaviour. It is desirable to capitalize on the differences and thereby upgrade each.)
9   Solutions suggested by the leader are improperly evaluated and tend either to be accepted or rejected.

MINORITY INFLUENCE

Minorities can influence the consensus reached by a majority in a group if they turn the processes of social influence to their own advantage. According to Moscovici and Lage (1976) and Moscovici (1980), a minority can undermine confidence in the majority consensus if they agree among themselves, remain consistent over time and offer a positive social identity, in other words being a member of a group that is highly regarded in the respective society with implications on individual self-esteem and behaviour. However, the minority's consistency may be interpreted as rigidity if it is taken too far and may thus be ineffective. Moscovici suggests that minority dissent promotes a systematic processing of information as the minority's suggested alternatives create uncertainty about reality as interpreted by the majority which in turn stimulates deeper reflection among majority members. More systematic processing can lead to private acceptance of attitude change but not necessarily to overt agreement with the minority.

Integrating mechanisms of communication

Faced with the complex consequences of group diversity, groups should adopt the mode of 'learning organizations', that is action should be based on available knowledge and take into account new knowledge generated in the process (Dodgson, 1993; Starbuck, 1983). For an effective decision-making process it is essential to construct a view of the negotiation process that is shared by all participants (Maznevski, 1994, p539).[6]

Group members should be made aware by the facilitating body of the communication process and of the role of communication in group performance. In addition, group members should be provided with specific information on the effects of the types of diversity that are relevant to their group. Understanding differences is the first step to managing them synergistically – acknowledging that the result of a cooperative effort between different parties can produce a stronger outcome than parties working in separation.

These findings refer to a need for meta-communication: space for communicating about the way the group communicates. Members of decision-making groups can improve their effectiveness by satisfying the preconditions for communication. Therefore, they should be provided with specific information on the effects of diversity on communication to understand effective and ineffective communication behaviours (Maznevski, 1994).

COHESIVENESS

An inherent feature of decision-making processes in diverse groups is the expression and discussion of alternative or conflicting opinions and perspectives. Exposure to alternative views allegedly improves the learning process of the group and the quality of argumentation. However, dissent and disagreement often arouse negative emotional reactions, impeding the problem-solving process (Nemeth and Staw, 1989).

For decision-making groups, studies of how positive feelings influence negotiations are of particular interest. Group dynamics[7] stresses the role of cohesiveness – the result of the feeling of mutual regard and the commitment to the group and its activities. Without cohesiveness, the group will fall apart. It may translate into greater motivation to contribute and perform well as a means of gaining approval and recognition and thus lead to greater productivity of the group as a whole (Festinger et al, 1950). Emotions are likely to be particularly beneficial for improving performance where flexible and creative thinking can lead to more effective resolutions than compromise (Jackson, 1996). A very high degree of cohesiveness, on the other hand, can have harmful effects.

Groupthink

When loyalty as a correlate of cohesiveness becomes the paramount aim, when groups become more concerned with reaching consensus than with making the right decision, 'groupthink' can be the result. Irving Janis (1972, 1982) applied the term groupthink to situations in which the drive to reach consensus at any cost outweighs the desire to assess adequately alternative courses of action and thus interferes with effective decision-making. The implementation of decisions is threatened.

There are several ways that might prevent groupthink without losing the benefit of cohesiveness (Janis, 1982; Smith, 1996). First, to ensure adequate consideration of alternatives, open enquiry and dissent should be actively encouraged. 'Devil's advocates' could be appointed to ensure that weaknesses in the group's favoured decision are pointed out and that the opposing views are heard. Second, outsiders can be brought in to validate the group's decision and look out for shared biases. Different groups with different perspectives could work simultaneously on the same problem or the group could break into subgroups that take different points of view. Third, to reduce conformity pressure, public votes should be the exception rather than the rule. The role of the leader should be minimized, and the expression of objections and doubts should be encouraged.

However, some of these solutions might prove impractical due to a lack of resources. Also, some of these 'solutions' might again have undesirable and corrosive side effects such as prolonged debates, damaged feelings caused by too open criticisms or a lack of loyalty to the final decision due to break-up groups. This discussion shows again some of the complexities of group dynamics. As discussed above, a learning approach should be adopted to account for the idiosyncrasies of each situation and specific group composition. Meta-communication should be encouraged to make group members aware of underlying group processes and possible implications.

Forms of diversity

When intergroup contact is established, pre-existing categories of, say, ethnicity or gender are likely to be overlaid by other dimensions of categorization – for example, the new emerging category of a working group. Cooperation provides repeated opportunity to challenge certain stereotypes. Doise (1978) has argued that discrimination with regard to the original category will be reduced. A common identity becomes salient, that is more prominent, subsuming the – often problematic – division. This form of recategorization might be a crucial step in achieving a general attitude change (Brown, 2000, p344).

Gender, age and ethnic group membership are the most salient characteristics of a person. Therefore, these characteristics have a relatively great impact on how we perceive and explain people's behaviour. The same behaviour can be perceived differently if shown by a man or a woman, a young or an old person, a white or a black person. Hence, categories of ethnicity, age and gender in decision-making groups are high-impact categories. This impact is enhanced even further as members of minorities are usually underrepresented in decision-making groups (women, Indigenous Peoples, black Americans in the US, youth, among others). This effect may reinforce the impact of stereotypes on people's perception and judgement so that the behaviour and opinions of stereotypes is perceived even more to be the result of their being female, black, young, and so on (eg Ashmore and DelBoca, 1986).

The goal of understanding multicultural and gender-specific group processes is both to maximize advantages such as multiple perspectives and creativity, and to minimize weaknesses such as mistrust and miscommunication.

GENDER DIFFERENCES

Despite the fact that women are said to perform a more integrating style of communication and leadership than men and often act as 'informal peacemakers' in cases of organizational conflict (Kolb, 1992), in many cases they are not in a position to fulfil their potential in decision-making groups. We have to consider a multitude of factors to understand this seeming contradiction.

Prejudice against women is one of the main factors. According to stereotypic beliefs women are less competent in management qualities such as initiative, strategic thinking, tactical skills, assertiveness and authority. In addition, the stereotypic belief about women being emotional possibly causes men to mistrust women and expect them not stay calm and rational in critical situations. Stereotypic beliefs that women are unpredictable and therefore less trustworthy are equally harmful (Kuepper, 1994; Hemmati, 2000b).

Numerous psychological studies have demonstrated differences between women and men with regard to their communicative behaviour and their styles of collaboration in groups (Dion, 1985). However, differences in the overt behaviour of women and men are less prevalent than stereotypes might suggest. This is also true for men's and women's leadership behaviour (Friedel-Howe, 1990; Rustemeyer, 1988).

In gender-mixed meetings, women speak less often and more briefly, interrupt others less, and are interrupted more often. Women express their feelings more often than men who show a rather factual, technical and unemotional style of communication (Dion, 1985). This does not mean that women are in fact more emotional, but it can be a reason why they are less likely to be perceived as skilful and self-controlled strategists. The tendency of women to behave less competitively in groups often makes their contributions seem less important. Men are often more visible in teams because they tend spontaneously to take a leading role.

It has also been shown that the same kind of behaviour will be judged as perfectly 'normal' and 'acceptable' when shown by a man but will be judged differently when exhibited by a woman – not only will it be perceived as non-feminine but also as more extreme in its aggressiveness or assertiveness (Friedel-Howe, 1990; Ashmore and DelBoca, 1986; Wintermantel, 1993).

Women and men also differ with regard to resources of power and ways of exercising power. Female strategies of exercising power are usually indirect. In organizational or micropolitics women often employ 'soft' strategies such as showing friendliness, empathy, sympathy and loyalty or demonstrating devotion (Dick, 1993). These behavioural responses, however, are not very functional in order to succeed as well as having success attributed to oneself (Hemmati, 2000b).

CREATING EFFECTIVE GENDER-BALANCED GROUPS

The dynamics in the communication process of the diverse groups described above may lead to experiences of exclusion, having effects on the quality of instrumental exchanges, self-censorship and withdrawal (Elsass and Graves, 1997). Vital information may become lost in the process as judgements may not be expressed.

The salience of social categories – for example, demographic characteristics such as gender – is dependent on the context and the proportion of representatives in a group. One way to realize that the category of gender loses some of its salience so that women are less associated with gender stereotypes is to raise the percentage of women involved above the 'critical level' of about 15–20 per cent (Friedel-Howe, 1990; Wintermantel, 1993). This rule-of-thumb also applies to other social categories/minorities.

However, group members do not belong just to one but to multiple relevant categories. Social categories overlap. Depending on the context, a different category apart from gender might come to the fore and thus influence the perception and judgement of other group members.

CULTURAL DIVERSITY

As stated above, group membership does not exist in a vacuum, but depends on the cultural context. Hofstede (1980, 1991) defines culture as 'the collective programming of the mind, which distinguishes the members of one human group from another' (1980, p1). Until recently, social psychological research into small groups has been conducted mostly in North America (and other Western societies) with the assumption, usually implicit, that findings are representative of other cultures. A focus on cultural diversity within North American society as well as experiences of an increasing number of international work groups in the organizational context have revealed this cultural bias more clearly.

According to Hofstede's results, the US is the most individualistic nation in a study comparing 53 nations and thus is the most atypical nation (Smith and Noakes, 1996). Individualism, Collectivism and Power Distance have been identified as key dimensions that describe differences between cultures in social behaviour patterns.

Power Distance indicates the degree of maintaining a respectful distance from superiors to having more informal and equal relationships with superiors (Smith and Noakes, 1996, p480).

Groups in collectivist cultures are more concerned with long-term commitment, are more deferential towards authority and are more concerned with harmony in the group, but are just as competitive with the outside (Triandis, 1989, 1995). Collectivist or interdependent cultures, like most in Asia, South America and Africa, foster and reinforce views of the self in group terms (Markus et al, 1997). People from these cultures tend to see themselves as members of larger groups. In contrast, people in more individualistic cultures think of themselves in more idiosyncratic terms.

It is important to note that NGOs, business and industry, Indigenous Peoples, trade unions and the like are also 'cultures' (see Hofstede's definition above) which (can) differ with regard to these characteristics. Multi-stakeholder processes are ones of cultural diversity.

Another view of culture that can be helpful in working with MSPs conceives of culture as 'the way we do things around here'. Members of a culture understand those ways and generally honour them, although without necessarily being conscious of doing so. Since MSPs bring people with different cultural orientations into interaction with one another, sensitivity to cultural differences is essential. More precisely, cultural sensitivity involves awareness of norms (standards of behaviour) and beliefs (assumptions about the way things are) and values (standards of importance) on which the cultural norms are based.

CREATING EFFECTIVE CULTURALLY DIVERSE GROUPS

In addition to the dilemmas facing monocultural groups, multicultural groups initially must overcome language problems and differing understandings of how to get to know one another. At a later stage, alliances of those who share cultural norms may form, which may impede effective decision-making. Reliance on stereotyped expectations also will be strongest during the early phase of group development. The challenge for the group is to move beyond stereotypical expectations, enabling individuals to become more aware of their own and others' assumptions and to use the information given. This process will be impeded if some team members experience their status (for example national or stakeholder group) as being privileged over others, thereby determining whose opinions are sought and acted upon. Feelings of inequalities and mistrust can originate from colonial history, historical antagonisms and the economic dependence of some countries on others (Smith and Noakes, 1996, p491, referring to studies by Bartlett and Ghosal, 1987 and Ohmae, 1990). It is vital to take these underlying feelings into account, particularly in multi-stakeholder processes, as they impact more or less directly on the relations of different stakeholder groups.

Adaptation can be accomplished best by appreciating the cultural relativity of conceptions and practices within the group, while creating a sensitivity at the individual and group level, sometimes referred to as 'valuing difference'. If these problems are dealt with effectively, the group may then capitalize upon its diversity rather than be obstructed by it (Smith and Noakes, 1996, p495). People should be aware that most of what we experience as 'natural' is actually culturally specific. Again, meta-communication as part of the discussion and decision-making process can be suggested as a way forward, as well as other joint activities in which sharing information about one's culture is made possible in a more informal environment.

COMMUNICATION CHANNELS

Another important issue is the choice of communication channels: switching from face-to-face to electronic communication, for example, can provide a good basis for neutralizing differences in status and personality, as related to gender, age and ethnicity. Non-verbal stimuli like personal characteristics – for example, charisma, mimicry and gesticulation – can be displayed less effectively in the process of communication and thus be less successful in preventing others from contributing/contradicting (Kiesler et al 1988; Hiltz and Turoff, 1993). Representatives of groups with less status, such as women or members of ethnic minorities, would benefit primarily from this filtering of personal characteristics. Without participants being physically present, more attention can be given to the contents of the communicative act (Turkle, 1995; Geser, 1996).

Research suggests that information technology supported communication is more suitable for producing heterogeneity. Thus, the internet could be the ideal tool for collecting suggestions to a given problem in a brainstorming or for getting an overview of the diversity of opinions on a given subject matter. If the goal is to convince others or to generate unanimity, the internet would not be the most useful tool (Geser, 1996; Kerr and Hiltz, 1982; Sproull and Kiesler, 1993).

Status and power

Behaviour in decision-making teams reflects status and power differentials within the group. Numerous studies have investigated the effects of socially defined status, that is status based on age, gender, ethnicity, profession, income level, and so on. Status usually correlates with demographic characteristics that are not necessarily relevant to performance in the group (Ridgeway, 1987).

There are wide-ranging behavioural differences between people of different social status:

> *Compared to those with lower status, higher status persons display more assertive non-verbal behaviours during communication; speak more often; criticize more; state more commands and interrupt others more often; have more opportunity to exert influence, attempt to exert influence more, and actually are more influential.* (Jackson, 1996, p62)

If lower status is not based on task-relevant attributes, differences in status appear to contribute to process losses because the expertise of lower-status members is not used fully.

In a review of formal group discussion procedures, Pavitt (1993) looks at the impact of formal procedures on small group decision-making. A formal discussion procedure (such as reflective thinking; brainstorming as a method of proposal generation; 'nominal group technique' or NGT; devil's advocacy; dialectic inquiry) consists of an ordered sequence of steps for decision-making groups to follow in their discussions (see Implementation, below). To ensure more equitable discussion, formal group discussion procedures like NGT encourage equal participation for all members of the group regardless of power and status. NGT (Delbecq et al, 1975) is characterized by the limitations of group discussions to exchanges between group members and an official group leader. After group members silently generate proposals on paper, the content of subsequent discussion is limited to the presentation and clarification of proposals, discouraging verbal clashes of differing ideas, the criteria for an ideal solution and the extent to which proposals meet these criteria. Thus, NGT emphasizes individual decision-making over group interaction (see Pavitt, 1993, p219).

The method of reflective thinking (Dewey, 1910) which has been the starting point for the development of many other procedures for discussion and problem-solving, gives equal opportunity to all proposals. It proceeds through a sequence of decision-making steps:

1 analysis of the causes and implications of the problem;
2 consideration of the criteria for an ideal solution;
3 proposition of a set of possible solutions;
4 evaluation of the extent to which each proposal meets the criteria for an ideal solution; and
5 choosing and implementing of the proposal that best meets the criteria.

According to Pavitt, 'formal discussion procedures can be a force for democracy in decision-making, and this fact alone may warrant their employment in institutions in which democracy is valued' (1993, p232). However, during the described stages of a formal procedure, appropriate chairing and facilitation needs to ensure equal and universal participation.

Implementation

The fundamental task facing decision-makers is how to go about developing a prescription for action and get it implemented. Most of the studies on diversity in groups are conducted in laboratory settings in which teams have to come to solutions and agree on courses of action. In this regard the actual implementation of decisions receives little attention. If diversity of perspectives makes consensus-reaching difficult, groups might try to accommodate opposing perspectives through compromise and majority rule instead of persisting to reach a creative solution by consensus. Reliance on compromise or majority rule may decrease group members' acceptance of the team's resolution and thus be an obstacle to effective implementation (Jackson, 1996).

Pavitt (1993) states that the impact of formal group procedures on the quality of the decision-making process is unclear. There is no firm basis for recommendations to practitioners. However, it is possible that formal procedures improve individual and, in turn, group performance. Referring to White et al (1980), he concludes that groups using formal procedures tend to be more satisfied with their decision and are therefore more committed to its implementation (Pavitt, 1993).

Further research suggests that agreements produced through mediation are characterized by very high rates of implementation (see below, Mediation) and negotiation. According to Bingham (1987), the most significant factor in determining the likelihood of implementing a mediated agreement appears to be direct participation in the negotiation process of those with authority to implement the decision. For a mediated agreement to stay in effect over time, a monitoring group should be established to ensure implementation (see Baughman, 1995).

To conclude, the implementation of a consensual agreement depends on a sense of ownership by all participants, be it those with high or low degrees of authority and power. To achieve and strengthen that sense of ownership, representatives participating in negotiations should also have opportunities to report back to their constituencies to ensure their backing and support.

Levels of representation

In contrast to personal decision-making, a commitment to a particular course of action within a group does not necessarily provide decision-makers with the possibility of complete control over the consequences of their decision.

Vary et al (unpublished manuscript) emphasize that the assumption of a shared understanding of the problem by all the stakeholders cannot be taken for granted. To ensure a jointly shaped and shared representation of the problem, the objectives and the goals of a group process, the following points should be kept in mind: first, the similarities and differences of the problem representation of the stakeholders should be acknowledged; second, divergences should be discussed; and third, the group should aim, if possible, to develop a common definition and view. Tools that help to develop a common problem definition include addressing still open and possibly already decided questions and the background knowledge underlying the problem (Vary et al). Hence a group needs to be open to revisit explicitly the first stages of problem definitions if differences become apparent.

Humphreys (1998) points out that different representations also arise at different hierarchical levels. He describes the discourses employed in decision-making by identifying these different levels of representations of the issue under discussion. These levels set constraints on what can be talked about at the next level, thus establishing a common representation about the situation, by means of which a prescription for action may be legitimated. The decision-making group, in order to act, must limit the number of problem representations until a common course of action is prescribed and can actually be embarked upon.

Therefore, working towards a shared definition of the problem needs to be the first step of all problem-solving procedures. Cultural differences and constraints due to hierarchical levels between representatives of the same stakeholder groups need to be kept in mind when working towards shared representation.

Leadership

Leadership can be defined as a process in which a group member is granted the power to influence and motivate others to help attain the group goals (Forsyth, 1999; Smith and Mackie, 1995). It is important to note that leadership is defined as a process (not a fact or stable position) and that the definition now prevalent in the social sciences explicitly acknowledges that leadership is being granted by the ones being led – without that, there is no leadership (but control, dictatorship, and so on) (see Neuberger, 1990).

Leaders have a disproportionate influence on team dynamics. Through their attitudes and behaviour, leaders may amplify, nullify or moderate some of the natural consequences of diversity. They can shape informal norms and structure the process used for decision-making (Jackson, 1996, p70).

Effective leadership ideally involves both enhancing group performance and maintaining cohesion (task- versus relationship-focused style). A high degree of quality and acceptance of the decision is needed for effective decisions. Therefore, the effective leader must recognize and distinguish between facts/ideas and feelings/biases – a distinction not easily made, as feelings/biases are often veiled behind made-up reasons or rationalizations. Hence, diagnostic skill is another important leadership requirement (Maier, 1970).

There has been substantial disagreement over the years with regard to the most effective leadership style, with some studies favouring democratic over autocratic leadership and vice versa and others finding no significant effects of different styles at all (see review in Wheelan, 1994, p111). A learning approach, as described above, may be most likely to succeed if the group has a leader with strong leadership skills, ie being supportive and participatory but not too directive. Fiedler's 'contingency model of leadership' (Fiedler, 1958) was a starting point for a lot of research, including new kinds of analysis, for example factor and cluster analysis, which have become possible through the development of computer-based statistics. Based on that large body of research examining Fiedler's model, it seems that effective leaders vary their styles to meet the demands of the situation. The essence of good leadership may therefore be the flexibility to adapt to the needs of the group and the respective problem.

Mediation and negotiation

A number of studies on mediation has emerged over the last two decades. For example, the University of Washington's Institute for Environmental Mediation describes mediation as

*a voluntary process in which those involved in a dis-
pute jointly explore and reconcile their differences. The
mediator has no authority to impose a settlement. His
or her strength lies in the ability to assist in settling
their own differences. The mediated dispute is settled
when the parties themselves reach what they consider
to be a workable solution.* (Cormick, 1987, in Baughman, 1995, p254)

To attain consensual agreements, the focus in mediation lies upon
collective rather than individual interests. Mediators often work with
the different stakeholders individually to determine both the differences
in values that parties place upon the issue under discussion and the
range within which each party is able or willing to negotiate. This
enables the mediator to create alternative solutions, and group discussions may then focus on commonalities rather than differences. It is
therefore one of the tasks of the mediator to limit discussions to the
extent that it appears to serve the achievement of consensus (Baughman, 1995).

A study of local governmental mediation in municipal boundary
disputes in Virginia, US, by Richman et al (1986) describes dispute
resolution processes and the role of mediation in settling these,
providing valuable information for other negotiation processes. One
aspect is an analysis of the non-explicit and non-rational dynamics
involved in negotiations. Contrary to the dominant impression, negotiations are not necessarily a purely cognitive and emotionally 'cool'
process in which people focus on their immediate stakes on the matter
under discussion. Reality seldom fits this rational image.

In the negotiation process, the bottom line of each party is usually
determined by a sense of vital interests or wants which it seeks to
satisfy. Bottom lines are usually more ambiguous and vague and, though
stakes are felt to be immutable, almost always difficult to be translated
into concrete negotiable positions. According to Richman, one reason
for this is that Western culture – capitalistic and competitive as it is –
teaches not to identify and seek what one wants but to get as much as
one possibly can. Attention is turned toward the external situation and
the focus lies on how to outdo the other side (Richman, 1986, p129).
Here the mediator can manage the process by improving communication, and increasing comfort with the other:

*As comfort with the negotiating relationship grows, so
does trust. The bottom line payoff of mediation is that
it nurtures the trust required as a foundation for the
parties' moving to dialogue at the level of vital interests
and wants.* (Richman, 1986, p140)

Interactive conflict resolution

Ronald J Fisher (1997) analyses how interactive methods can influence decision-making processes and policy formation at the intercommunal and international levels. He defines the method of interactive conflict resolution as involving small-group, problem-solving discussions between unofficial representatives of parties (groups, communities, states) engaged in protracted social conflict, mediated by a third party. The analysis takes a social-psychological approach by asserting that relational issues (of misperceptions, miscommunication, distrust) must be addressed and that satisfactory solutions will be attained only through joint interaction. It is therefore seen as a complex process that allows for new mechanisms to develop to achieve constructive dialogue. The overall goal of the intervention is to transform a mutually hostile 'win-lose' orientation into a collaborative 'win–win' scenario. Numerous interventions described as dialogue can be considered as applications of interactive conflict resolution (Fisher, 1997).

The methodology of dialogue can be regarded as a prerequisite to other processes, such as negotiation or problem-solving. It puts emphasis on simply understanding the other party and acknowledging the conflict as a mutual problem. The goal is to discover new ways out of complex problems in which integrative solutions emerge that were not at first perceived by anyone, leading to consensus (see above; Fisher, 1997).

Seibold (1999) describes a range of procedures that helps groups to agree. He lists six rules for a non-competitive method of reaching a group decision in which all members eventually agree to agree, notwithstanding individual preferences:

1 Avoid arguing for favourite proposals.
2 Avoid using 'against-them' statements.
3 Avoid agreeing just to avoid conflict.
4 Reject specific decision rules.
5 View differences as helpful.
6 View initial agreements as premature and suspect.

Based on the review of findings in this chapter on effective communication and decision-making processes in groups of high diversity, considering and utilizing these rules to achieve consensus may have the potential to equalize participation and integrate many of the benefits of diverse decision-making groups.

CONCLUSIONS

Multi-stakeholder processes of any type are a novel approach to public participation, be they informing, monitoring or full decision-making processes. Creative and innovative solutions have to be found for a process that has not occurred in that same form before. It is important to appreciate the setting in which such processes should take place and optimum decisions would be reached. The setting is a competitive, knowledge-rich and complex world in which our decisions affect the world either in some momentary way or in a way that has global and lasting proportions, and in which it is often difficult to determine the consequences of our actions because of the increasing interconnectedness of people, organizations, corporations and states. Each decision, therefore, requires the use of a maximum of knowledge of all kinds. Even dialogues 'only' aiming at informing decision-makers deliver more than information given by each of stakeholder group separately. As a result of following the discussions that are taking place among stakeholders, rather than by asking each group individually, participants gain additional insights and more clarity about the differences and commonalities between stakeholder groups. Multi-stakeholder processes have a great potential to assemble, transform, multiply and spread necessary knowledge and to reach implementable solutions.

Several points emerge clearly from the review of social and organizational psychological research. There are strong arguments that any MSP should take a learning approach towards its procedures and, in some cases, to issues developing over time. Preset agendas, timetables, definitions of issues, group composition, goals, procedures of communication and decision-making will not work. Participants also need to take a learning approach – to be prepared to learn from and about others (new knowledge; overcoming stereotypes) and to 'teach' others about their views (assembly bonus effect). The same applies to facilitators who need to be able to respond flexibly to a group's needs and developments.

Several points emerge as the guiding lines for group composition:

1 Aim for sufficient diversity of views.
2 Aim for an equitable distribution of views, endeavouring to create a symmetry of power (at least of some sort).
3 Include at least two representatives of each stakeholder group (gender balanced).
4 Do not invite people to represent more than one stakeholder group.
5 Avoid groupthink by checking that a significant number of participants are not dependent on another member (who would easily assume leadership and dominate the process).

The human being is not a *Homo oeconomicus*. Communication and decision-making are not merely rational processes and should not be approached as such. People's feelings, attitudes, irrationalities in information processing, and so on, need to be taken into account and respected. Discussions need to be based on factual knowledge. However, cultural values, ideals, fears and stereotyping (positive and negative) are human, too, and should not be ridiculed.

Trust building is an essential prerequisite of successful groups of high diversity. There are a number of fundaments for building trust, above all honesty and the integrity of participants, fairness, transparency and equity of the process. The necessary processes of overcoming prejudice and stereotyping need to take place before people are able to truly 'dialogue'; they take time and concrete experience.

Employing formal procedures of communication and decision-making within groups of high diversity is certainly beneficial, for several reasons. First, they raise communication standards (being clear; speaking equitably; listening to others; taking each other seriously etc). Second, they ensure that everybody gets the same amount of speaking time, helping to create more equitable discussion. They can thus help to keep in check factors of social influence such as power and status, charisma, eloquence, and so on. For MSPs, such procedures need to be agreed by participants. One option is for the group initiating the process (ideally a stakeholder mixed group) to present possible procedures to potential participants and to include discussion and decision-making on procedures in the (common) MSP design process. Formal procedures can make a group process more task-oriented, but successful groups need socio-emotional components, too. The challenge will be not to over-formalize a process and to keep it flexible, while at the same time reaping the benefits of formal procedures.

Several reasons make it advisable to create space for meta-communication in MSPs. Groups increase their effectiveness if they work on the basis of an agreed set of rules – hence they need to communicate about the way they communicate. Meta-communication also allows space for dealing with problems which arise when members feel that others are not playing by the rules. In culturally mixed contexts (such as many MSPs), it enables participants to discover what are indeed cultural differences, perhaps more than we tend to believe.

6

The Practice: Examples of
Multi-stakeholder Processes

Related to an increased interest in public participation and to the implementation of Agenda 21, numerous examples of multi-stakeholder processes have been conducted over the last few decades. Not surprisingly, since the 1990s there has been a significant increase of such processes within the area of environment and sustainable development. We have looked at a number of examples of various issues, objectives, diversity of participants, scope and time lines.

We developed a set of questions which were used to obtain a systematic overview of the various processes (see Appendix 1). In order to analyse these examples we sought answers to these questions by:

- Using publicly available material (documents, websites). Much of the process-design related information which we were looking for was available on the respective websites and in printed reports.
- Interviewing people from different stakeholder groups who were/ are involved in the respective processes. In most cases, some relevant information was not available in publications. We therefore conducted interviews either in person, over the telephone or via email.

In most of the cases presented, we used a combination of literature research and interviewing. Studying the examples was not intended to analyse a representative sample or to give a full assessment or evaluation via a representative group of people being interviewed. The goal of studying literature and interviewing people was to obtain a descriptive analysis of the respective MSPs.[1]

OVERVIEW

Among the large number of possible examples, we picked primarily ones that are directly related to sustainable development and Agenda 21, and/or are conducted around intergovernmental processes. We also included examples that are initiated by a group or organizations as well as those initiated and carried out by one single organization. There are numerous varieties with regard to many of the questions we looked at – ways of designing the MSP, identifying relevant stakeholders and participants, preparing meetings, documents, and so on. The variety of examples also demonstrates the variety of projects and processes which are being called multi-stakeholder dialogues or processes (hence Chapter 2 covering terms and variety).

The following is meant to provide an overview of the examples studied, based on the questions we looked at.

General Information

Issues The MSP examples we looked at address a wide range of issues: environment, development, sustainable development, human rights, labour and gender equality.

Goals A variety of goals are listed in publications and by interviewees which can be grouped as follows:

Opening the space for stakeholder interaction: bring people together to develop constructive dialogue in an area of conflict; improve the understanding of stakeholders, governments and donors; enter into a dialogue with government representatives; open up a closed process; generate stakeholder involvement (eg Brent Spar process; Global Environment Facility, Country Dialogue Work (GEF CDW) OECD Conference).

Informing policy-making: inform and impact a policy-making process; inform an intergovernmental body; inform stakeholders (eg Beijing+5 online discussions; CSD stakeholder dialogues; Financing for Development (FfD) Hearings; WHO Conference; GEF CDW).

Produce information from an independent source: produce an independent assessment; conduct a rigorous review and develop recommendations and guidelines for future decision-making; develop and disseminate guidelines (eg for reporting), (eg Mining, Minerals and Sustainable Development (MMSD); Paper Initiative; the Global Reporting Initiative (GRI); the World Commission on Dams (WCD)).

MSPs as a political strategy: create a counterpoint to a planning proposal; support a global initiative and campaign (eg Lower Columbia River Basin process; MMSD).

Towards implementation: generate commitment by stakeholders to enact principles through joint activities or individually (eg UN Global Compact; GRI).

Specific goals of businesses: provide reputation management for companies; support alignment of businesses' internal/global policy; enable further identification of employees with a company (eg UN Global Compact, Novartis Forum).

Participating stakeholders MSP examples include a variety of stakeholders. In the examples studied, processes included three or more stakeholder groups. Definitions of stakeholder groups vary, from being based on the Major Groups identified in Agenda 21 (Chapters 24–33) to being identified specifically for an MSP, depending on the issues and scope. The following were listed: various UN entities (DESA units, SG's office, among others); various UN agencies; other intergovernmental bodies; governments; NGOs (in various definitions: environmental NGOs, community groups, development NGOs, etc); academics/scientists; women's groups; farmers; business and industry; trade unions; local authorities; Indigenous Peoples; technical experts; ethics specialists; professional associations; media; water and forestry districts; affected people.

Time-frame Time-frames vary considerably, depending on the scope, level and goals of a process. Many are one-off events for which there is a preparatory period before the actual event and a period afterwards to produce reports and publications.

Most of the example processes which are related to one-off events take five to ten months to carry out, eg CSD stakeholder dialogues; Bergen ministerial dialogue; FfD Hearings; Online Discussion of the World Bank Report 2000; Beijing+5 Online Discussions.

Some one-off events develop into follow-up processes which may be scheduled for one or two years, such as follow-up processes of CSD stakeholder dialogues (voluntary initiatives; tourism; agriculture).

Processes which include several meetings at various levels, commissioned research, separate working groups, reviewed background papers and other input, run for about two years or more, such as the World Commission on Dams; the Mining, Minerals and Sustainable Development process; Local Agenda 21 processes.

Finally, there are ongoing processes which do not have a planned closure date (or an extended one) but annual agenda items and other steps within the process, such as UN Global Compact, Global Reporting Initiative.

Classification

We have aimed to describe processes by issues, objectives, participants, scope and time lines.

Issues We listed the issues the MSP was addressing.

Objectives Most of the examples focus on informing a policy-making process, a particular intergovernmental body, and the like. These can be either 'only' dialogues or they can aim at consensus-building and agreement on positions, strategies, and/or output documents. In that case they are still informing but include mechanisms of reaching agreements and making decisions. The processes which involve some kind of consensus-building and/or decision-making also show a great variety: some are part of policy-making (Aarhus Convention), some are (partly) planning processes (LA21), others take an advising role (Brent Spar process). Others are developing tools (GRI), or independent analyses (MMSD; WCD) to be agreed within the process.

Participants Participants and the diversity of stakeholders involved in the examples vary greatly; numbers of participating stakeholders (including governments and intergovernmental bodies) range from at least three up to ten and more. Some processes work on the basis of the definition of Major Groups in Agenda 21 (for example CSD stakeholder dialogues, UN Global Compact).

Scope Most of the example processes are international (12); some are regional (5), national (8), subnational (3) and local (3). Some examples include subentities and processes at several levels (such as regional processes which feed into international ones).

Time lines Many processes are single events which, however, are sometimes extensively prepared over the course of several months (CSD Dialogues); others involve commissioning research, hearings and meetings at several levels (WCD; MMSD). Generally, it seems that ongoing processes allow the groups to build more trust and closer relationships, which should be associated with greater success (a judgement that we did not aim to make).

Procedural aspects

Designing the MSP: How was the process designed? And by whom? Were there consultations with stakeholders on the design?
    Various strategies are employed in the MSP examples. These can be grouped according to the level of stakeholder involvement; some employ a multi-stakeholder approach to the design.

One organization initiates, designs, facilitates and carries out the whole process; this can be a UN body or agency, such as the United Nations Economic Council for Europe (UNECE), the UN Division for the Advancement of Women (DAW) and the Division for Sustainable Development (DSD), FfD, another intergovernmental body (eg WHO), an individual company (eg Novartis), or another single institution (eg local authorities).

In some cases, the initiating body designs the process in consultation with stakeholders – one, two or more groups can be involved, either in separate consultations or via group consultation.

Sometimes, NGOs, multi-stakeholder organizations or professional facilitating organizations are contracted to carry out the process. In these cases, the process is often designed in consultation between the contracting partners. This can be carried out including further stakeholder consultation or not. For example, the initiative can come from a host country government who contracts an organization (Norway contracted the UNED Forum for the Bergen Ministerial Dialogues); or a company may contract a professional facilitator (Shell and The Environment Council).

Many processes have taken a step-by-step approach to designing and facilitating: initial scoping or planning meetings are initiated by one or more organizations. These meetings result in the founding of some kind of a steering committee (or task force, facilitating group, coordinating group, advisory group) which is usually made up of various stakeholder groups' representatives. This group then engages in further designing the process and often adding new members on the way in order to ensure diversity and inclusiveness. Often coordinating groups also develop the terms and principles of the process, appropriate levels, working groups, criteria for inclusion and balanced participation, and so on.

In some cases, NGOs approach a decision-making body and suggest an MSP. This can then be negotiated further with the body in question, involving or not involving more stakeholder groups (for example World Bank report online discussions).

As our sample of examples is not a representative one, we cannot identify a most common approach. It seems, however, that efforts to design a process together, as an MSP itself, have recently become more common. This could be based on the often reported experience that participants' commitment to a process largely depends on their involvement in the process from the outset, including the design.

Identifying the issues to be addressed in an MSP: Who identifies the issues and how?

The issues addressed by many of the examples are set by an international agreement (Beijing+5) or determined by the decision of an intergovernmental body (such as the UN General Assembly, UNECE, DAW), or by a single initiating organization (say a company or intergovernmental body). However, often issues are further defined and differentiated through the process. This can lead to a need to pose more precise questions instead of putting a broadly defined issue to a group process. This is being done by the initiating body alone or in more or less transparent consultation with stakeholder groups.

Sometimes, potential participants are presented with a number of issues or questions and they can choose which ones they want to address in their contribution (eg FfD Hearings). In other cases, issues have been defined by an initial draft document but have been broadened through the multi-stakeholder debate.

Where a process is designed to feed into an official, for example intergovernmental event, issues and agenda tend to be set by the agenda of that event. The multi-stakeholder participation process is then designed in accordance with that official process.

In cases where a coordinating group or similar body takes on the task of designing the process, it also works on defining the issues to be addressed (eg WCD, MMSD). Again, this can be done, including further consultation with non-members. Diverse coordinating groups seem to be more inclusive when the issues are being defined. This is, however, also a question of available time (see below). Yet other processes are based on a process framework and issues vary by country (eg GEF CDW) or year (eg CSD stakeholder dialogues).

Identifying relevant stakeholders: Who identifies relevant stakeholders? And how?

Sometimes stakeholder groups are predefined by international agreements (as Major Groups in Agenda 21), but there is still a choice to be made among them. And in many cases, stakeholder groups which are relevant to the issue at hand need to be identified. Some processes are by invitation only, others are semi-open, based on set numbers and definitions of stakeholder groups, while others are completely open.

Many MSPs with a single initiating body (intergovernmental body or company), it will also be the one identifying relevant stakeholder groups for participation (eg CSD stakeholder dialogues; Novartis Forum). This can be done in consultation with stakeholder groups' representatives, a contracted NGO or other body (eg MMSD), or via an initial coordinating group which can result in a wide outreach (eg GRI, WCD). Sometimes, particular efforts are undertaken to ensure participation by some stakeholder groups. Some processes engage in ongoing outreach throughout the process, sometimes supported by outreach and background material. In other cases, a kick-off event organized by one body or an initial coordinating group is used to increase stakeholder involvement. Such events reportedly benefit from some well-known people attending (eg LA21).

In longer term processes which involve various activities at several levels or in several working groups, very often the stakeholder base will increase over time as activities develop and more groups become interested (eg GRI). Stakeholder participation is sometimes limited by a governmental or intergovernmental body's decision; the reason given is that only a small number of participants can be accommodated in a limited space or time (eg CSD stakeholder dialogues, Bergen ministerial dialogues).

The activities related to identifying stakeholder groups often seem rather ad hoc and the criteria employed are sometimes not available. In contrast, some processes operate on the basis of publicized criteria which have been developed within a coordinating group of high stakeholder diversity.

Identifying MSP participants: Who identifies participants and how? It is possibly different for the various participating stakeholder groups

In most examples that we looked at, identifying the participants within a stakeholder group is up to the group itself; they elect or appoint their representatives to the process. Processes of election or appointment can be more or less transparent. Often, identification processes are most transparent among NGOs involved (eg CSD stakeholder dialogues).

In other cases, the participation of stakeholder representatives is by invitation by the initiating body only (eg OECD Conference). However, this is often done in consultation with stakeholder groups in order to ensure some level of representativeness. Or the process does not aim at stakeholder groups being represented by their chosen representatives and organizers invite members of stakeholder groups at their own discretion (eg Novartis Forum).

Particularly, online discussions tend to keep access completely open and there are no access controls. However, in these cases people are participating in an individual capacity and not on behalf of an organization or stakeholder group, and are asked to identify themselves so that the group position can be identified (eg Beijing+5 online discussions; WB Report online discussion; GRI). These processes also involve massive outreach efforts which can be specifically targeted to ensure regional or gender balance.

Many processes employ some kind of monitoring of numbers to ensure balanced participation by the various stakeholder groups involved (eg Brent Spar process).

Sometimes it seems necessary to reach out actively to potential participants (eg FfD regarding business representatives). Small stakeholder groups can share one representative to a process (Lower

Columbia River Basin process). Aiming at a very broad process but an overseeable group size, the WCD opted for a two-tiered approach of a small Commission (12 members) and a large Forum which served as a 'sounding board'.

Setting the goals of an MSP: Who sets the goals and how? Can goals develop over the course of the MSP, say from an informing process into a dialogue/consensus-building process; from mere exchange of views to implementation?

Goals can be set from the outset by one initiating organization with or without consultation with stakeholders or a coordinating group (eg Beijing+5 online discussions, Novartis Forum, FfD Hearings, OECD Conference). In processes around intergovernmental bodies, these are often based on existing international agreements. Goals can also develop over time through the MSP itself (eg GRI, WCD, MMSD, Local Agenda 21, Paper Initiative). Some MSPs have a mix of preset goals and goals developing over time, beyond the given set (eg UN Global Compact).

Choices with regard to goal development can be due to time limits, such as when a process has to deliver a certain input according to an official agenda and timetable (eg WHO Conference, WB Report online discussion). Sometimes the way that goals develop will depend on the way a chair chooses to facilitate a dialogue meeting – towards identifying common ground or contentious issues (eg CSD stakeholder dialogues).

Do participants have opportunities to check back with their constituencies when changes are being proposed?

This seems to depend mostly on the time-frame and the resources available. Checking back with constituencies is usually possible in MSPs involving several meetings or allowing for input and comments into draft documents within a reasonable time period. At one-off events, involving constituencies is only possible in the preparatory period. With regard to resources, groups with easy access to the internet, resources for communication and meetings find it much easier to check back with their constituencies than those lacking those resources.

Setting the agenda: Who sets the agenda? And how? Do participants have opportunities to check back with their constituencies when changes are being proposed?

The agenda – preparations for a one-off event or a long-term process – can be set by an initiating body alone or in consultation with stakeholder groups. Sometimes it is not quite clear how that was done or various sources contradict each other.

Agenda-setting can be facilitated through a contracted body organizing the process (eg Brent Spar process) and/or a more or less diverse coordinating group (eg GRI). In some cases, the process of developing the agenda is not predictable – it might or might not be carried out with stakeholder consultation or it has initially been developed in consultation and recurs in regular intervals based on the same scheme (eg CSD stakeholder dialogues).

In MSPs around intergovernmental meetings, agenda is largely dependent on the official agenda (preparatory meetings, deadlines for background papers, and so on). In processes steered by a diverse group and going on over a longer period of time, agenda-setting is part of that group process, and in many cases can change, adapt and develop over time, which makes the agenda of the process itself the result of an MSP (eg GRI, WCD). Where MSPs comprise various strands of work in different working groups, these often develop their agenda themselves (eg MMSD). In the UN Global Compact, for example, we find a mixture of a preset agenda (eg annual requirements) and an agenda developing through the process (eg issue dialogues).

Setting the timetable: Who sets the timetable and how?

In MSPs around intergovernmental meetings, timetables are determined by the official schedule (eg UNECE, Beijing+5, FfD, CSD). Independent processes that aim at impacting policy-making in a particular political process set their timetable accordingly (such as MMSD for Earth Summit 2002; WB Report online discussions). MSPs organized by a single entity mostly have their timetables set by that entity (eg Novartis Forum, OECD Conference).

In some cases, facilitating bodies propose a timetable which is then discussed and in some form adopted by the group (eg Brent Spar process, Bergen Ministerial Dialogues). Ongoing processes with a (diverse) coordinating group sometimes see timetables developing over time, mostly within a given overall deadline (eg WCD).

Preparatory process: How is the dialogue prepared (consultations within constituencies; papers; initial positions, etc)? Are preparations within stakeholder groups monitored somehow?

There is a great variety of preparatory processes within the sample we looked at. Choices largely depend on the objectives, size, scope and time lines, and on whether the processes involve consensus-building and decision-making or not.

One-off event MSPs are often prepared via various kinds of communications, bilateral or involving representatives of all participant groups. Some MSPs involve the preparation of initial stakeholder background or position papers (eg FfD Hearings). Such preparatory papers are submitted in advance to a dialogue meeting which some-times works and sometimes does not. In some cases, these are analysed and compared to prepare further for a meeting (eg CSD stakeholder dialogues, Bergen Ministerial Dialogues). Preparatory material can also be produced to help stakeholders decide if they want to participate (eg Brent Spar process: CD-ROM, user-friendly documents).

MSPs that aim to produce a common agreed document require different procedures. Drafts can be prepared by a coordinating group, a secretariat or facilitating body (eg WCD; Brent Spar) and put out for comments to all participants. Upon redrafting, documents can be put to a plenary meeting for final discussion and adoption, either by consensus or voting mechanisms. Such procedures can involve several layers, perhaps moving bottom-up from country to global level (eg MMSD, National Strategies for Sustainable Development (NSSD)).

In MSPs initiated and organized by one body, preparations often involve informal discussions about issues and schedules, between the inviting body, consultants, invited speakers and other stakeholder representatives (eg Novartis Forum, OECD Conference).

Larger processes tend to engage in a multitude of multi-stakeholder meetings and sub-processes at different levels and on specific issues. Each of these can have a separate preparatory process. Some long-term processes involve the commissioning of background or research papers, sometimes including their submission for comments to all participants. MSPs that involve small group work often hold large strategy meetings and produce newsletters to keep everybody informed about the different strands of ongoing work (eg WHO Conference).

Preparations of different participants of online discussions can vary significantly – some might not prepare at all, some might hold national meetings to prepare (eg Beijing+5, WB Report).

The amount of consultation within stakeholder groups which are preparing for a dialogue varies; in some cases or for some groups, there is a lot of consultation. Preparations within stakeholder groups do not seem to be monitored in any 'official' way, although NGOs in some cases carry out a consultation in a publicly accessible manner (eg via list serves).

Communication process: How is the communication conducted?

Nearly all examples make intensive use of web-based communication, some report 'huge email traffic', and most publish their (draft) material on websites which are often developed for the process itself. Web-based communication also allows a large number of people to be involved, is relatively cheap for many people and very quick. It allows transparency through open list servers and publicly accessible websites and archives. The downside, which is mentioned by many interviewees, is the large gaps in internet access, particularly between South and North.

Only online discussions operate without any face-to-face meetings, and thus completely exclude people who do not have internet access. The lack of face-to-face feedback can also make communication more difficult.

MSPs involving a one-off event are often prepared via email, but also use telephone or video conferencing or pre-meetings. One-off events mostly involve a mixture of formal and informal meetings in preparation.

Longer-term or multi-layered MSPs often involve a mix of national or regional meetings and fewer international ones. These are often flanked by (electronic or printed) newsletters, brochures and other publications. Some make use of CD-ROMs.

Small working groups within larger processes, particularly international ones, also tend primarily to use email. Local processes involve many face-to-face meetings but also use a whole array of other communication channels.

Face-to-face dialogues are often conducted with a mixture of presentations, question and answers and discussion. They can also involve a mixture of plenary and small working groups meetings, presentations, panel discussions, side events with more information communications, and the like. More elaborate working group techniques such as phases of brainstorming and discussion, and meta-plan, are also used.

Dealing with power gaps: Are there power gaps between participating stakeholder groups? How are they being addressed/dealt with?

These questions are rarely addressed in published material and do not necessarily come out in written interviews. Where they are addressed, most people asserted that there are indeed power gaps, for example between governments and NGOs, between NGOs and business, between the MSP group and the decision-making body it was aiming to inform or impact. Power gaps are also due to differences in internet access – checking back with constituencies, consultations within stakeholder groups and keeping track of developments is much more difficult if you don't have regular and easy internet access.

People perceive that power gaps are rarely openly addressed. In some cases, they are dealt with explicitly by giving each group the same number of seats and support those in need with funding for travel, the production of preparatory material or communication (eg CSD stakeholder dialogues). Some MSPs aim to balance power by balancing the numbers of participants who are presumably in favour, against or neutral towards the issue or question at hand (eg OECD Conference).

People also noted that different groups have different bases of power, such as access to information, decision-making power, presumption of good intentions ('moral advantage'), access to building coalitions, the ability to take quick decisions. It was said that these different power sources might create a balance, which is less obvious than when looking at only one power base such as decision-making power or financial resources. Interestingly, some interviewees said that power gaps were balanced through lack of interest, preparation or coordination on the side of a potentially very powerful group.

Are there mechanisms of meta-communication during the process? What kind?

Mechanisms for meta-communication – communicating about the way we communicate and the process we are involved in – are rare components of MSPs. In some cases, people reported that there was spontaneous meta-communication in an informal manner. Many interviewees asserted that it would have been beneficial for the process if there had been encouragement and some kind of formal and transparent mechanism for meta-communication. This question also goes back to the initial design issue. If there is a coordinating group designing the process, it is more likely that this group also addresses the communication process, how to deal with power gaps, how to deal with deadends in decision-making and so on.

Decision-making process: Procedures of agreement (depending on the type of MSP). Is agreement being sought? If so, how is that conducted and by whom?

In many examples, no agreement was sought so the question was not applicable. MSPs can, however, spontaneously develop into consensus-building. This question also shows the importance of facilitating: even dialogue-only processes can be facilitated towards identifying common ground and possible (eg future) agreement, or they can be facilitated towards identifying areas of conflict (eg CSD stakeholder dialogues on agriculture in 2000).

Larger processes that aim to develop a consensus document often involve a multi-layered approach to consensus-building. Some agreement is often built within small working groups who then submit their outcomes to all participants for further comments and final agreement. Often, such agreement is sought at a final plenary meeting. Some processes intentionally avoid voting procedures and work to find consensus (eg GRI), some involve voting procedures or allow minority positions to be reflected in an outcome document (eg NGO preparations for CSD stakeholder dialogues; to some extent the WCD report).

Some MSPs rely on a professional facilitator or an experienced chair to identify the appropriate time for seeking agreement by the whole group (eg Brent Spar process).

Implementation process: Depending on the type of MSP, how is implementation decided/planned/conducted and by whom?

In most of the examples, no implementation was sought, at least not at the time. In the case of informing processes around intergovernmental bodies, the implementation of any consensus depends on the inter-governmental process taking MSP outcomes into account and into the official decision, and subsequently the appropriate bodies to initiate implementation (eg MMSD).

Some ongoing processes which emerged from CSD stakeholder dialogues are supposed to look at implementation (such as in the form of joint implementation projects) and to report back to the CSD within a given time-frame. In the case of the Aarhus Convention, implementa-tion is now, after its adoption, a case for national governments, and NGOs are expected to play a key role in the implementation process as well as to monitor national implementation efforts. In the Brent Spar process, potential implementers (such as potential contractors of Shell) were part of the process. In the GRI process, implementation will depend on the companies' activities, a process which is also expected to initiate redesigning of the reporting guidelines which have been developed. With regard to Local Agenda 21 (LA21) processes, it was observed that there are no objective studies to assess their implementa-tion. In the case of the UN Global Compact, there is disagreement about whether the process involves implementation or not – critics claim that it does not, while some business partners report that it does produce changes within their companies.

Closing the MSP: How and when does the process conclude? Who makes the decision and how?

MSPs around intergovernmental processes and/or aiming at a particular event close within the schedule of that official process or given event (eg Beijing+5 and WB Report online discussions, WHO and OECD Conferences, Novartis Forum events). Interviewees sometimes report that an MSP was planned as a one-off event but may inspire more such processes subsequently, or has led to ongoing processes (eg WHO Conference, Bergen Ministerial Dialogue, CSD stakeholder dialogues). Other processes close with a final meeting which has been scheduled when setting the timetable within the process (eg WCD, MMSD) but often involve follow-up processes at various levels, mostly aimed at feeding the outcomes into official decision-making. Ongoing processes do not report a closure but expect to develop over time, into such processes as monitoring and implementation (eg GRI).

Structural aspects

Structures/institutions of the MSP: Secretariat? Facilitating body? Board/Forum?

Many processes are supported by a secretariat or similar body (eg WomenWatch for the Beijing+5 online discussions, CSD Secretariat, FfD Secretariat, OECD, WHO, Novartis). In other cases, an initiating body contracts an NGO, a professional facilitator, or a multi-stakeholder organization to organize and back up an MSP.

Some longer term processes have given themselves their own base (eg WCD, GRI). Such bodies can develop their own constitution or function in an ad hoc manner with bylaws. Diverse governing boards or executive committees are meant to ensure adequate representation of all participants' views in the governance of the body and the process. Multi-layered processes might work with various bodies at local, regional and international levels. Some processes include diverse coordinating groups guiding the affairs which are primarily organized by one or a small number of organizations.

UNECE had a working group for the Aarhus Convention process, plus a 'Friends of the Secretariat' group. WCD worked with a special Secretariat, a small Commission and a large Forum. Local authorities will mostly organize LA21 but sometimes create a body for that purpose which can also be a mix of local government and independent or multi-stakeholder institution.

Within stakeholder groups, coordination is provided by associations (eg the ICC, the World Business Council for Sustainable Development (WBCSD) and the ICFTU), networks and steering committees (eg NGO Steering Committee, caucuses), and umbrella institutions active in the area of interest (eg the ICLEI for local authorities).

Facilitation: Who facilitates the MSP? What is the exact role of a facilitating body? How does the facilitating organization work with stakeholders? Does that include secretariat services?

These questions were understood as inquiring about the actual facilitation or chairing of meetings. Online discussions are regularly moderated, with messages being screened for length and relevance. Moderators communicate directly with participants whose messages need to be reformulated; they are often taken on as external consultants.

Around official intergovernmental processes, officials such as chairs of the Bureau tend to facilitate stakeholder dialogue meetings (eg CSD, FfD). Joint chairing by government representatives and NGOs also takes place (eg Bergen Ministerial Dialogues). Within LA21s, local authority representatives usually chair meetings. One-off events organized by a single body usually appoint chairpersons from among various stakeholder groups (eg OECD Conference) or other professions (eg journalists at Novartis Forum events). Pre-meetings tend to be prepared and facilitated by the body coordinating the process. Interviewees reported that using professional facilitators was beneficial but that having a charismatic, respected chair was equally successful.

Documentation: Rapporteuring from meetings; summarizing outcomes; publication of documentation – by whom, when and how?

Many MSPs report that a large number of documents are produced over time as drafts are commented on and redrafted; meetings are minuted; additional background and research material is submitted, and so on. In many processes, pre-final documents or meeting minutes are only distributed electronically via email and/or website.

Online discussions are often fully archived on the internet and publicly accessible. Summary documents of such discussions are produced by the organizing body and made available in electronic and printed format.

There are various mechanisms for rapporteuring: in most processes, minutes are taken by members of the organizing body (eg Brent Spar process, FfD hearings, CSD dialogues), and draft reports might be forwarded to participants for amendments and comments. Minutes can also be taken by different stakeholders on a rotating basis and publications produced by one of the facilitating bodies involved on a rotating basis (eg Lower Columbia River Basin process).

Depending on agreement being sought or not, MSPs might work towards a consensus, an endorsed document which usually goes through several stages of drafting and redrafting (eg GRI, LA21). Another option is chair's summaries which can be presented for comments but don't need endorsement (eg CSD stakeholder dialogues, Bergen ministerial meeting). In MSPs initiated and organized by one body, summaries and reports are often produced by that body alone (eg Novartis Forum, OECD Conference).

The question of rapporteuring and documentation is also linked to the question of linkage into official decision-making. The ways in which documents are produced and fed into the process can make them effectively impact the official process, or not (see below).

MSPs might also produce extensive material that is publicly available, preparatory or reflecting the outcome – interactive websites,

CD-ROMs, background and issue papers, and knowledge management systems are such options (eg Brent Spar process, MMSD).

Relating to non-participating stakeholders: Do other stakeholders know about the process? Can they feed into the process and how?

Answers to these questions depend on the objectives, the resources and time available, and the limitations sometimes set by governments or intergovernmental bodies.

In many cases, interviewees regret that there is not enough information available for other stakeholders except those who are aware of the process because of general or previous involvement (eg the Aarhus Convention).

Many processes rely more or less on publishing their material on the internet; sometimes they engage in outreach activities to make other stakeholders aware of the process. Open processes often continuously work to involve more stakeholders through proactive outreach activities (eg GRI). Media-related activities are mostly used to inform the general public (see below). The extensive use of specialist language or UN jargon reportedly often hinders involvement of stakeholder groups.

Most processes, however, do not have formal mechanisms for non-participating stakeholders to be informed and/or to get involved – it depends on them showing interest and approaching the facilitating body. Non-participating stakeholders can sometimes feed into the process through linking up with participating stakeholders. This can be difficult due to tight time lines (eg Bergen Ministerial Dialogues). Online discussions are mostly not limited to particular stakeholder groups, but of course access depends on access to the technology.

Most of the examples studied here have been held in English – a reflection of the reality of many international processes but also of the authors' common language being English. The online discussions on the draft WB Report allowed contributions in French and Spanish which were, however, not translated due to lack of resources.

Relating to the general public: What kind of information about the MSP is available to the public? Via which channels? Who provides that information? Can the public comment/ask questions/feed in and how?

Many interviewees stressed the need to convey the message of the respective MSP to the public in plain language, and often reported the difficulties in doing so. Limited time, highly specialized issues and financial constraints further limit public outreach.

Many processes rely on their material being publicly available on a website. However, this is reportedly not being seen as ensuring public access due to the lack of information about the site and jargon-loaded language. This is most often the case with MSPs dealing with specialized or highly technical issues. Some MSPs produce various materials for public dissemination. Press releases and conferences are the most common. School packs, brochures, CD-ROMs and videos are less commonplace. Reports are often widely disseminated but feeding into the process remains difficult for the general public. Local Agenda processes often use local media such as newspapers and radio to inform and to generate increased involvement. LA21s also seem to be the processes that are most easily accessible by the general public. Press coverage of one-off events is often ensured by inviting journalists to attend (eg WCD, GRI) or to participate actively at an event, perhaps as facilitators (eg Novartis Forum).

Some processes engage in public media-related activities, most frequently towards the end of the process, launching an outcome document. Launch events can be big public events involving celebrities (eg WCD). Media work is most often done by the coordinating organization. If there is a lot of public interest in an issue, it will be in the news. This is most often the case when contentious issues are being addressed (eg Brent Spar process).

Linkage into official decision-making process: Is the MSP linked to an official decision-making process? Of governments, intergovernmental bodies, other stakeholders? Via which mechanisms? How transparent and predictable are these mechanisms? Can stakeholders impact the mechanisms and how?

These are particularly important questions as most MSP examples aim to impact policy-making and implementation. Around official decision-making processes, MSPs can have various forms of linkage mechanisms. Principally, it is up to governments or intergovernmental bodies to take up outcomes of an MSP meant to inform their deliberations (eg MMSD, WB Report online discussion, WHO Conference). For the Beijing+5 online discussions, a summary was prepared as a background document for the next PrepComm. For the FfD Hearings, summaries were submitted to the 2nd PrepComm as official reports to the meeting. At the Bergen ministerial meeting, a chair's summary of the Dialogues was taken to the closed official meeting the next morning. For the CSD stakeholder dialogues, the CSD Secretariat has in recent years produced a summary in the chair's name which is then handed to negotiators for the CSD decision, along with the summary of the CSD High Level Segment. In the preparations for the Aarhus Convention, the multi-stakeholder involvement was part of the official process. In the NSSD process, outcomes feed into OECD preparations for 2002 and a OECD

High Level meeting. With regard to the UN Global Compact, interviewees disagreed as regards linkage into official decision-making.

Independent processes work with their participants to take on the outcomes and implement them. However, such processes may spark government interest which may lead to impacting official decision-making (eg GRI). The WCD uses the outcome report to impact governments reviewing their policies on large dams.

Some interviewees report that processes were not sufficiently linked into official decision-making and that this could have been designed better to increase impact. Some MSPs have to rely on ad hoc linkage mechanisms. They can be impacted by stakeholders but governments are not formally agreeing a regular procedure. Others rely on lobbying based on their outcomes and seek government involvement to facilitate linkage into official decision-making.

Funding: Is the process being funded? By whom? Who is fundraising? How much does it cost? What impact do funders have on process, structures and outcomes?

Some processes being facilitated by the UN or other bodies are funded through their core budget (which can be a trust fund for a particular process, eg FfD) and additional travel funding, particularly for NGOs and representatives from developing countries (eg FfD Hearings, CSD stakeholder dialogues). Funds are often generated short-term from individual governments. Other participating stakeholder groups fund their participation themselves, particularly business. One-off events initiated and organized by one body are often completely funded by that same body (eg Novartis Forum, Bergen Ministerial Dialogues, OECD Conference, LA21s by local authorities).

Many processes rely on various funding sources from the UN Foundation, other private foundations, UN agencies, individual governments, donor organizations, multilateral development banks, private sector associations or individual companies, NGOs and/or research institutions.

Funding without contributions from the private sector tends to be perceived as lending an MSP more credibility, and arranging for multiple funding sources is regarded as allowing for independence. Within our sample, there is only one example where the process itself agreed a fund-raising strategy and carried it out via its facilitating body, the WCD.

Many MSPs report that insufficient funds are impeding the process and its impact. Overall costs vary significantly.

Additional comments and recommendations by interviewees

Interviewees and MSP reports raised a number of additional issues and comments which are relevant to the task at hand.

Types of MSPs Ongoing processes are seen by some people as more successful than one-off events. However, one-off events can reportedly serve as starting points and build the necessary trust to continue engagement.

Defining the issues Over-simplifying the issue in the beginning of an MSP can create problems of addressing the questions which would need further development. A sufficient problem identification phase in the beginning is the key. In a similar vein, keeping the agenda-setting process open allows further crucial issues to be identified through the process. Sometimes it takes time for these to emerge, such as social, economic and equity questions within primarily environmentally focused processes.

Stakeholder participation Some MSPs reportedly benefited in terms of decreased power gaps because of the lack of participation, preparation or coordination by a potentially powerful stakeholder group. MSPs need to take care not to lose those who cannot easily become involved in further discussions, working groups, and so on due to a lack of time and resources. The early involvement of those who need to be involved is beneficial, otherwise the process can lack credibility and have less impact. As a general rule, one should note that participation processes take more time than expected. Many processes seem to have key people who acted as drivers and persisted in pushing the envelope and keeping others involved.

Power gaps It is recommended that people should keep in mind that power can be based on various kinds of resources. Power gaps do exist but different groups have different advantages (access to information, decision-making power, presumption of good intentions, access to building coalitions, ability to take quick decisions). The challenge is to identify one's power base and work with that – for example, community organizations and NGOs often succeed in bringing the media on their side which reduces the actual power of business and governments. MSPs tend to make those in power feel threatened, an issue which needs to be addressed by carefully defining the desired role of the MSP.

Chairing and facilitation Independent facilitation is regarded as better than facilitation being provided by a stakeholder or body which is not seen as independent.

Outcome documents MSP output should be summarized in short documents to ensure wider readership.

Meta-communication Many processes do not have such mechanisms and would reportedly benefit from them.

Consensus-building and decision-making Is consensus compromise by another name? Many people would not want to see an MSP leading to compromise but to consensus which integrates various views. Agreeing ground rules for decision-making is crucial.

Rapporteuring It is important that every stakeholder has an opportunity to record decisions taken – for example, minutes can be taken on a rotating basis.

Implementation If one sector leads an MSP, there is a danger that all others will look to the leading sector for implementation.

Closure/follow-up As decisions not to do something are almost always revisited, the advantage goes to those organizations who have staying-power.

MSP effects MSPs can help to build trust between participating stakeholders, for example between government or local governments and communities. This is perceived as very important as there is reportedly often a lack of trust.

Costs and funding MSPs are expensive and need a solid, well-prepared funding base to function properly and according to the ideals of inclusiveness, equity and transparency.

REPORTED PROBLEMS AND CONCLUSIONS

Some of the examples studied might not be MSPs in the strict sense according to our definition, because they a) did only involve two stakeholder groups plus governments and b) did not involve direct interaction of several stakeholder groups (eg FfD Hearings).

It appears that in some cases, there are different views on a process, its strengths and weaknesses. This is only natural as MSPs are about working in an area where there is a wide range of views and diverse actors. Differences arise, for example, with regard to the perception of power gaps (more on the side of weaker groups), of transparency (higher on the side of organizers), and so on. This also reflects different basic values or hierarchies of values. Whereas for many NGOs, for example, transparency and equity are high priorities, some businesses and governments can place more importance on quickening processes and producing outcome in a short time period. Our analyses have been limited as regards the numbers of people interviewed and more representative samples would most certainly generate an even wider range of views.

Multi-stakeholder nature of processes that have involved a diverse group of stakeholders from the start (say as an initial coordinating group) can better take into account the different viewpoints throughout the process. This is understandable as they are likely to have been designed with a strong view to inclusiveness, transparency, equity, and so on. But this is also an issue of increased commitment (and active input) of participants who have been involved right from the start. Where stakeholders have not been involved from the beginning, they sometimes question whether much effort has been made to be inclusive.

Issues and goals MSPs need specific objectives. Investing sufficient time into problem identification and agreeing issues and goals is key. A lack of agreed, specific objectives can impede an MSP's effectiveness, or at least can make it be perceived as less effective. It was recommended that MSPs should always tackle the easiest objectives and common ground first in order to build trust and pull out some real initial achievements; then it can start to face the more contentious areas. Focusing on the issues and creating a problem-solving group culture is an important prerequisite for success.

Capacity One commentator observed that lack of capacity is the first major problem of MSPs – lack of human and financial resources, time, and information and knowledge to enable meaningful participation. There is a need to ensure equitable capacity for participation. This has to be taken into account when designing an MSP, including its fundraising strategies and targets. The question of who is to design and provide human capacity-building also needs to be addressed.

Stakeholder participation MSPs seem often to be in a 'chicken and egg situation': 'So you start the work and then expose the work to a wider group of people or do you start with a very open process and get pulled in 20 directions immediately'? (Church, 2001). Step-by-step ways of increasing stakeholder involvement in the design process seem to be commonplace in cases where design is done through a body or process which involves several stakeholders. New participants joining the process always require additional attention as they will have a less strong sense of ownership of the principle elements that already exist. In general, many processes lack gender balance and many lack regional balance.

Linkage to constituencies Over the course of an MSP, some participants reportedly do not work well with their constituencies which creates problems for the process. They might tend to check with their organizations but not the broader constituency. Checking back with constituencies also depends on enough time and resources being available – differences can create power gaps. Another problem is what The Environment Council has called 'constituency drift': it may occur when stakeholder representatives take part in a process and learn through it, while their constituencies have not had that experience and do not necessarily agree with changes regarding views or strategies. This demonstrates the need for participants to work closely with their constituencies, particularly in MSPs which aim at agreements and implementation. The need to check back with constituencies can, however, reportedly also be (mis-)used as a veto-power or at least to stall a process of consensus-building and decision-making.

Preparations MSPs seem to benefit from preparatory material such as stakeholder position papers being available well in advance. It helps to make best use of the usually limited time available for multi-stakeholder meetings. This needs to be part of the design process and commitment to meet deadlines for submissions will be increased if participants have been part of the design process.

Formal procedures or communication, consensus-building and decision-making In general, it can be said that such formal ground rules seem to help an MSP. They also help to create transparency about processes which is sometimes lacking – whether because information is not publicized or is not easily accessible.

Consensus-building and decision-making Agreeing the ground rules for communication, particularly for seeking consensus and making decisions, is a crucial component of processes which aim at some kind of agreements. Concealing conflict can be used to achieve consensus-building which is not worthy of the name. An MSP can be rendered meaningless if the diversity of views and requirements leads to rather vague language in the outcome documents rather than acknowledging differences and working on them (at least towards agreement on disagreement). Open, honest, respectful and equitable communication and sufficient time will help to avoid concealing conflict for the benefit of the process.

Power gaps This issue seems in many processes not to be sufficiently addressed. It is certainly among the most difficult questions. In some examples, it is mentioned that lack of participation, preparation or coordination of governments, intergovernmental bodies or business has benefited the process through making a potentially dominating group less powerful. Some NGOs feel that strong and well-coordinated business involvement, for example, tends to dominate an MSP and lead to biased outcomes.

Dealing with power gaps needs to be given serious attention when designing an MSP and throughout the process (see also meta-communication, below). Some processes deal with the problem by assigning the same number of seats to all groups. Yet this is not the only aspect – differences in resources, capacities, education, eloquence, language skills, and so on impact on power balances.

Meta-communication, in other words communication by a group about its own processes, is reportedly lacking in most cases, and people say that more meta-communication would have been beneficial. Informal meta-communications can impede (perceived) transparency; therefore, some formal or plenary mechanism should be developed to help the group communicate about the way it communicates.

Linkage into official decision-making processes is another crucial point. In many cases, there is a lack of transparency in this regard, and governments and intergovernmental bodies are often reluctant to outline in more detail how processes feed into their decision-making. Creating transparent linkages is an important question in the design phase. The early involvement of decision-makers and potential implementers is recommended.

Coordinating organizations It is questionable whether processes that are entirely designed by one body can be developed into true dialogue processes which the participants can take some ownership of. (Sometimes, this is of course not the priority goal.) They are more likely to be perceived as lacking transparency and legitimacy. Particularly in cases where companies or government bodies create dialogue processes in such a way, they can easily be discredited as mere public relations jobs.

NGOs are (increasingly?) being taken on to facilitate processes – by businesses, business associations, governments, intergovernmental bodies. In such cases, the contracted organization tends to aim at openness, inclusiveness, transparency, equity and other key characteristics of MSPs which ensure increased credibility. It might be feasible to promote such practice. However, contracted organizations which become fully dependent on funding through MSP facilitation eventually become consultancies. It might not be a bad thing for NGOs to develop a consultancy part of their operation but this needs to be taken into account.

Time lines A number of problems arise from time constraints. However, people also assert the need to work within time lines to keep an MSP focused. Compressing MSPs into the timetables of official decision-making processes can be frustrating and a barrier to establishing a transparent, democratic and inclusive process. Often, decisions to include some kind of MSP in the preparations for an official meeting come late in the process. The reported fear of many (inter)governmental bodies towards developing 'never-ending', expensive processes also needs to be dealt with by making realistic suggestions and agreeing dates of closure and reporting-back mechanisms. Time limits are also a barrier towards increased involvement by other stakeholders and the public and/or consultation within constituencies. Stakeholder groups have different cultures and different requirements due to their different structures and mechanisms of decision-making, access to information and communication, and human and financial resources. Learning and acknowledging each other's positions, looking for a way to integrate them and building trust take time; hence time limits are a barrier to real dialogue.

Implementation There is general criticism of voluntary initiatives such as MSPs, particularly from NGOs. MSPs can be criticized as 'talk-shops' and for being misused as legitimization while not having to do anything. Monitoring MSP follow-up is important, otherwise the process may not lead to much result. There is a question, however, regarding who should take on the role of monitoring an MSP outcome/implementation process.

Building on previous experiences This seems to be done in some processes and not in others. Little information is available with regard to how processes build on or learn from previous experiences. It is more likely if the same initiating or coordinating bodies are involved. There is need for more networking and exchange between processes and documenting lessons learnt for future MSPs.

Funding Many MSPs report funding problems; process constraints and weaknesses can develop due to a lack of funding. It is important that MSPs are sufficiently funded and that developing fund-raising strategies and targets are part of the design process, taking into account the requirements of various stakeholder groups. The WCD seems to be an exceptional case in this regard and is being flagged by many as a leading example.

TWENTY EXAMPLES

The following presents a brief summary of the examples. Points where no information was available were left out. The literature we used is listed in the References section; interviewees were not named with the examples for reasons of confidentiality.

Although we aimed at a purely descriptive analysis, interviewees tended to make evaluations and comments and draw conclusions. Some of them have been included in the presentations, not because we share them but because they added to the picture. Where they present conclusions, as based on analysis undertaken by the interviewee, we have noted them. Where they are assessments which contradict other people's opinions, we have aimed to include several of those opposing views.

Also note that the information provided is dated April 2001; the ongoing processes will have developed further by the time of publication, and some of the finished processes will have had further impact and follow-up. For up-to-date information, please refer to the contact details and URLs given for each example:

1   Aarhus Convention Process
2   Beijing+5 Global Forum / Online Discussions (1999/2000)
3   CSD Multi-stakeholder Dialogues (1997–2000)
4   Environment Council: Brent Spar Dialogue Process (1996–1997)
5   Finance for Development Civil Society Hearings (2000)
6   Global Reporting Initiative (since 1997)
7   Local Agenda 21 Process A: Cooperation for Sustainable Development in the Lower Columbia River Basin (since 1999)
8   Local Agenda 21 Process B: Local Agenda 21 Processes (in the UK and elsewhere) (since 1992)
9   Multi-stakeholder Dialogues at the 8th Informal Environment Ministers Meeting, Bergen (2000)
10   Novartis Forum Events (1997–1999)
11   OECD/Biotechnology (1999–2000)
12   Processes Developing National Strategies on Sustainable Development A: National Strategies for Sustainable Development/International Institute for Environmental Development (IIED)
13   Processes Developing National Strategies on Sustainable Development B: Creation of National Councils for Sustainable Development/ Earth Council
14   UN Global Compact (since 1999)
15   WBCSD/IIED Mining, Minerals and Sustainable Development (1999–2001)
16   WBCSD/IIED Paper Initiative (1997)
17   WHO European Health and Environment Conference (1999)
18   WB World Development Report/Online Discussion of Draft Report (2000)
19   WB GEF Country Dialogue Workshops Program
20   WCD (1998–2000)

AARHUS CONVENTION PROCESS

The UNECE regional convention on access to information, public participation in decision-making, and access to justice in environmental matters

'The Aarhus Convention is a new kind of environmental agreement. It links environmental right and human rights. It acknowledges that we owe an obligation to future generations. It establishes that sustainable development can be achieved only through the involvement of all stakeholders. It links government accountability and environmental protection. It focuses on the interactions between the public and public authorities in a democratic context and it is forging a new process for public participation in the negotiation and implementation of international agreements' (UNECE, 2000).

Issues Public right to know, right to participate in environmental decision-making, right to justice in environmental matters. It links environment right and human rights.

Objectives Enhancing government accountability, transparency and responsiveness. Assisting civil society participation and helping to create participatory democracy for sustainable development in Europe.

Participants UNECE (forum of 55 countries of North America, Western, Central and Eastern Europe, and Central Asia); bodies involved in 'Environment for Europe' process (a framework bringing together environment ministers, institutions and organizations, including environmental citizens' groups); other relevant international organizations; environmental NGOs; other NGOs.

Scope Although legalities will only apply within the UNECE region, it has global implications and potentially could serve as a framework for strengthening citizens' environmental rights. Kofi Annan described it as the 'most impressive elaboration of Principle 10 of the Rio Declaration, which stresses the need for citizens' participation in environmental issues and for access to information on the environment held by public authorities'.

Time lines Full preparatory process culminating in adoption at the Fourth Ministerial Conference 'Environment for Europe' in Aarhus, Denmark, 25 June 1998; ongoing time-frame to implement.

Contact, URL Official process UNECE, Geneva; www.unece.org

Procedural aspects

Designing the MSP It evolved partly as a result of being one of the first major programmes to significantly involve NGOs at that stage. Design was done by UNECE, with three staff members. NGOs provided process advice, too. The governing body, the Committee on Environmental Policy, established a Working Group for the preparation of the Convention (January 1996) and also formed a 'Friends of the Secretariat' group to assist the process, based on the Sofia Guidelines (see below).

Identifying the issues Issues were concerned with the development of the Aarhus Convention, an idea that emerged from the 'Environment for Europe' process. The Convention has provoked interest when compared to other environment conventions because it focuses on the processes by which environmental decisions are made. The emphasis on process rather than on outcome provides an innovative model of multilateral policy-making. Specific issues flagged as requiring further attention under the auspices of the Convention are: genetically modified organisms (GMOs); the development of pollution registers; new forms of information, including electronic, and compliance issues.

Identifying relevant stakeholders Questions remain over whether there was any real attempt to identify relevant stakeholders. NGOs were invited to participate and went on to play a central and unprecedented role in negotiations drafting the Convention itself. This raises questions about the role of NGOs as opposed to the general public, as opposed to the broader voluntary sector. The Convention process differed from other official processes as NGOs assumed the practical status of full and equal partners. It was a government process with NGO involvement.

The UNECE process was well established, with a history of NGO involvement, for example parallel forums at the Sophia and Lucerne meetings, and a record of involving NGOs from Eastern Europe and the Newly Independent States (NIS). There was a good base for the Aarhus process. Timing was interesting, too, as UNECE were involving Eastern Europeans at a time when people was talking about engaging civil society. One problem was that it was clearly a ministerial 'Environment for Europe' conference, so there was a big emphasis on environment groups, with less on the social or economic development side. The Convention covers these broader interests, however.

Identifying participants An expert group of NGOs was involved and then a major strategy planning meeting took place attended by 100 NGOs. It was dominated, however, by a handful of Western NGOs with a very clear agenda. They dominated but could justify this by saying that the smaller organizations lacked the capacity. It is also questionable how far the process went beyond governments and NGOs. It is unclear what discussions UNECE had with business. There was academic involvement, with the lawyers/academics being mostly on the side of the NGOs.

Setting the goals The Aarhus Convention involves a long-term goal. The whole Environment for Europe process aims to strengthen environmental institutions, legislation, and so on. Aarhus was just the development of a convention. Comment: the elite of the NGOs did have opportunities to check back with their constituencies and to consult electronically via list servers and in other ways.

Setting the agenda There was a strong preparatory process, far stronger than anything in Europe up until that time, which in its way was groundbreaking. Also notable was the fact that during the ministerial conference, the NGOs had an afternoon where they set the agenda and booked the speakers. It was an important symbolic moment, with ministers sitting down and talking on an NGO agenda.

Setting the timetable The timetable was defined by setting the Aarhus meeting. The Convention was to be discussed there so all preparations had to be completed within the timetable. Two years of negotiations with inputs from countries and NGOs throughout the UNECE region.

Preparatory process The preparatory process included a large strategy meeting and some newsletters. It was mostly small group work which, considering it was a fairly arcane area of policy-making, is not surprising. The Convention is now completed.

Communication There is a question over how much consensus-building actually took place, although there was plenty of dialogue. Communication was conducted mostly in small groups and people were involved in these. Small group discussions were facilitated. Power gaps did exist but because the process was about the politics of participation, it would have benefited from more discussion about the process itself. The situation was dominated by a small group of NGOs working within a tight time-frame. Although there was time for reflection in between meetings, the process was heading towards one particular point.

Implementation As a policy-making process, implementation is now happening at a national level, with some monitoring and feedback to the international level, for example the Dubrovnik Review Conference (July 2000), attuned by ministers and NGOs. The UK Government has held a workshop on national and local implementation. NGOs are expected to play a major role in implementation processes.

Closure The process will not conclude for a long while yet. For example, the UK has only just (November, 2000) given royal assent to its Freedom of Information Act which 'directly supports sustainable development by providing enhanced access to information held by public authorities about their responsibilities and activities. This will be used to produce a culture of greater openness so that decisions taken are more transparent and, as a consequence, public authorities are more accountable for their actions' (DETR, 2001).

When the process does close there will be a need for ongoing monitoring. Given the crisis in implementation in so many conventions, there is a lot of NGO scepticism over how much difference this can really make.

NGO comment It will probably, ultimately, need to be challenged in the courts – hardly an example of good MSP practice!

Structural aspects

Institutional back-up and facilitation Secretariat – the UNECE is theoretically the facilitating body. The European Eco Forum (a coalition of environmental NGOs from across the UNECE region) coordinated the NGO response. It was a government process with NGOs there to some extent on sufferance, but recognizing that this was their chance. The whole process changed massively and is still going on, but the main body of work happened before the Aarhus conference.

Documentation There were huge amounts of documentation. Country reports were coordinated by the REC (Regional Environment Center for Central and Eastern Europe); small work groups produced reports, and so on. An Implementation Guide was published by the UNECE in 2000.

Relating to non-participating stakeholders Many stakeholders still don't know about the Convention, especially if stakeholders are defined as anyone who is going to be affected by it. For example, once the Convention is in force, any major developer putting in a planning application will, have to provide a lot more information to the public in a way that did not necessarily happen before. Post-Aarhus, European environmental citizens' organizations are calling for a pan-European campaign for transparency and participation to ensure that the Aarhus Convention and the UNECE Guidelines on Access to Environmental Information and Public Participation in Environmental Decision-making, endorsed in Sofia (October, 1995) by European Environment ministers, are fully implemented.

NGO comment The process would have benefited from more private sector involvement, but one reason that it did work was that the private sector paid it little attention.

Relating to the general public A great deal of information is available; the internet was widely used by stakeholders. However, very little is of relevance to the general public although the follow-up conference in 1999 tried to provide information that is relevant. It is now an information exercise and thus up to national governments.

For example, the UK DETR position is that as an agency it does not engage in specific MSPs; instead, it undertakes very general public consultation exercises in response to new proposals. It was suggested that the Environment Agency, working at a lower level, might do more innovative work. In its latest Annual Report reviewing progress towards sustainable development, the UK Government refers to the Aarhus Convention as 'strengthening the existing public access regime for environmental information and making it more liberal and more responsive'. The Report goes on to state that the Government 'is committed to improving public access to environmental information . . . New Regulations to bring the access regime up to this more demanding standard will be laid in most parts of the UK in 2001, well ahead of European Community legislation' (DETR, 2001).

Linkage into official decision-making The MSP was linked to the official decision-making process of developing a UNECE Regional Convention. The question now is how much implementation there will be. The Aarhus Convention is not yet ratified by enough countries for it to come into law (39 countries and the European Community have signed it). The original goal was for the Convention to come into force by the end of 2000.

Funding NGOs received funding from national governments (not all).

BEIJING+5 GLOBAL FORUM ONLINE DISCUSSIONS

Issues 12 areas of concern of the Beijing Platform for Action.

Objective Informing the preparations for Beijing+5.

Participants Open to anyone – participation by NGOs, UN, governments, researchers.

Scope global.

Time lines Scheduled online discussions of four to six weeks each.

Contact details, URL UN Division for the Advancement of Women (UN DAW), New York; www.un.org/womenwatch

During 1999, WomenWatch held global online working groups to gather information on the implementation of the 12 critical areas of concern of the Beijing Platform for Action (PfA). The 'Global Forum' was part of the UN Division for the Advancement of Women's (DAW) strategies to take women's NGOs contributions into account throughout the process of preparing for Beijing+5. It consisted of 12 scheduled online discussion groups addressing each of the PfA sections and open for all stakeholders to participate.

Procedural aspects

Identifying the issues Issues were the Beijing PfA 12 Areas of Concern. Within these areas, DAW developed a set of questions for each of the dialogues which were fed in week by week. The working groups focused on identifying:

1 Policies, legislation, strategies and partnerships that have been successfully furthering women's equality.
2 Case studies, best practices and examples of successful government, business and civil society efforts as well as lessons learned.
3 Remaining obstacles to progress and how they can be overcome.

Some of the topics generated much interest in the discussions, while others did not.

Identifying relevant stakeholders The UN DAW decided that they wanted participation from NGOs and others; invitations mostly targeted NGOs (DAW database, list servers, and so on).

Identifying participants Access was completely open. The 12 discussions had about 10,000 participants from over 120 countries altogether – mostly NGOs and government representatives, intergovernmental organizations and researchers. Participants were allowed to participate in as many debates as they wished.

Setting the goals, agenda and timetable DAW

Preparatory process Weekly questions were developed by experts within DAW.

There was no monitoring of preparations within stakeholder groups or by individual participants. Participants were not asked to speak for a particular group or body. Consultations among constituencies were possible, but no information is available summarizing such activities by participants.

Communication Email only. DAW were aware of power gaps arising from differences in Internet access but these were not addressed.

Decision-making No agreements sought.

Closure Set through the schedule by DAW.

Structural aspects

Institutional back-up The online discussions were facilitated by WomenWatch. 'WomenWatch is the UN gateway to global information about women's concerns, progress and equality. It was initiated by the Division for the Advancement of Women (DAW), the United Nations Development Fund for Women (UNIFEM) and the International Research and Training Institute for the Advancement of Women (INSTRAW). WomenWatch is an inter-agency activity involving the participation of many United Nations organisations.' (WomenWatch, 2000)

Facilitation Facilitation by DAW. One external moderator for each group was to screen the messages, the criteria being the relevance of the questions on each topic per week, and clarifying messages with people if necessary. There was an ongoing dialogue within DAW and WomenWatch throughout the process, with experts within the organizations, between them and the moderators, and so on.

Documentation The online discussions have been archived on the WomenWatch website and are publicly accessible. DAW also produced a summary document as a background document to the 3rd PrepComm for Beijing+5, United Nations: E/CN.6/2000/CRP.1.

Relating to non-participating stakeholders and to the general public Full archive and summaries available at www.un.org/women watch.

Linkage into official decision-making The background document was not discussed as such but was mentioned in the outcome document several times. Many NGOs felt that this exercise had not informed the process or had any impact on the Beijing+5 outcome document because they were not aware that anyone had used it to develop their positions.

Funding Funding came out of the DAW budget for Beijing+5. This was about US$600,000 from the UN Foundation, plus UNDP. The online discussions were part of the whole package.

Additional remarks This was an expensive process; hiring moderators required substantive funding. Holding online discussions for six weeks might be too long (and is expensive); reducing them to two to three weeks would be an option. It was commented that the online discussions were useful in terms of building and educating a constituency. It would be better to link in all stakeholders rather than only NGOs. Involved UN bodies such as UNIFEM were satisfied because it connected them with the public.

In general, online discussions should be summarized in a short report to be recommended, otherwise nobody will read it. The report should focus on the issues being highlighted – the important information for governments and others (to learn who thinks what). It might be good to conduct such discussions on issues that people are not yet debating to generate interest and initiate exchange.

UN COMMISSION ON SUSTAINABLE DEVELOPMENT MULTI-STAKEHOLDER DIALOGUES (MSD)

Issues Various, depending on the UN CSD agenda (1998: industry; 1999: tourism; 2000: sustainable agriculture; 2001: energy and transport).

Objectives To Inform the UN CSD negotiations.

Participants Over the past four years (1997–2000) trade unions, industry, local government, NGOs (including women and Indigenous Peoples), farmers.

Scope International.

Time lines 4 dialogue sessions over 2–3 days on 4 issues each year with a 6-month preparatory period.

Contact, URL UN Division for Sustainable Development, New York; www.un.org/dsd and www.un.org/esa/sustdev. Each stakeholder group may put it on their website.

Procedural aspects

Designing the MSP Done in consultation with stakeholder groups. NGOs' recommendations are the basis for the present design. The Secretariat presented it to the Bureau for agreement. Representatives of stakeholder groups (multi-stakeholder steering committee) before the first, second and third dialogues were involved in redesigning the process.

Identifying the issues The issues in the second multi-stakeholder dialogue (MSD) were defined by the stakeholders and agreed by the Bureau; the third was proposed by the Secretariat and comments by stakeholder groups; the fourth was defined by the Secretariat. In each case that means a broad description of issues but not the substance of subjects to be discussed. Generally, the Secretariat recommends to the Bureau.

Identifying relevant stakeholders The Secretariat recommends to the Bureau – there is no consultation.

Identifying participants Participants are identified by the stakeholder groups under their own processes: NGOs through consultation, with criteria such as expertise, gender and regional balance; trade unions on the basis of case studies submitted and on gender and regional balance.

Setting the goals In the third MSD the chair and his staff took a role in facilitating a process of stakeholders developing the goals together. They tried to find common ground and to build on this to make the MSD move into concrete areas of action beyond the dialogue. For the fourth dialogue the chair looked at disagreements and that impacted on the possibility of moving forward together.

Prior to the dialogues there is considerable consultation with constituencies. For the third dialogues the NGOs discussed whether to agree (or not) to the proposed basic outcomes the day before the dialogues started. Trade unions set their goals through an international working party.

Setting the agenda The agenda is set by the Bureau and the chair and also depends on the approach the chair takes. For the third dialogue there was considerable consultation with the stakeholders. Some stakeholders regularly submit suggestions.

Setting the timetable The timetable is set by the UN (the General Assembly Special Session (UNGASS), 1997, defined the ultimate timetable and everyone has worked to this).

Preparatory process When the topics are agreed stakeholders consult within their constituencies to prepare. Stakeholders employ various mechanisms of drafting and redrafting. By November/December groups complete draft papers for peer review before handing them into the UN Secretariat in mid-January (dialogues are in April). The coordinating bodies monitor what is happening within stakeholder groups. There is limited monitoring by the CSD Secretariat. The NGOs put material out into the public domain but they are the only group to do so.

Communication Various channels of communication are used – mostly email. Telephone conferences are held regularly to update on preparation. There are one or two face-to-face meetings per year. Power gaps are addressed by giving each group the same number of seats, and for NGOs and trade unions there is some travel funding.

Decision-making This depends on the chair. At the second and third MSDs agreement was sought. At the fourth meeting the chair was looking at disagreements, although finding agreement depends on the dialogues that take place among the stakeholders themselves.

The process is mostly geared towards influencing the chair, which in turn will affect the subsequent negotiations, and influencing participating governments.

Implementation If no follow-up is sought in the CSD decision, the process concludes at the CSD meeting itself. The CSD decisions following the MSDs in 1998–2000 did set up ongoing processes to implement parts of the agreements. Agreements to do this were taken by governments and the requirement is to report back to them. Coordination is given to particular UN agencies. There are different views as to the progress of the follow-up processes.

Closure Closure is fixed in advance but processes carry on informally. MSDs often form the beginning of an informal process. MSD follow-ups as of CSD decisions have formal reporting back mechanisms.

Structural aspects

Institutional back-up The CSD Secretariat facilitates the dialogues in consultation with stakeholder groups, but as these can change each year it puts the Secretariat in a strong position.

Facilitation The CSD Secretariat facilitates the interface between the stakeholders and the CSD Bureau. It facilitates the stakeholder preparations with each other and the dialogues themselves with the CSD chair. The Secretariat produces a UN document with the stakeholders' background papers and distributes it. The minutes from the Dialogue Sessions are taken by the Secretariat and produced into a chair's text. In many cases, the chair also has someone who shadows this.

Documentation The CSD chairs facilitate the dialogues. The summaries come out in their name, usually for the high-level ministerial meeting; if not, then for the negotiations the following week, which should draw on the chair's summary and the CSD intersessional meeting outcome.

Relating to non-participating stakeholders Information about the MSDs is available to other stakeholders if they are aware of the CSD information on the UN website and other websites of stakeholders and sometimes the chair. The CSD Secretariat also produces a printed newsletter.

Relating to the general public As above. The NGOs have open access to listen on the list servers preparing for the dialogues. The public cannot comment as it is a dialogue between stakeholder groups.

Linkage into official decision-making The MDS are linked to the official CSD process, through the high-level ministerial meeting and/or the negotiations the following week, which should draw on the chair's summary and the CSD intersessional meeting outcome. These linkage mechanisms are not transparent and there is no note to stakeholder groups or the chair – it depends on the Secretariat to tell them. This puts stakeholder groups who are new to the process into a disadvantageous position. Stakeholders can impact if they understand the timetable and work on the government members of the Bureau. For example, this happened for the third dialogue session only (1999) and was successful.

Funding The CSD Secretariat bears the costs; there is limited funding for stakeholders to attend the dialogues.

THE ENVIRONMENT COUNCIL/SHELL –
BRENT SPAR PROJECT

Issues How to dispose of an oil storage buoy that was provoking international attention and incidents.

Objectives To find a suitable disposal option and contractor to implement the decommissioning of the Brent Spar, an agreed decommissioning plan that all stakeholders could support; advising Shell on a decision they had to present to the UK Government.

Participants Central and local government, NGOs and pressure groups, ethics specialists, academics, technical experts and contractors, Shell staff.

Scope Regional: Europe-wide. UK Government decision.

Time lines November 1996–December 1997 (actual decommissioning finished on schedule January 2000).

Contact, URL The Environment Council, UK; www.the-environment-council.org.uk

> *The 'Brent Spar Project' was Shell's constructive and participative approach following its dispute with Greenpeace in 1995. Convened by the EC, the company sat down with a large number of its stakeholders and worked through a stakeholder dialogue process which enabled a new recommendation for the fate of the Spar as a quay extension in Norway.* (The Environment Council, 2001)

A real dialogue must be a two-way conversation. We must listen, engage and respond to our stakeholders. We will be judged by our actions rather than our fine words. (Harry Roels, Shell Services International, Shell Report, 2000; www.shell.com/royal-en/content)

Procedural aspects

Designing the MSP Initially a professional facilitator (The Environment Council) designed the process in consultation with the project manager from Shell, talking closely to some other stakeholders. Once the process was started, the stakeholders fed back on both content and process and they too shaped the design.

The facilitator had tried the process out on Shell staff and some other stakeholders to make sure she was prepared and that the process was robust.

Identifying the issues The stakeholders were given free rein with the issues which were generated at the workshop, in small, facilitated groups.

Identifying relevant stakeholders The Environment Council, through its experience of dialogue, identifies organizations and sometimes individuals, then asks the question 'Is there anybody not on our list that you think really should be?' The list stays open. The rule for the Brent Spar was that every person who attended the dialogue workshops needed to represent a 'constituency' to which they must report back and feed any constituency thoughts into the dialogue process. That way many more people were reached than were able physically to be there. In The Environment Council's experience participants often needed help when dealing with their constituencies.

Identifying participants If, when the stakeholders have been invited and a disproportionate number of one particular type – say, industry representatives – respond, then The Environment Council will actively chase stakeholders from other sectors to balance the numbers.

Setting the goals Content goals were not set. A question was posed. It was not 'Where do you want to decommission the Brent Spar?' but 'How can we decommission the Brent Spar in a way that all stakeholders can support?'

Often the funder (in this case Shell) has a need (to dispose of the Brent Spar), and the goal is to keep the question as broad as possible. Many thought Shell still wanted to 'dump', as they called it, because it was the cheapest option. Funders need to be aware that goals are likely to develop – they are likely to hear things in the dialogue that make them want to change their goals when a quicker or less conflictual path becomes apparent. It is often something nobody has thought of before, because the 'intelligence' has never been brought together in this way before. This happened with the Brent Spar. It went from being a piece of waste that Shell had to dispose of to a highly valued bit of steel which a number of development projects would dearly have loved to acquire.

Setting the agenda The agenda in terms of process is set by the Core Group (in this case The Environment Council facilitator and Shell staff). In terms of substance, it is up to the participants. The outline is provided by the facilitators; participants provide the filling and therefore the kind of outcome.

Setting the timetable Facilitators had an idea of a timetable, but this was open to change.

Preparatory process Many papers, a CD-ROM and other user-friendly documents were produced and distributed to the stakeholders to help them decide if they wanted to be part of the dialogue process. Central records of all meetings are kept by the Project Coordinator at The Environment Council. This is usually in the form of photographic reports of meetings which are written on flip-chart paper.

Communication In the beginning, a lot of one-to-one telephone work is required to build the list of stakeholders. Then invitations and information are sent out, followed by joining instructions and finally the workshop. This was the first time that some had met, while others had met in confrontational situations such as on television news programmes. If there is high conflict there are facilitators to facilitate small groups. They ensure that voices are heard, and thoughts and values are translated into words on the flip-chart. It is an essential part of planning a process that people of all types are able to contribute towards. For those who have a problem talking in large plenary groups, there are smaller group exercises.

Decision-making Consensus was sought by asking appropriate questions and choosing appropriate techniques to ensure that there was a level of understanding among the participants, enabling them to make decisions based on technical information, and the values and needs of their constituencies. The facilitator designed this process and intervened to ask questions that aimed to get to consensus agreements. The key to this was to get the participants at workshops in London, Copenhagen, Holland and Germany to come up with criteria that any proposed option should meet. Thus, if Shell chose a disposal option which met these criteria, the stakeholders would be happy.

Implementation Enabling the 'right' action/implementation was the goal of the dialogue. The potential contractors were well aware of that and at some points were involved in the dialogue.

Closure The process concluded when there was a final stakeholder workshop and the participants agreed that they were happy for Shell to make a final decision based on the criteria developed, and on specific pointers and concerns around each option that were highlighted at that workshop. The participants were asked to theoretically choose, in small groups, which option they would like. The difference in opinion was striking, and some groups strongly disliked the exercise. This demonstrated the difficulty in the decision-making process.

Structural aspects

Institutional back-up The Environment Council managed the whole process and had many planning meetings with Shell to make sure that everyone was up to date and that the material going out was in plain English (not engineering speak), and so on. The Council also arranged events, invitations and venues. This was a highly political issue at the time, and Council's coordinator and facilitator acted as 'honest brokers' at times with parties who had difficulty contributing to, understanding and/or trusting the process. Workshops were used to gain input from participants and to put dilemmas to participants, in order to inform Shell of stakeholder needs, and to inform stakeholders of Shell's constraints in choosing options (there was, for example, a hole in the structure which made it unsafe).

Facilitation By The Environment Council.

Documentation Reporting was done verbatim from flip-charts and Post-it notes used at the events. Reports were also transcribed with nothing changed. Stakeholders could then share the outcomes of the workshops with their constituents to get their feedback and comment on the process. The reports were put on the web and made available to anybody in document form, too.

Relating to non-participating stakeholders The facilitator was constantly on call to all participants who felt they might have difficulty relating why they had made the decisions they did at the dialogue workshop. Sometimes a stakeholder may go back to their constituency and, after the learning experience of the workshop, have a different opinion from that held previously. The constituency has not had this learning experience which might cause difficulty at this stage ('constituency drift').

Relating to the general public Schools packs were produced, a competition was set up to see who had good ideas for the decommissioning of the Brent Spar, a website and a CD-ROM were created, as well as many other forms of communication. The press were particularly interested in this project, so disseminating the decisions of the process was very easy (eg the *Six O'Clock News*).

Linkage into official decision-making Shell needed to present a recommendation to the Government. The Government could reject their recommendation, but since there was a wide range of stakeholder support for the final decision, this was highly unlikely. The UK Government welcomes processes that produce consensus between a wide range of stakeholders because it makes ministers' jobs easier – they know that no key stakeholder will object to the decision they make.

Funding Shell paid – on the polluter pays principle. Shell were definitely the problem holder, having had a flawed decision-making process the first time around. (Although it was not legally flawed, it was not a legitimate decision and the public would not let them implement it.) The process cost £450,000.

Additional remarks The Brent Spar episode is perceived by industry and government as a 'defining moment' in the relationship with environmental groups and the general public. It marked a shift towards seeking more open dialogue, and for campaigning groups it was a move towards solutions-oriented campaigning. In 1995, following a Greenpeace direct action campaign and Shell's subsequent decision not to use the ocean for disposing of the unwanted Brent Spar, pending further discussion regarding options, Greenpeace commented that it was to Shell's credit that it had had a sea change in its attitudes. Greenpeace analysed its own tactics following the 'Brent Spar experience' at their 'Brent Spar and After' conference in September 1996, trying to work out what the 'defining moment' meant in practice.

UN FINANCING FOR DEVELOPMENT HEARINGS (FFD)

Issues Financing for development and sub-issues.

Objectives Informing FfD negotiations; identify viable proposals, innovative ideas, action-oriented suggestions for the FfD process.

Participants NGOs, business.

Scope International.

Time lines July–November 2000 (Hearings) – February 2001 2nd Prep-Comm (summary reports) – September 2001 (UNU book publication).

Contact, URL Financing for Development Coordinating Secretariat, New York; http://www.un.org/esa/ffd

Procedural aspects

Designing the MSP The initial idea was sparked by a precedent: before the General Assembly (GA) decision on FfD, there were formal hearings in the GA 2nd Committee (in 1998–99). At the organizational 1st PrepComm, the Secretariat suggested modalities of civil society involvement in the process: dialogues (modelled after CSD dialogues) or hearings. Nobody pushed the CSD model because nobody was really familiar with it. There was also concern about the amount of resources required to run a dialogue process similar to CSD, and concerns about the burden put on delegates in terms of preparatory papers, and so on.

It is questionable if this is an MSP as hearings with NGOs and business were held separately.

Identifying the issues Issues were predefined as the issues of the FfD process, based on decisions by the GA and the FfD Bureau. Participants chose which of these issues they wanted to address.

Identifying relevant stakeholders This was based on a broad definition of civil society by the FfD Bureau; included were NGOs (who included women), business, trade unions and academics.

Identifying participants Slightly different strategies were necessary to identify participants from the NGO and the business communities. The process started by identifying possible panellists via the following means, starting on July 2000:

1 contacting the network of NGOs (small at that time), mostly those who participated at the 1st PrepComm (ten NGOs);
2 sending information to relevant list serves; and
3 issuing personal invitations (20 to 35) to people identified by the Secretariat (DESA), UNDP, WB and the Non-governmental Liaison Service (NGLS).

People took some time to respond; by September 2000 there were few confirmations – a rather frantic time followed to find panellists and alternates between September and November 2000. Potential participants were then required to submit outlines of their planned presentations. These were reviewed within the FfD Secretariat by the NGO Focal Point and colleagues knowledgeable on the various issues. Selection criteria were: critical approaches; innovative ideas; possible policy recommendations; balance by gender and region. The Secretariat made suggestions into which panel potential participants would fit. The decision was taken by the FfD Bureau.

NGOs: there were 23 panellists, including one trade union representative and one academic (of an initially longer list of academics), and women.

Business: achieving the goal of regional and gender balance was difficult, particularly because the process was supposed to be very open. Getting successful *and* available business representatives to participate is difficult (it is usually either/or). After submission of the first drafted list, the Bureau required that more developing countries' business representatives should be identified. In the end, only one North American business representative was present at the hearings. The process of identifying business people was more top-down than with the NGOs; there was more active search required. It was difficult to find interested business people (in the traditional sense) and people who would trigger ideas rather than make requests.

Setting the goals The goals were set by the 1st PrepComm, the FfD Bureau and Secretariat (making suggestions). The goals were to have a process as broad and as open as possible. The hearings organized by the GA in 1994 served as the model. No new organizational grounds were covered; hence the process was labelled a 'hearing'.

Setting the agenda The FfD Bureau set the agenda. The NGO format was that all panellists spoke, followed by questions and answers. In the business format, questions and answers occurred after each panellist's presentation.

Setting the timetable The initial idea was to invite both groups, NGOs and business, for the same dates. There was resistance from the business community towards that idea, so it was decided to hold the NGO and business hearings separately.

Preparatory process Participants were required to send their papers well in advance and about 50 per cent of them did so. It would have been better if more of the presentations had been circulated well in advance.

Communication Hearings were held as face-to-face meetings with questions and answers following the presentations. Room for discussion was limited as some presentations were too long so that little time was left. As stakeholder groups did not participate at the same time (business and NGO hearings were separate), no dialogue took place between business and NGO representatives at the hearings. There are diverse views regarding government participation – some view it as little (with no real interaction), some as significant. The assessment also seems to depend on the respective issues being addressed. Some governments feel they do not need to enter discussions at the hearings as they perceive the process as an informative input into intergovernmental negotiations. The process did not have space for meta-communication (but some people said that would have been good).

Decision-making No agreement was sought; it was an informative process providing input into subsequent intergovernmental deliberations.

Implementation No implementation process is being sought at this point. Implementation will depend upon decisions coming out of the intergovernmental FfD process, to be finalized by March 2002.

Closure The FfD hearings were single events. However, most likely the process of civil society input is not over. There might be more, maybe at the international, maybe at regional levels. This will depend on decisions to be taken at the 2nd PrepComm and what requests it will generate towards the FfD Secretariat to organize further procedures of stakeholder involvement, such as round-tables on certain issues (for further exploration) or panels on issues where the documents are rather weak so far. The FfD Bureau is discussing the idea of a 'task force on business' which would aim to design a follow-up process with the private sector.

Structural aspects

Institutional back-up UN DESA/Financing for Development Secretariat.

Facilitation The FfD process has a 15-member Bureau, with 2 co-chairs at ambassador level. The co-chairs alternated at hearings. The co-chairs and other Bureau members worked all week on these, starting Sunday morning with a four-hour briefing with participants, with Bureau members making presentations; then there were the hearings themselves followed by more events. This was viewed as very significant engagement and involvement of the governments present. The hearings also triggered increased NGO involvement (10 at the 1st PrepComm; 100 registered for the 2nd PrepComm by January 2001). In the FfD Secretariat, one person is working on this process (NGO Focal Point), with help from a person in NGLS and from people within the Secretariat who are knowledgeable on certain issues, to help review submitted outlines of presentations.

Documentation The goal is to publish the hearings' outcomes as objectively as possible. Documentation is as follows: the FfD Secretariat produced two summaries of business and NGO hearings respectively, which were official reports to the 2nd PrepComm (not background papers, which was viewed as a success), translated into all UN languages. A UN university book publication is planned for September 2001, to make the material publicly available (targeting, for example, NGOs, academia) and to provide delegates. The book will be much more widely accessible than UN papers.

Relating to non-participating stakeholders Information is publicly available via the FfD website. NGOs have been disseminating information to their constituencies and networks. Feeding into the preparations of presentations was possible but dependent on the process of preparation chosen by the participants. There was more or less consultation, but it is difficult to assess as this information was not requested by the process.

Relating to the general public FfD website. Feeding into the process by the general public is difficult; interested people would need to get in touch with those already involved.

Linkage into official decision-making The hearings have been the starting point of bringing substance into the FfD process; the 1st PrepComm was only organizational. It is for government delegates to pick up what the summary reports offer (as is true for the Steering Group (SG) reports). It is up to the intergovernmental process to bring the initiatives together. People who judge the hearings as well attended them believe that the reports will be used. There was also sometimes a sense of complicity between G77 countries and NGOs, but it is not foreseeable how that will play out in the negotiations. NGOs have been organizing briefings to increase understanding of certain issues, especially for delegates; steps forward are possible and likely, but it does not depend only on the preparatory papers – negotiations are different.

Funding The hearings were funded out of the FfD Trust Fund and by Nordic country governments. The UNDP provided travel funding for three panellists, the FfD Secretariat for seven. The UK Government supported panellists' with a daily allowance and funded seven to eight NGOs to attend. Business representatives from developing countries were also funded (four to five people).

GLOBAL REPORTING INITIATIVE (GRI)

Issues Developing consensus on a global framework for corporate environmental/sustainability reporting. Multi-stakeholder perspectives.

Objectives To develop and disseminate globally applicable sustainability reporting guidelines for voluntary use by organizations reporting on the economic, environmental and social dimensions of their activities, products and services. GRI is a long-term, multi-stakeholder, international undertaking, focused on the corporate sector, with possible extensions to other organization types in future, such as local municipalities, NGOs.

Participants The Coalition for Environmentally Responsible Economies (CERES); NGOs; accountants; business; international organizations such as UNEP.

Scope International/national. International processes may spark off national or local level MSPs.

Time lines Initiated in late 1997, ongoing, developing process.

Contact details, URL: www.globalreporting.org

Procedural aspects

Designing the MSP The Coalition for Environmentally Responsible Economies (CERES), in collaboration with the Tellus Institute, convened the GRI in late 1997. (CERES is the coalition of environmentally concerned groups that sponsors the ten-point CERES principles.) The UNEP then joined as a key partner. Encouragement was given to others to become part of the process.

    The GRI has two main components:

1 To develop a multi-stakeholder, global consultation process based on the principles of transparency and inclusiveness.
2 The development and dissemination of the GRI's Sustainability Reporting Guidelines.

The process for the initiative was fairly organic. Initially, an informal group of like-minded people developed the concept, then a more formal group was set up (also involving new individuals) as a Steering Committee (SC) to develop the Mission Statement. The SC has membership from 7 countries and 17 organizations and has guided the GRI to date. The statement was open to comment and change for others outside the SC. Now it is fairly defined, although it is still open to change. The core principle is to allow anyone interested and committed to the process to participate, that is no stakeholder is being excluded. Also, if a party should decide not to participate, then they can still receive regular updates and reports on the process for purposes of transparency and openness.

The opportunity for GRI arose in response to rising expectations for greater corporate accountability, transparency and encouragement for more companies to move towards sustainability reporting (as opposed to just financial reports).

Identifying the issues CERES identified potential SC members to kick-start the process. The Steering Committee had the initial idea and then widened the discussion. GRI meetings were held in more than 15 countries – 35 countries have been involved so far. The GRI process developed through working groups, briefings, conferences and communications. The GRI's Sustainability Reporting Guidelines were released in a draft format in March 1999, and opened to comments and testing. The Revised Guidelines released in June 2000 were developed with the help of representatives from business, NGOs and governments across the world.

Identifying relevant stakeholders The process of identification began informally, then through a more coordinated structure (SC). Alliances were built, eg John Elkington (SustainAbility), Roger Adams (from the UK Association of Chartered Certified Accountants – ACCA) and working groups and programmes developed. The SC meet quarterly and less frequent 'open meetings' are held to identify the focus of a working group, eg Social Development Indicators. Governments, NGOs, businesses, business associations, labour organizations and human rights groups are involved to date.

Identifying participants The GRI is open to all individuals and organizations interested in sustainability reporting. There is particular targeting of multinational corporations in this phase. The GRI clearly states that it will not enter formal alliances, partnerships or ventures with commercial firms. Altogether, 21 companies pilot tested the draft guidelines, published in 1999 – about half volunteered and the rest were recruited after the gaps became obvious. They were selected on the basis of various criteria, such as geographical balance, diversity in size, reporting experience, and so on. Many other stakeholders – corporate and non-corporate – provided feedback. Several companies have already published GRI reports.

Setting the goals The GRI Steering Group in partnership with stakeholders has guided developments so far. The vision aims to move, over time, from an informing process to one that brings together disparate reporting initiatives into a new multi-stakeholder, global process, with ramifications for disclosure, investment and business responsibility. Set out in a mission statement (defined by the SC) and refined through ongoing dialogue and consultation (largely via the internet and email).

Setting the agenda The GRI in collaboration with stakeholders. An open process, so checking back is possible. Process in steps: stewardship (consolidation), tools (identification issues) to application (use and implementation). Set by the SC and open meeting.

Setting the timetable The process is ongoing. This band of activities will finish in 2002. The timing is led by the SC, the Secretariat and Transitions Director.

Preparatory process The GRI describe the process as intensive, multi-stakeholder and international. As well as from input from business and governments, the June 2000 release benefited from the thinking of labour organizations, human rights, environmental and investor groups. The GRI identifies initiatives, invites them into the process and tries to find common elements across the programmes. It optimizes the use of email, regional meetings and video conferences to ensure a top-down, bottom-up balance. It uses the internet for grass-roots and NGO monitoring and feedback. People are involved more in a personal capacity and less on behalf of organizations, so consultation is less relevant and anyone can be involved. However, where contentious issues arise people can go away and assess.

Communication Extensive use of electronic reporting to facilitate dialogue dissemination. Email, meetings, conferences, international symposia, for example Washington. The process seeks to be neutral as far as possible. Careful and strong chairing in a meeting is essential. The GRI offers an opportunity to NGOs to deliver their message to industry and government actors. The GRI view the process as one which enhances and disseminates the Guidelines through ongoing consultation and stakeholder engagement.

Decision-making Agreement is sought through working groups; careful wording and clarification of definitions is often necessary. Groups work by consensus, not by majority.

Implementation The Guidelines will be a useful resource for any company wishing to use them. They were described by Roger Adams of the ACCA as 'a major step towards a generally accepted, global framework for sustainability reporting' (DETR, 2001). The test of whether the GRI succeeds in improving the quality of company reporting will depend on the number of companies adopting the

Guidelines. The process is constantly redefined (this is an integral part of the GRI process) and redesigned through an iterative, open process (rather like software development – version 1.0, 2.0, and so on).

Closure The process is still in its early stages. The Guidelines will be further tested and refined. Work is to be done on strengthening and increasing stakeholder engagement. The SC decides with open meeting consultation.

Structural aspects

Institutional back-up The SC, Secretariat, working groups, open forum (largely internet-based). The interim Steering Committee reflects the GRI's multidisciplinary and international dimension. Set up in early 1998 and currently based in Boston, US. Efforts are under way to build a permanent GRI institution, governed by a Board of Directors and involving multi-party technical and stakeholder groups to ensure the continuation of the GRI's core values of inclusiveness and transparency.

Facilitation The GRI Secretariat, in partnership with CERES (GRI base) and the UNEP. Offers research, meeting, drafting, coordination services.

Documentation There is extensive use of the (internet; reports, frameworks and so on are being produced – the first draft of the GRI Guidelines in 2000.

Relating to non-participating stakeholders The June 2000 release of the GRI's Sustainability Reporting Guidelines attracted widespread attention. The Guidelines can be used by any relevant institutions and the UK Department of Trade and Industry for example, is currently seeking independent advice on the feasibility of their reporting against the Guidelines. The GRI is now working to strengthen stakeholder engagement and can receive information, comment and input at any opportunity.

Relating to the general public The GRI is not really a public forum but the process is open to comments from relevant individuals. Information is available via the internet. The GRI Guidelines provide reporters and users of reports with guidance on reporting principles and recommendations for report content. They also include indicators covering the 'triple bottom line' issues – environmental, social and economic issues – which will make it easier for users of reports, such as investors, to compare performance across organizations. Information is available through brochures, the internet, and the press.

Linkage into official decision-making The GRI is a voluntary initiative and a non-governmental process. The agreed principle initially was that government involvement at too early a stage could slow down the process and be potentially hazardous. Now, however, government interest is growing and the GRI is often consulted in other processes, the EU Disclosure guidelines, such as the OECD equivalent, by the International Organization for Standardization (ISO), UNEP, GC, UN, ILO, and the High Commission for Human Rights. The GRI is assisting the processes of standard reporting.

Funding The GRI is funded mainly by foundations including the United Nations Foundation, Ford Foundation, MacArthur Foundation, CS Mott Foundation, as well as Spencor T Oil (US), the US Environmental Protection Agency and one Danish funder (undeclared). A business plan to secure future growth is under way. Independence is an issue. The budget is around US$3–4 million for the first three years. Requirements will grow to US$4–5 million per year. The proposal in the future is to create a trust, ensuring transparency. Funders will have no control or influence over the distribution of their funds.

LOCAL AGENDA 21 PROCESSES A: COOPERATION FOR SUSTAINABLE DEVELOPMENT IN THE LOWER COLUMBIA RIVER BASIN

Issues Urbanization, agricultural and forest practices, fisheries practices, economic development and navigation.

Objectives Informing and defining processes to create a community-based political counterpoint to a proposal from the United States Corps of Engineers to dredge the Columbia River channel from the Pacific Ocean to the Port of Portland, Oregon. To build on this issue a specific coalition to create an ongoing bi-state local community involvement strategy towards sustainable development of the lower Columbia River basin.

Participants The National Oceanic and Atmospheric Administration's (NOAA) Office of Sustainable Communities through the consultancy Sustainable Strategies & Solutions, Inc, the City of Astoria, Oregon, Port of Astoria, Astoria News, a variety of local governments from both Washington State and Oregon, including port districts, cities, counties, water districts and forestry districts, regional environmental NGOs, chambers of commerce, and the Governors' offices from both Washington and Oregon.

Scope The proposal involved national, state, regional (counties) and local authorities, and coastal communities on both shores of the final 150 miles of the Columbia River. It needed to bring together a variety of data centres and plans.

Time lines: Ongoing since mid-1999.

Contact, URL: Gary Lawrence, Sustainable Strategies and Solutions, Inc. Email: jgarylawrence1@home.com

Procedural aspects

Designing the MSP The process in which a broader outreach was to be accomplished was designed by a team representing the City of Astoria, representatives of local economic development organizations and regional environmental NGOs, with assistance from the NOAA which provided a consultant. Advice was solicited from the media, the League of Women Voters and political party organizations.

Identifying the issues The catalysing issue, dredging the Columbia River channel, was proposed by the Port of Portland, agricultural interests in eastern Washington and Oregon, Idaho and Montana in conjunction with the US Corps of Engineers. A great oversimplification of the core issue was that it was a fight for survival in which fisheries' interests were pitted against agricultural interests.

Identifying relevant stakeholders Some of the relevant stakeholders – local and state governments – were obvious. Many of the environmental and business stakeholders were identified through their participation in litigation and public information campaigns. Community organizations such as churches, welfare organizations and social clubs were identified through consultation with local newspapers and radio reporters. There is a continuing attempt to broaden the stakeholder base to include urban constituencies in major media markets.

Identifying participants It was left to each organization to choose their representative. Smaller organizations were offered assistance in organizing local meetings in case they wanted to appoint shared representatives. When particular participants, by personality or history, were perceived by other organizations to be barriers to progress, the consultant was asked to work with the organization to find a different representative. It was important that stakeholders' viewpoints were considered objectively, and some representatives had histories that made hearing their points of view difficult.

Setting the goals Goals were proposed by the instigating group (NOAA, Astoria, Columbia River Watershed Alliance) and changed or adjusted at the first and second organizing meeting. The group tried to function as a consensus organization, although 'mission creep', a gradual broadening of goals, was resisted in order to keep scarce resources and limited energy focused on the initial priorities. Participants were encouraged to check back with their constituents regularly. Some participants did not work well with their own constituents, and this was a problem. Also, some attempted to exercise veto power at critical junctures by declaring a need to check back even after there had been ample opportunity to get direction earlier.

Setting the agenda For the initial issue – proposals to dredge – the agenda and time lines were determined by the Corps of Engineers' submission of an application for review under the US National Environmental Policy Act (NEPA). There is ample time under the review calendar of NEPA for those who follow the processes closely to check back *if* communications channels and communication coordination is established within the organization up front. A loosely run system in which reviewers feel no time pressure will not work. After failure to agree upon clear, outcome related goals, poor information management that does not establish personal responsibility or take into account different learning styles, is a fundamental barrier to success.

Setting the timetable The timetable was established by the initiating partners – Astoria et al – to ensure compliance with the legislatively established project review and comment requirements. Even the time line for legal appeals is covered in NEPA.

Comment It is often the case that stakeholder processes must be compressed in order to comply with legislatively mandated time limits, as frustrating as that can sometimes be.

Preparatory process The more formal dialogue (newsletters, and so on) was prepared by a consultant who listened to the informal dialogue within and among stakeholder groups and then fed back to the groups, in non-jargon language, what he interpreted to be the important issues. The stakeholders group did some editing and then approved the effort.

Comment To my knowledge, there is no programme to monitor for either faithfulness to the agreed dialogue or the effectiveness of the dialogue in educating the public. It is always a struggle when specific interests are trying to act like a group. Priorities, language, the need to satisfy constituencies, and so on, result in a lot of 'word-smithing' and, if one is not careful, it can render the dialogue meaningless.

Communication Within the smaller communities involved, communication is mostly face-to-face or through small, informal meetings. In the larger communities and in the larger interest groups, the communication takes place through meetings, newsletters and the telephone.

There are significant differences in power. Federal and state governments have information, access and staying power that is unavailable to community organizations. The private sector has the ability to take its decisions more quickly and in private, contrary to the public meeting requirements of local government. The community organizations have the advantage of a 'presumption of good intentions' that makes it easy to question the statements and findings of government. In this case, the local governments, community organizations and local media are all in tune so that they can present forceful arguments through public media to individuals who count on the local constituency for re-election. The local communities, in this case, also have an advantage of federal and local law and regulation that gives them a standing in court when the legal process starts.

Populism is the predominant political ethic in the Pacific Northwest part of the US. Laws codify the rights of individuals to participate in governmental decision-making, and the public almost always bring the power of the public media to their side. This tends to reduce the willingness of elected officials to overuse their statutory authority. Community organizations, especially through environmental laws, can often stop or modify projects through their power to slow things down while, with the support of the media, taking the 'moral high-ground.'

Decision-making The efforts started by Astoria et al are intended to reach agreement among other compatible stakeholders so that no agreement is possible with the proposal to dredge the river channel. A steering committee of stakeholders is responsible for this area.

Implementation Not applicable at this time.

Closure It is likely that, as a result of lawsuits and legal appeals, elections, and so on, a final decision to dredge or not to dredge based on the current application will take a few years. Then, if the decision is not to dredge, the issue will come up again in a decade or so and the entire process will restart. Decisions not to do something are almost always revisited. Ultimately, the advantage goes to those organizations that have staying power.

Structural aspects

Institutional back-up The stakeholders group has not been formulated as a legal organization. This effort is ad hoc and built upon a fragile trust rather than bylaws.

Facilitation Two members of the Astoria City Council facilitate the process. City Council members are elected to serve part-time on the assumption that their income will come from full-time jobs in the community. One member is director of an environmental stakeholder and another is involved with a local economic development organization. They use City of Astoria staff for meetings arrangement, mailings, etc – a common practice in the Pacific Northwest of the US.

Documentation The minutes from meetings are taken by different stakeholders on a rotating basis. Publications are produced by one of the local governments on a rotating basis.

Comment It is important that every stakeholder has an opportunity to be the recorder of decisions taken.

Relating to non-participating stakeholders Other stakeholders know about the process. Participants are all trying to extend their constituencies through this process. Most of the formal outreach comes through the editorial page of the regional newspaper and through solicitation of comments at public meetings. A more formal outreach process in a time-limited process with ad hoc stakeholder collaborations is difficult. In this particular case, the applicants for permission to dredge are required by law to have public meetings and public written comment periods. They are also required to record public comments and their responses. Ultimately, all of this is included as information for review if and when the project review moves to the courts.

Comment As always, the right to be heard does not result in any obligation to be heeded. The comments need to expose flaws in the environmental findings and proposed mitigation.

Relating to the general public Only what the newspaper and radio chooses to cover, statements recorded in public meetings, reports from meetings and word of mouth, is available to the public. Information is provided by all the stakeholders working off an agreed-upon focus document. There is no controlled comment requirement.

Linkage into official decision-making This entire MSP is driven by the notion that there is strength in collaboration when providing opposing views in a formal National Environmental Policy Act process. The US Army Corp of Engineers is the project applicant, along with freight, aluminium and agricultural interests, who see the river as a means of transport that gives the products a competitive cost advantage. The law prescribes formal input mechanisms. There are informal mechanisms, designed to affect the weighting that decision-makers give environmental considerations versus economic interests. The formal mechanisms are completely transparent. Informal mechanisms are as transparent as either party cares to make them or as transparent as the media can make them.

Funding Funding comes from each stakeholder in support of their participation. In this case, local governments are subsidizing the participation of community-based organizations by paying for meeting rooms, supplying facilitators and producing publications.

Comment Unless there is some cost loading on organizations with taxing power and resources in place, most small NGOs will get left out.

LOCAL AGENDA 21 PROCESSES B: LOCAL AGENDA 21 (IN THE UK AND ELSEWHERE)

Issues equity, strong partnership, community participation, improving people's quality of life; environment + social issues + economic issues = sustainability.

Objectives Partly awareness-raising/informing, partly planning; developing and implementing an action plan, based on shared visions, for local sustainable development.

Participants Local authorities, civic society, NGOs, community-based organisations, business and more

Scope Local/regional, sparked off by an international process.

Time lines Initiated Earth Summit 1992, ongoing.

Contact Jan McHarry, London, email: jmcharry@earthsummit2002.org; Chris Church, London, email: cjchurch@geo2.poptel.org.uk

Procedural aspects

Designing the MSP The process has never been designed around a single template; as a result, 'a thousand flowers have bloomed'. Some have become genuine attempts at better community planning, others little more than environmental awareness exercises. The UK Local Government Management Board (now the Improvement and Development Agency) issued guidance – *Local Agenda 21: Principles and Process. A Step by Step Guide* (1994) – but this was not really about process design. In fact, virtue was made of the fact that all LA21s were going to be different, which is one of the problems for evaluation. The consultation procedures were often designed by people looking upwards, rather than starting at the grass-roots, which was why much consultation did not break out of the traditional mould, did little to empower people or communities, but carried on the 'business as usual' approach.

The ICLEI has, over the years, run a variety of MSPs, such as the European Local Agenda 21 Round-table Programme. Stakeholder representatives are identified through networks, the ICLEI database and wide-ranging participation – from faith groups to business, from women to youth to local authorities. Participants are identified as 'experts' involved at the European level or concerned with urban sustainability. This can be a broad swathe of people – churches, elderly people, cyclists – depending on the issue. The round-table is essentially a brainstorming, with results now disseminated by the web (for economy and effectiveness). Usually the ICLEI tries to get the host city to make a declaration or recommendation.

Identifying the issues Local Agenda 21 is the process of developing local policies for sustainable development and building partnerships between local authorities and other sectors to implement them. It is a crucial part of the move towards sustainability. LA21 is a continuing process rather than a single activity, event or document. There is no single 'tick-list' of things you must do or cover for LA21. Instead, the process involves a range of activities, tools and approaches from which local partners, including the local authority, can choose according to local priorities and circumstances.

Identifying relevant stakeholders The process varies enormously. Within two to three years of LA21 starting, information was available to guide anyone who wanted to have serious input from, and dialogue with a range of stakeholders, but many processes remained based within the local authority, relying on their mailing lists. The traditional way of involving people was to ask them to participate. The stakeholders were largely defined by LA21.

In their analysis of LA21s from around the world, the Women's Environment and Development Organizations (WEDO) state that the

> *cases clearly demonstrated that to a large extent there has not been an explicit approach to gender in most countries as part of LA 21; however, they showed there is ample room for development of such an approach.* (WEDO, 2000)

The report goes on to identify barriers to women's participation and strategies to overcome them.

Identifying MSP participants Many local authority processes are initiated by asking 'known' people to attend a launch conference. Those that do have the opportunity become involved in further discussions, working groups, and so on; those that do not are often 'lost' to the process.

Setting the goals Set internationally by Agenda 21. There was some confusion as to whether LA21 was about community empowerment or about a programme of better environmental management. This lack of clarity about the purpose is not surprising given that LA21 was a fundamentally new approach to local development with no established procedures and it was not a statutory duty. The original aim, as set by Agenda 21, was a local plan for sustainable development that would focus on key issues, including poverty, health and livelihoods, as well as resource and environmental issues. Goals did develop and processes moved into a dialogue situation.

Conflict – Consensus The basic principles of LA21 call on councils to achieve 'a consensus' with their community. This led to increased interest in consensus and mediation techniques by councils, backed by active promotion from local government support organizations. However, many NGOs and community networks remain sceptical about consensus, seeing it as compromise by another name. A number of flawed or inconclusive exercises provide evidence to support this view, as does the way in which some authorities have set the frameworks for consensus-building exercises in ways which meant that areas of conflict have been concealed rather than openly discussed and resolved.

Comment Those who said it was a consensus-building process had not asked the right people to be involved. Very few Local Agenda 21s have done realistic or credible work on consensus-building, but that does mean that there has not been a substantial consensus.

Evaluation Right from the start, questions were asked as to what impact LA21 might have. This led to interest in local indicators to track progress. It is probably too late to evaluate LA21 successfully. Much of the very rich seam of material has probably been discarded or 'fallen down the back of filing cabinets'. In 1997, some NGOs supported the '3 Ps' model which poses insightful questions (Church, 1997):

Process Has the process of consultation been designed to ensure that all stakeholders had a genuine opportunity to take part and have an input?

Projects Are things actually happening in the locality as a result of the LA21 process?

Policies Are the policies of local authorities and other affected bodies changing as a result of the LA21 process in ways that support moves towards sustainable development?

Participants have had endless opportunities to check back with their constituencies, but there are real questions as to whether this ever happened as effectively as it might. People within working groups tend to become members of that group, rather than representatives of an organization. If they checked back, they tended to do it with the organization they had come from, rather than with their broader constituency. People don't know how to do this properly, and often end up representing an artificially large constituency – an environmental group might represent the community sector (where in a large city they could be faced with contacting several hundred groups they have no knowledge of).

Legitimacy issue NGOs and councils frequently claim to speak for local people, but often there is little legitimacy for this claim. Some NGOs may represent the broad long-term interests of local people, but claims by participative groups to be representatives for specific communities are often founded on nothing more than wishes and anecdotal evidence. The most positive approaches are where each viewpoint has acknowledged the other and has agreed on the need to link these different processes in a well-defined and transparent manner. Dialogue like this takes time to build.

Community empowerment has to be a precursor to more issue-focused work if that work is to be sustainable over the long term. Much local action is only effective up to a certain point, after which institutional and political problems prevent it from achieving its full potential.

Setting the agenda The best LA21s were open processes using the initial stages to see what expertise people had and what they wanted to do. This was how many processes changed from being purely environmental initiatives. For example, the issue of equalities arose early in the London Borough of Redbridge's process and it has developed into one of the few LA21s with a meaningful statement and subsequent action on this.

Setting the timetable Timetables are usually set by the local authority, and lately have been set to coincide with the revised target of having an LA21 strategy in place by the end of 2000. The ICLEI is coordinating local government preparations and input into the Earth Summit 2002. One element is a worldwide survey of LA21 in practice (in association with UN CSD Capacity21/UNDP).

Preparatory process A multitude of approaches, but the standard technique is to have an initial conference, the use of working groups and some kind of cross-sectoral body monitoring it all. This might be a steering group or, in the case of Redbridge, an ongoing panel which represents all sectors, rather than individual issues. Many programmes, when questioned about what they might do differently on this issue, reply that they would make more strenuous efforts to widen the steering group to involve other key organizations so that ownership, representation and the platform for action is widened.

In many LA21s the involvement of various sectors – notably business or an institution such as an education authority – has tailed off as the process has got under way. Stages can be described, therefore, as a public participation exercise, agreeing a more detailed vision, and specific actions plans in response to the needs identified. This process can take two to four years for trust building and partnership to evolve. A frequent comment is that the participation work always takes more time and persistence than originally expected.

Creating better dialogue round-table format (as defined by the Canadian experience), not one-off meetings; composed of senior representatives of government, business and environmental interests; active at a range of scales; non-hierarchical and meeting on terms of equality, so as not to be 'owned' or dominated by any one partner.

Strong partnerships Experience from the ICLEI member, Puerto Princesca City, the Philippines, demonstrates that even communities that have suffered severe environmental degradation in the name of economic development can reverse the trend and become a role model for sustainable development, as long as a strong partnership is developed between the local government and its citizens. People power made a difference. While the Puerto Princesca Watch originated as a special task force unit under the office of the mayor, it grew eventually into a multisectoral movement that involved the air and police force and joined forces with civilian volunteers to apprehend perpetrators of marine and forest-related crimes. Among the lessons learned for smooth process and programme implementation is the need for strong political will coupled with broad-based support from all key sectors.

Communication Primarily face-to-face contact, meetings, newsletters, publications and events. There is less reliance on electronic means (due to the time-frame when LA21 was initiated), but this is picking up now. A mixture of participation routes works better than one medium; together they provide a mixture of credibility and creativity. Other tools for creating involvement include visioning, planning for real, village appraisals and parish maps. The better designed processes had independent facilitation, especially for external meetings. The spirit of LA21 initiatives has ranged from 'can do' to 'must do', depending on the local authority person coordinating it. This is a key point for most of the LA21 processes – the professional involved does an enormous amount to 'shape' the atmosphere of it. This is something that needs to be explored in more detail as success depends on it. Identical processes in different boroughs and neighbouring towns can have hugely different rates of success which is often down to just one key person. Power gaps exist by the very nature of the process. Recent evaluations suggest that in very few places have the power relationships changed as a result of LA21 (Young and Church, 2000).

Participation – representation question With any interest in partici-pation comes concern from those in authority about real or imagined loss of power (Abbot, 1996).

In many cases the total failure of MSPs to involve different disci-plines is a significant failure. They are clearly more democratic than authorities simply, saying 'This is what we are going to do'. As a lesson in democracy, LA21 has been very good at mobilizing white, educated middle-classes. Its nature – jargon-laden, with lots of meetings taking place in people's relatively rare spare time, and a requirement (to be effective) of knowing how local authorities work – leads it to people who are well educated, employed and so on. This issue lies at the bottom of most LA21 problems – and is exploited by chief executives who label them as 'middle-class chatter-shops', which is unfortunate as it ignores some of the very good work that has been done.

There are numerous opportunities to review issues and often an annual conference is used.

Decision-making Often sketchy and ill-thought-out; relatively few LA21s had coordinated 'ground rules'. They might have a day where a facilitator who had been brought into the process stressed the need for 'ground rules', but on many occasions they have been forgotten by the next committee meeting (because people are human).

Implementation A classic case is if one sector leads an MSP, all the other sectors look to it to implement the results rather than taking on ownership themselves. This occurs partly as a result of the big power gaps because local authorities have a huge role as guardians/stewards of the local environment. One internationally recognized example of LA21 implementation is the MAMA-86 Drinking Water Project in the Ukraine which brought together community activists from different parts of the country, representatives of other stakeholder groups and government officials to facilitate an integrated approach to discussions on water quality and its impact on health. Communication work on these issues and public participation underpin their work. MAMA-86 (a grass-roots NGO set up after the Chernobyl disaster) uses inter-national forums/agreements (events associated with Agenda 21, the WHO Conference on Environment and Health, the CSD among others) to publicize its work. It believes that this tactic increases the role of NGOs and major stakeholders and the possibilities for cooperation with foreign partners in the implementation of Agenda 21.

Closure LA21 was never intended to be a process with an indefinite future: Chapter 28 of Agenda 21 set an initial target of 1996 for the production of plans. The UK has a revised target of 2000. Some plans are still ongoing and evolving with a new agenda to 'mainstream' sustainable development; some closed; some just collapsed and died when a local authority withdrew funding, or LA21 staff posts were not filled, or there was a lack of political commitment, or when something else came along to grab attention, such as Community Planning (part of the modernization of UK local government). Note that many of the innovative tools under development to assure greater democracy have been used by LA21 initiatives previously. It has been suggested that LA21 practitioners should be happy to stand back and not insist on taking credit for their own innovations (Christie, 1999).

Comment It is difficult to think of LA21s that have just ended (Manchester pulled the plug when NGOs walked out). Other local authorities, like Gloucester, have handed over the responsibility for running the process to an external body (this could be seen as devolving ownership but cynics also say that it relieves the authority of responsibility if the process goes wrong).

Structural aspects

Institutional back-up/facilitation Local authorities often assume overall facilitation and an enabling role.

Documentation Varying ways and levels of reporting.

Relating to non-participating stakeholders and the general public Other stakeholders do know about the process because theoretically it is open to anyone. The lack of people 'buying in' to LA21, the lack of publicity and comprehension by the media meant that it became hard to get publicity out. LA21 is full of jargon – it doesn't 'speak' the language of people on the street. Most processes have not engaged people; LA21 is seen as something designed to empower the middle classes. But the best processes have set targets for public awareness and made all efforts to reach out to different stakeholder groups, often the traditionally hard to reach. Specific areas of concern have been the under-involvement of black and ethnic minority communities, poorer or disadvantaged communities, youth and the aged. 'Non-involvement of such groups is a common failing of participative processes that have developed with little forward planning or policy' (Taylor, 1995). Strengthening civil society can be seen as a process of building social capital, of building confidence and trust between citizens and institutions. This is extremely relevant to local councils which are often mistrusted by their local populations. Much work done through LA21 processes directly relates to building social capital.

Using mass media to convey messages is far more effective than other means. Many far-reaching claims have been made for LA21 processes, but there is no doubt that

> *tens of thousands of people have taken part in a process that developed both their environmental awareness and their perceptions of how such issues are related to broader social issues. In the best cases, there has been capacity and confidence building, and the creation of new local structures that seem to be self-sustaining ... LA21 has opened up new ways of working nationally, locally and even globally: what is less clear is how far it has helped deliver the key objectives of Agenda 21.* (Church, 2000)

Linkage into official decision-making The LA21 MSP is not clearly linked to an official decision-making process, so as a non-mandatory process it is all the more remarkable that it has gone so far. But as a non-mandatory process, there is a question as to how much it will deliver. Perhaps its influence on other processes will be a more important and lasting legacy. While many individual LA21 initiatives have been disappointing in their failure to deliver what was expected, some extremely good work has been done and the best initiatives have certainly provided very valuable information on how sustainable development can be taken forward at the local level.

Funding There are different funding arrangements, depending on the situation. This is mainly under the control of local authorities which, as facilitators, have an ongoing role in initiating, running and implementing LA21 processes.

Additional Information

The ICLEI is involved in a number of MSP-related projects:

1 One very specific project, a region in Germany where ICLEI representatives go to assist; ongoing, it will last two to three years. There is no evaluating work to date.
2 Evaluation of Local Agenda 21 in Europe: the Local Authorities' Self-assessment of Local Agenda 21 (LASALA) Project will provide an overview of what is going on in Europe and will help LA21s to self-assess their actions; it also offers training on the internet.

3 Research is under way on a number of issues to discover facts and conditions and prerequisites for urban sustainability, and to see how LA21 can contribute to employment action plans.
4 Round-table formats, consisting of dialogue between stakeholders.

All these programmes aim, on different levels, to engender urban sustainability and action plans. International Council for Local Environmental Initiatives (ICLEI) website: www.iclei.org.

Multi-stakeholder Dialogue Session at the 8th Informal Environment Ministers' Meeting, Bergen, Norway

Issues water for basic needs; energy for a sustainable future; multi-stakeholder participation.

Objectives To facilitate a multi-stakeholder input and dialogue with ministers, with a view ahead to 2002, in order to inform ministerial deliberations.

Participants Environment ministers (worldwide); high-ranking UN officials; leading civil society representatives (local government, trade unions, women, business and industry, Indigenous Peoples)

Scope International.

Time lines 15 September 2000 (six months' project: five months' preparations, reporting one month).

Contact, URL UNED Forum, London; www.earthsummit2002.org/es/2002/bergen/bergen.pdf. Ministry for Environment, Government of Norway; http://odin.dep.no/md/engelsk

Procedural aspects

Designing the MSP The initiative to incorporate an MSP into the usually closed ministerial meeting came from the Norwegian Government which decided that it might advance participatory discussions at the international level. UNED Forum was invited to coordinate the three-hour dialogue session. It was the first time that civil society participation had been allowed at this annual meeting.

Identifying the issues The major issues – water and energy – were among the issues on the agenda of the ministerial meeting. The Steering

Committee, working with stakeholders, chose to focus on water and energy for strategic reasons, given that the target audience was ministers. The Steering Committee identified the overarching theme and topics for dialogue according to the following criteria. It should be:

- Manageable in 90 minutes and be cross-sectoral.
- Relevant to each of the stakeholders with potential for common ground and collaboration.
- Relevant to issues on the agenda for CSD-9 or the Earth Summit 2002 process.

Specific topics and sector viewpoints were decided by participating groups in the preparatory process. Umbrella organizations represented business, local government, trade unions, NGOs, Indigenous Peoples and women.

Identifying relevant stakeholders The UNED Forum working with umbrella organizations via their own networks, contact and experience. Major groups approved for this meeting were limited to:

- Business and industry – coordinated by International Chamber of Commerce and the World Business Council for Sustainable Development;
- Trade Unions – International Federation of Free Trade Unions;
- Local Government – International Council for Local Environmental Initiatives; and
- NGO Group – coordinated by UNED (NGOs), CSD Women's Caucus, and CSD Indigenous Peoples Caucus.

Identifying participants The UNED Forum and umbrella organizations via their networks and expertise. The numbers were limited due to the nature of the event and the time-frame for dialogue (a three-hour session).

Setting the goals The dialogue with ministers was perceived as being a useful background and complementing forthcoming preparations for other international policy processes, such as the International Freshwater Review Conference 2001; energy at CSD-9 (also with multi-stakeholder dialogue sessions); Earth Summit 2002.

Setting the agenda A Steering Group according to the criteria mentioned above.

Setting the timetable Set by the schedule drawn up by ministerial meeting.

Preparatory process A one-off event, allowing about five months for preparations. A thorough preparatory process involving a range of civil society groups from all regions. Once the overall themes had been chosen, they were narrowed down further. They were carefully framed to provide a focus for a short dialogue to be cross-cutting and inclusive in scope so that each stakeholder group could make a positive contribution. A common methodological framework was agreed for writing the background papers, allowing for a useful comparison of the positions of each group. (Business and industry diverged from this, with agreement.) Papers were prepared in consultation within stakeholder groups. NGOs were to absorb the input from women and Indigenous Peoples. However, the time lines were too short for Indigenous Peoples to conduct a consultation within their constituency. However, they participated at the dialogue itself. A comparative summary of the different papers was prepared (in table format) highlighting areas of divergence and convergence. This and background papers went to all the participants before the meeting. The participants reported back that they had found the preparatory process a valuable cooperative learning experience of working with other stakeholder groups. The summary tables clearly demonstrated that there were several points of convergence between the groups. UNED reports that, given a longer preparatory process, areas of convergence and conflict highlighted in the papers could have been explored more substantially. Stakeholders – as potential agents of change – have a responsibility to continue this dialogue and to explore the common ground.

Communication During the preparatory phase via telephone conferences and email, the dialogue was a face-to-face meeting. Energy was addressed in the first half, followed by water. Sessions opened with brief presentations from civil society (business, trade union, local government, and NGO perspectives). Both women and Indigenous Peoples participated as well. Following civil society presentations, the proceedings were opened up to the ministers and other delegates. Discussion was lively as ministers were able to speak and participate without the need to reach a formulated outcome. They also sought input from civil society representatives as to what government strategies needed to be adopted to address the issues. It was an attempt at open and genuine dialogue and ministers were enthusiastic about the process. 'This has strengthened my view that interactive debate should be the way' (Siri Bjerke, 2000). There was particular interest by delegates from countries without a strong civil society presence.

Decision-making No formalized outcome was expected. The proceedings were more 'preparing the ground' and seeding topics for further discussion at relevant upcoming international meetings.

Implementation No implementation process was aimed at.

Closure A single event, but ramifications will ripple through to future discussions and agreements at ministerial level.

Structural aspects

Institutional back-up Steering Committee membership consisted of representatives from each of the participating stakeholder groups who hold appointed or elected coordinating positions within their groups.

Facilitation UNED provided preparatory material for telephone conferences and email discussions in the preparatory process. The dialogue was co-chaired by the Environment Minister of Norway, Siri Bjerke, and UNED Forum Chair Derek Osborn.

Documentation Background papers and results are available at www.earthsummit2002.org.

While the remainder of the ministers session was closed, conclusions taken from the chairpersons' reports were taken by UNED, written up overnight on consultation with stakeholder representatives and present and distributed to all ministers the next day.

Relating to non-participating stakeholders UNED disseminated information about the process during the preparatory phase. Participating stakeholder groups were agreed with the Norwegian Government and numbers were limited from their side.

Relating to the general public It was a specific and specialized debate. Information is available on the web. There was press coverage in Norwegian daily newspapers.

Linkage into official decision-making Not directly linked at this stage. Stakeholders urged ministers to consider how the process of stakeholder engagement at international meetings can be developed into a recognized, transparent mechanism which links into decision-making. This is of specific importance in the run-up to 2002 where openness and transparency depend, to some extent, on whether adequate time and resources for meaningful participation have been allocated.

Funding The Norwegian Government paid for the preparatory process and stakeholder representatives attending the meeting.

Novartis Forum Events

Issues Acceptance of GMOs (genetically modified plants for food production) in Germany (1997–1999; in 2000 the focus shifted to healthcare issues around ageing).

Objectives To create a platform for informed debate and to demonstrate the company's willingness to listen to stakeholders.

Participants Environmental NGOs, consumer groups, ethical and religious institutions, politicians, administrators, scientists, communications consultants, trade unions, representatives from different industries (all relevant to the issue), the media.

Scope National.

Time lines annual event since 1997, 1.5 days each.

Contact, URL Novartis Germany (contact Martina Bauer), www.de. novartis.com; Novartis International (contact Andreas Seiter), www. novartis.com

Procedural aspects

Designing the MSP Designed by the company, Novartis Germany (communications department) together with consultants.

Identifying the issues Defined by the company (related to Novartis' technology and products).

Identifying relevant stakeholders Novartis, in consultation with stakeholder groups.

Identifying participants Novartis either knew the relevant people (eg GMO expert in trade union) or asked stakeholder groups for advice ('Who in your institution is the expert on GMOs?').

Setting the goals There were no specific goals for the event which required agreement. The focus was on mutual listening and learning. A mix of presentations and discussion (panel, panel and full audience, group discussions). There were no company presentations; Novartis was in a listening role.

Setting the agenda and timetable The agenda was set by Novartis, consultants and speakers/chairpersons of the panel discussions.

Preparatory process Thorough pre-discussions between consultants, designated speakers and Novartis.

Communication The event started with presentations (different viewpoints on the issue), discussion, break-out groups. The evening was free to allow for informal discussions (a very important aspect). There was no formal meta-communication, but plenty of informal. There was a chance to talk to people who usually are not easily accessible.

Decision-making In discussions, one goal was to identify agreements and disagreements (Where do we need more debate?), but no formal agreement was sought on anything.

Implementation There was no formal implementation; experience shows that participants tend to return the invitation if they organize dialogue events – the debate continues, proceeds faster and smoother as before.

Closure An open process, ongoing but adapting to the current issues; it focused on (potential) conflict areas between the company and society.

Structural aspects

Institutional back-up Provided by Novartis; consultants helped to approach speakers or identify important stakeholder representatives and to assist in briefing speakers.

Facilitation Provided by Novartis. The moderation of the event was shared between a senior company executive and an outside chairperson. Journalists typically acted as facilitators of workshops.

Documentation The company puts together a written report and sends it to the participants and everybody else who want to be informed.

Relating to non-participating stakeholders Only by word of mouth; the event is not widely announced. Experience shows that several people register spontaneously without being invited.

Relating to the general public There was no direct link with the meeting, but journalists are always present who are encouraged to write about it.

Linkage with official decision-making There was no formal link with the decision-making process.

Funding Entirely funded by Novartis.

OECD/BIOTECHNOLOGY

The OECD Edinburgh Conference on the scientific and health aspects of genetically modified foods (2000)/OECD consultation with non-governmental organizations on biotechnology and other aspects of food safety (1999)

Issues The scientific and health aspects of GM food.

Objectives To bring together a diverse group of participants for a constructive dialogue on the safety of GM food.

Participants Organisation for Economic Co-operation and Development (OECD); governments; industry; scientists; civil society organizations such as Greenpeace International, Friends of the Earth, GeneWatch; consumer groups.

Scope International/national.

Time lines OECD Conference, 2000; OECD first NGO consultation process 1999.

Contact, URL OECD, Paris; www.oecd.org/subject/biotech/edinburgh. htm and www.oecd.org/subject/biotech/ngoconsultation.htm

Procedural aspects

Designing the MSP 1999: Consultation process initiated by OECD with over 50 invited NGOs with the purpose of hearing/understanding their views.

2000: OECD Conference, hosted by UK Government as part of an ongoing programme of work at the OECD on biotechnology.

NGOs did not have input into the conference planning process. However, it is possible that the 1999 consultation impacted the design of the conference.

Identifying the issues The initiative arose out of a request from the G8 Heads of State and Government that the OECD 'undertake a study of the implications of biotechnology and other aspects of food safety' (G8 Summit, Cologne, June 1999). The conference focus was GM food safety and human health. There was discussion of the science (including social science of consumer attitudes) with agreement from the chair, Sir John Krebs (Professor of Zoology, Oxford University and Chair

Designate of the future UK Food Standards Agency) that other 'non-scientific issues eg values and beliefs' should not be excluded from the debate.

From an NGO perspective, it appeared that the government felt it needed to constrain the dialogue to health. The debate was then constrained by the fact that unless evidence was peer-reviewed, issues could not be raised. Therefore, scientists who had peer-reviewed work were able to dominate and much of that benefited biotechnology.

Identifying relevant stakeholders The OECD Directorate for Science, Technology and Industry (DSTI) responded to concerns of the OECD Council and the Secretary-General that 'communication with the public and representatives of the many concerned elements of civil society is crucial to promoting progress in the fields of biotechnology and food safety'. Civil society participants included scientists, business, industry, agriculture, labour, consumer groups and a few environmental organizations, plus a number of representatives from developing countries.

Identifying participants The conference was attended by approximately 400 invitees from more than 25 countries. The aim was to be inclusive, to encourage a wide diversity of views both on the platform and in the audience. NGOs included Greenpeace International, Friends of the Earth, GeneWatch, Soil Association, the Royal Society for the Protection of Birds. There were also health professionals but no opportunities to overlap.

Setting the goals The purpose of the three-day event was to bring together a diverse group of participants for 'a constructive dialogue on the safety of GM food', with an emphasis on the underlying science and on human health.

Setting the agenda The OECD set the agenda.

Setting the timetable The OECD set the timetable in response to the request from the G8 Industrialized Countries' Heads of State and Government (1999) and OECD mandates.

Communication A one-off event which was in conference format with short introductory presentations to each section. Panel members then offered their comments before the discussion was opened to the audience. There was, however, an informal segment during the event which would have allowed for a mixing of the different groups and more side-line discussions.

It was NGOs' view that the format – a large conference hall with no possibility of clusters/sector groupings – was not appropriate. There was very little evidence of MSP dialogue – it was more a 'showpiece' event. With an 80/20 ratio of pro/con participations, there was no real cause for concern. Others said that the speakers and panellists were, in approximately equal numbers, proponents of GM, opponents, and those who were neutral. Presenters came from a wide range of developed and developing countries; they were primarily scientists, regulators, NGOs and industry representatives. It was recognized that the debate needs to become more open, transparent and inclusive.

The conference organizers perceived that there was a strong sense of the need to rebuild trust between the various actors, particularly governments, industry, scientists, regulatory agencies and the public.

Industry commented that at an unofficial side event organized by a Scottish environmentalist group, the debate was more informal and addressed more of the fundamental philosophical issues; the impression was that this was a step towards overcoming the usual hostilities.

NGOs were not happy with the process, described as a 'complete abuse' of what an MSP ought to be, compared with other events like the World Conservation Congress. NGOs said they would not participate in this kind of set-up again. The view of some industry representatives was that some activist groups were not happy with the format because it did not work in their favour; they had problems in responding to the chair's repeated explicit invitation to support their anti-GMO claims with evidence, whether it was scientific or anecdotal. This made them look stupid so that even the press reacted negatively at the Greenpeace press conference. Industry also commented that there was a deserved degree of discomfort among some people who tried to stick to their preapproved corporate speak in a setting which would have required a more open, flexible approach. There were interesting internal discussions on the industry side.

Decision-making The conference did not aim at consensus, rather it identified 'areas of greater agreement, of divergence of opinion, and of uncertainty due to lack of knowledge'. The chair's report suggested that 'the most significant aspect of the Edinburgh conference was that it included all sides of the debate surrounding GM foods and nevertheless identified certain areas of agreement ... It also succeeded in separating out issues which are subject to scientific analysis and those which are related to political factors, beliefs and values' (OECD, 2000).

Implementation No implementation process aimed at.

Closure There was support for continuing the process to deal with other parts of the debate. The chair recommended that an international forum be created. One possible model is that of the Intergovernmental Panel on Climate Change (IPCC) which informs but does not make policy and acknowledges minority scientific views. The IPCC reports, however, come under the scrutiny of governments before publication. For a similar process on GMOs, wider stakeholder involvement and a global scope would be required.

Structural aspects

Institutional back-up The OECD as Secretariat and in a facilitating role.

Facilitation The OECD; facilitation of panel discussions by conference chair.

Documentation The OECD summarized and produced a report on the findings. It states clearly that, unlike other OECD reports, these outcomes do not necessarily represent the official views of member governments; instead, they 'reflect broader and sometimes conflicting views of civil society, indicate areas of agreement and disagreement, and attempt to show a way forward towards resolving some of the controversies raised by genetically modified foods' (OECD, 2000). The report was published in hard copy and electronically.

Relating to non-participating stakeholders Participation was by invitation only.

Relating to the general public The reports are available on the OECD website. The proceedings acknowledged the need for trust building. 'The general public – consumers and citizens – not only have a right to know, but they also have valid points of view, which need to be effectively voiced, understood and given weight in the decision-making and policy making process. A range of good practice examples were put forward for public engagement' (OECD, 2000).

Linkage into official decision-making Linkage arose from an official request from G8 leaders; the linkage of outcomes into decision-making is unclear – it is an informative process. It will be up to governments to use the conference report.

Funding The conference was hosted and funded by the UK Government. The NGO consultation meeting (1999) was hosted by the OECD.

PROCESSES FOR DEVELOPING NATIONAL STRATEGIES ON SUSTAINABLE DEVELOPMENT, A: NATIONAL STRATEGIES FOR SUSTAINABLE DEVELOPMENT (NSSD)

Donor – Developing Country Dialogues on National Strategies for Sustainable Development

Issues National strategic planning for sustainable development, participatory dialogues.

Objectives To improve international understanding of the key challenges involved in developing and implementing NSSDs, and examine, through good practice examples, how donors can best assist developing countries in such processes.

Participants OECD/Development Assistance Committee (DAC), UK Department for International Development (DFID), European Commission, IIED, pilot countries and communities.

Scope international/national multi-donor initiative.

Time lines Phase 1, October 1999; Phase 4, February 2001.

Contact, URL www.nssd.net

Procedural aspects

Designing the MSP Building on previous discussions and agreements made by the OECD/DAC to review good practice to inform donors assisting developing countries, the IIED was approached in 1998 to coordinate and manage the overall project and provide technical support. The project is a collective effort of all the participants (developing countries and donors). The IIED has been coordinating, providing guidance and support, and assisting with analysis and synthesis. Country-based teams organized and facilitated the country dialogues on NSSDs with a view to documenting experiences, lessons learned and the effectiveness of NSSD approaches. The project focuses on the kinds of processes and conditions required to make NSSDs work in practice.

A scoping workshop was held in the UK in 1998 to help shape the project and a Task Force, led by the DFID and the European Commission, was established.

Participating countries: Bolivia; Burkina Faso; Nepal; Tanzania; Thailand. Three other 'parallel learning countries' – Ghana, Pakistan, Namibia – are participating through targeted reviews.

Identifying the issues In May 1999, DAC endorsed the definition of an NSSD as 'a strategic and participatory process of analysis, debate, capacity strengthening, planning and action towards sustainable development'.

NSSDs are therefore processes or mechanisms which enable better communication and informed debate among stakeholders; they seek to build consensus where possible and to facilitate better ways of working, leading to more effective action in planning for sustainability. An NSSD need not be something new.

Identifying relevant stakeholders Stakeholders: government, private sector, civil society.

Identifying MSP participants There were different procedures in different countries, depending on the circumstances, which aimed to allow input from all stakeholders. Country dialogues were implemented by country/regional institutions. More information was provided as www.nssd.net.

Setting the goals Set by the OECD/DAC – to develop a practical guidance and a source book for development cooperation on national strategies for sustainable development.

Setting the timetable The international timetable arose from the Programme of Action for the further implementation of Agenda 21 at the Special Session of the General Assembly (Earth Summit 11) in New York in 1997. This document states that 'by the year 2002 national strategies for sustainable development that reflect contributions and responsibilities of all interested parties should be completed in all countries' and that 'Local Agenda 21 and other sustainable development programmes should be actively encouraged'. The OECD/DAC set a further target of 2005 for NSSDs to be in the process of implementation. The timetable for the project was agreed by the participants (developing countries and donors). They viewed it as important to get the policy guidance before aid ministers at the DAC high-level meeting in April 2001 for endorsement, so that the DAC could use the guidance to lever a renewed focus on strategies and seek convergence around the principles in the guidance. Otherwise another year would have been lost (the high-level meeting only takes place once a year).

Preparatory process Five dialogues were held at the country level. One regional dialogue, in the Sahel, was planned but was not undertaken as it was found to be too complex in the available time-frame. Instead, there was more in-depth focus in the five dialogue countries. Each dialogue was implemented by a country or regional institution. In addition to the status review of all significant strategic planning processes that are current or recent, dialogues take place that involve stakeholder consultations, round-tables and workshops.

Communication There was constant communication via an email list and the website, and the IIED was in constant contact with all country teams and the donor Task Force. There was also considerable effort to establish in-country networks (and country websites). The process used focus groups, round-tables, national workshops (which vary according to local circumstances). Three review workshops took place during the time-span of the dialogue process – an initial planning meeting, mid-term and final workshop.

Decision-making With regard to the final document, the project worked with teams of authors and through workshops that discussed the documents. The DAC high-level meeting produced a statement based on the report (OECD, 2001).

Implementation The document will impact on donor decision-making and the country planning of NSSDs as the outcomes provide lessons learned and recommendations.

Closure The final workshop focused mainly on the main thrust and content of the policy guidance. The sourcebook was discussed in outline and will be developed between April and December 2001.

Structural aspects

Institutional back-up and facilitation The IIED facilitated and coordinated at the international level. Facilitation of the participatory dialogues is undertaken by local teams, guided by local steering committees.

Documentation Material was prepared by both the IIED and project participants. The NSSD website and CD-ROM were tools for project management and information sharing during the lifetime of the project and beyond; a detailed sourcebook was produced on NSSD processes and case examples; there was policy guidance for DAC members on good practice and support for developing countries. Various background and issues papers were also produced during the project's lifetime. These inform the process of developing NSSDs and comment on the processes used. The IIED developed the NSSD Knowledge Management System – an internet and CD-ROM tool. The website provides a forum for dialogue as well as background and reference material. The project maintains an email discussion list to facilitate dialogue and information exchange. Each country/region involved will prepare a status report and a dialogue report. The IIED will prepare a rolling Issues Paper, updated through the process, and a final report. A sourcebook, pulling together all the main issues and lessons from these reports, and guidelines for donors will also be published at end of project (OECD).

Linkage into official decision-making The results will be one of the main outputs from OECD/DAC to the Earth Summit 2002. It is likely to have other impacts in future national/international decision-making processes. The results will also go to a high-level OECD/DAC meeting in 2001.

Funding Multi-donor funded initiative.

PROCESSES DEVELOPING NATIONAL STRATEGIES ON SUSTAINABLE DEVELOPMENT, B: NATIONAL COUNCILS FOR SUSTAINABLE DEVELOPMENT (NCSD)

Issues Planning/implementing sustainable development strategies.

Objectives NCSDs are seeking to strengthen civic society participation in local and multi-stakeholder decision-making mechanisms and activities related to the implementation of the UNCED agreements. The Earth Council (an independent, international body) has, since 1992, been instrumental in promoting the creation and strengthening of NCSDs through greater civil participation. It has also facilitated the organization of regional networks of NCSDs (and similar entities) through a series of regional meetings held in Latin America, Europe, Africa and Asia.

Participants Governments, private enterprise, NGOs, civil society.

Scope National, regional and ultimately global.

Time lines The idea was introduced at the Earth Summit, 1992; it is ongoing.

Contact, URL www.ncsdnetwork.org

Procedural aspects

Designing the MSP Most countries have some form of focal point or mechanism at the national level to oversee the implementation of the Earth Summit agreements. Many of these are structured as multi-stakeholder and participatory mechanisms, usually referred to as National Councils for Sustainable Development (NCSD). The composition of each NCSD and the way it operates varies widely, reflecting the circumstances of each individual country. But key common features are their multi-stakeholder character and integrative approach.

Processes are designed through regional coordination. For example, in Latin America, there was national consultation after Rio+5 and some sub-regional groups. Specific multi-stakeholder processes are under way in two specific arenas:

1   Based on resolutions agreed at the International Forum for NCSDs April 2000, the global network is preparing to undertake a multi-stakeholder assessment of the Earth Summit commitments to feed into Rio+10 process.
2   With funding from GEF-UNDP, a pilot project is under way to 'develop methodologies to integrate global environmental priorities into sustainable development plans'. It will involve developing capacity-building strategies as appropriate to address weaknesses and barriers to change. The project is founded on the concept of Multi-stakeholder Integrative Sustainability Planning (MISP), based on the principles of broad participation, flexibility, dynamic, and promoting vertical and horizontal integration and empowerment. Countries involved include Mexico and the Philippines. Draft guidelines and information promoting good practice are available on the NCSD Knowledge Network website.

Identifying the issues The stakeholders identify the issues for the NCSD.

Identifying relevant stakeholders Initial contact occurs at global and regional meetings, through existing contacts with the Earth Council.

Identifying participants The Regional Coordinator (RC) makes unilateral visits to different groups within a country, then sets up a first group meeting.

Setting the goals and agenda The NCSD sets the goals and identifies priorities under the heading of sustainability, Agenda 21 and the Earth Charter. Goals develop over time, within a broad framework, and it usually takes over a year to develop strong foundations. As part of this process, participants need to check back with their constituencies. Continuity is hardest with governments.

Setting the timetable It is an ongoing process. Setting clear time-bound strategies for the implementation of priority areas is one of the most difficult aspects. Rio+10 Assessment: Preliminary results presented at CSD, April 2001; International NCSD Forum, December 2001.

Preparatory process The dialogue process is defined by the group, in consultation with, and via feedback from constituencies, municipalities, and so on. There is ongoing (internal) monitoring and reports of workshops (limited only by funds). The RC follows up issues and progress periodically.

Rio+10 Assessments NCSDs will identify the most appropriate ways to conduct these via workshops, working groups, issue identification techniques and national forums.

Communication Communication by the RC is initially through face-to-face meetings, then telephone contacts and mailing, with visits at critical points – RCs always revisit when there is a change of government. The need for additional support to engage and enable the participation of indigenous communities and other marginalized groups is addressed from the outset of an NCSD. The RC raises questions about NCSD and subnational groups resources (including financial) to enable their inclusion. An internet resource (NCSD Knowledge Network) has been developed to facilitate information exchange between NCSDs. Experiences and lessons learned are shared between countries within the region. Some countries have been in the process longer than others. Mexico is frequently cited as a good example for a region, with strong subnational groups and NCSD. The NCSD in Mexico is 50 per cent subnational representatives and 50 per cent national-level MSP.

The Philippines is perceived by many as the best global example. The Philippine Council for Sustainable Development (PCSD) was set up in 1992. It is a multi-stakeholder body involving government, civil society, business and labour sectors, practising consensus-building processes in decision-making. It already had a national plan for sustainable development before the development of the Philippine Agenda 21 (PA21). Through the PCSD, PA21 has been adopted as the nation's blueprint for sustainable development. This was published in 1996 after an extensive multi-level, multi-stakeholder consultation process. It covers a broad span of issues, including urban poverty, agriculture and labour, as well as a range of topics related to economics and technology. Specific reference was made to global governance and the need for financial assistance to developing countries to implement Agenda 21 commitments. In 1995, a regional NCSD meeting facilitated by the Earth Council and hosted by the PCSD, led to the formation of a network of NCSDs in Asia and the Pacific, called the Asia-Pacific National Councils for Sustainable Development (APNCSD). Outputs from this inclusive network include feedback into the Rio+5 Forum. It is currently investigating how it could strengthen existing mechanisms for communicating its message.

Decision-making Initially government driven, this is now evolving in many Latin American countries to be a more representative MSP. It is, by its very nature, a gradual process as it requires a change in the decision-making culture for many countries. The political, historical, traditional and cultural make-up of a country is crucial to how the NCSD structure is initiated and progresses. The move towards truly multi-stakeholder processes in decision-making for a region is a gradual one and requires considerable determination and belief in the underlying principles for the NCSD. As most NCSDs report back to a high-level position in government, often the head of state, they are in an ideal position to conduct participatory assessments of progress since Rio.

Implementation Using climate change as one example, the NCSDs work together, often in subgroups to build a strategy to implement the key principles in the Climate Change Convention, and also to undertake research and to implement and monitor progress.

Closure The NCSD is an ongoing structure, although priority issues may 'close'.

Structural aspects

Institutional back-up Each NCSD has its own secretariat. The secretariat and a steering committee or board meet regularly (every three to four months). They receive input from the subnational grouping (where they exist). Both secretariat and board are involved in facilitation. The Earth Council is tasked to design, strengthen and facilitate funding to establish national secretariats to support civil society participation within NCSDs and similar entities. It also facilitates regional networks of NCSDs.

Documentation The secretariat reports on the meetings. It produces National Agenda 21s (equivalent to National Strategies for Sustainable Development Reports).

Relating to not-participating stakeholders This issue is taken seriously. For example, in Mexico there are larger meetings and subnational meetings to incorporate views additional to the NCSD.

Relating to the general public Mexico produces occasional leaflets on key issues like climate change, as a strategy to help change public behaviour/attitudes. There is little money for massive outreach campaigns and wider public engagement. Work is dependent on government and stakeholder budgets.

Linkage into official decision-making There is a national link to Agenda 21; UN CSD and national reporting. There are also links to the UNEP and UNDP/Capacity21 (DESA). Experience highlights that in the initial stages, stakeholders are usually very sceptical/critical of large institutions, require clear reasons for getting involved, and need a deeper understanding of the process and their role in it. Developing an NCSD is by nature transparent. Stakeholders can impact the process considerably and challenge it throughout.

Funding The GEF, governments (for example The Netherlands, Canada, Scandinavian countries), Capacity21 (indirectly), UNEP.

Additional comments Discontinuity and inadequate funding are an ongoing problem, especially for engaging more local level input. For example, to get subnational representatives to a meeting in Brazil, participants must fly to one location, and on top of this resourcing, there is all the necessary reporting, administration and monitoring required. Local participants do so on a voluntary basis. One suggestion is to ensure that funding from external sources gets distributed evenly through all stakeholder groups and is not channelled through government first (as is current practice). This would also encourage each grouping to ensure that the other is managing their finances according to agreed strategies and programmes.

Some conflict exists with 'alternative processes', eg in Bolivia, where the Poverty Reduction Strategy Paper (PRSP) process (set up separately by the WB, directly linked to Heavily Indebted Poor Countries (HIPC) funds) is also under way. This financial incentive detracts attention from the NCSD process when actually it should be seen as one of the key elements for sustainable development.

UNITED NATIONS GLOBAL COMPACT

Issues Nine principles covering human rights, labour, environment.

Objectives Overall goals as defined by the Global Compact (GC) principles: business to 'enact the principles'. Individual companies' goals: reputation management; alignment of internal/global policy; alignment of global standards regarding human rights, labour relations and the environment; social component: identification of employers. Individual NGO goals: working on how to improve the transparency and answerability of business activity regarding the issues of the environment/sustainability to stakeholder networks. There are different views regarding what type of process this is – some view the GC as implementation oriented (through information), others as merely informative. Others say that the GC is an informing process at the moment; the process will have implications for future actions which this will lead to more concrete objectives.

Participants UN; industry; environment and human rights NGOs; trade unions.

Scope International/national (in-country activities).

Time lines started 1999 – open-ended; annual reporting.

Contact details, URL UN Global Contact Unit, UN Headquarters, New York; www.unglobalcompact.org

At the World Economic Forum, Davos, on 31 January 1999, UN Secretary-General Kofi Annan challenged world business leaders to 'embrace and enact' the GC, both in their individual corporate practices and by supporting appropriate public policies. These principles cover topics in human rights, labour and environment.

Procedural aspects

Designing the MSP The process started in 1999 with a series of bilateral meetings with business associations, then with individual companies, NGOs and trade unions, then defined the compact and what to do. The first GC meeting was held in May 2000. The UN is not only asking business to take action but to work with labour and NGOs; it is also asking labour and NGOs to work with business. The compact is not meant for business simply to carry out and include in the compact their own projects, but for business to change their practice. The compact process consists of several areas of work:

- business development (companies to join);
- learning forum (to share case studies, and so on, perhaps using the compact website);
- issues dialogues; and
- projects of companies with other UN agencies.

The GC is asking companies to join; the prerequisite for joining is that they agree with the nine compact principles plus the UN guidelines on working with the private sector, plus that they provide one good practice example per year to the UN. NGOs and labour have been invited; the prerequisite is that they have accepted to work with the companies. Activities in countries must be led by business and are not UN-initiated. The UN advises, including on NGO and labour involvement. A company wishing to engage in the GC can do so by sending a letter from the Chief Executive Officer to the UN Secretary-General, expressing support for the GC and commitment to take the following actions:

1 To issue a clear statement of support for the GC and its nine principles, and to publicly advocate it. This may include:
  - informing employees, shareholders, customers and suppliers;
  - integrating the GC and nine principles into the corporate development and training programme;

- incorporating the GC principles in the company's mission statement;
- including the GC commitment in the company's annual report and other public documents; and/or
- Issuing press releases to make the commitment public.
2 Provide, once a year, a concrete example of progress made or a lesson learned in implementing the principles, for posting on the GC website.

In addition, within the framework of the GC, a company may wish to:

- actively support the principles and broad UN goals by initiating and participating in projects in partnership with the United Nations; and/or
- participate in result-oriented Issue Dialogues related to the critical problems facing our world, for example The Role of Business in Zones of Conflict.

Companies have informal contacts with other GC partners; 'Local Compacts' might be established, for example in Switzerland, composed of Swiss businesses. Within some companies, working groups are being established (at Novartis: one executive committee member; one steering group member; and a working group; it is also planned to have a multi-stakeholder advisory group to monitor.) Some companies perceive the immediate effect of joining the GC to be that problems falling into the three areas of the GC are being brought on to the table within the company.

NGOs have criticized the GC, saying, for example, that it was designed haphazardly and that there is a lack of transparency about how it was designed. The code that affects the lives of people was not prepared by people, but by top elite within business and the UN, at a time when business was giving a lot of money for pieces of work to the UN. As a result, they received the UN imprint. It is also said that there is a lack of clarity about the agenda which was not defined from the outset, and that various partners pursue different agendas, not a common one.

Identifying the issues The nine principles came from the UN, stemming from intergovernmental negotiations. They are not to be negotiated with potential partners. Negotiations with partners focus on the implementation of the principles. Within industry partners, there are in some cases two levels (or layers) of the GC: with the UN as well as within the company. For example, Novartis has developed a set of parameters that function as a 'vulnerability check'. New issues (like issues of biodiversity, biosociety, healthcare, workforce) are being added to existing ones during the process as some of the GC issues do not seem applicable.

NGOs criticize the way the GC issues were identified by a core group that was established before proceedings were under way. Lack of commitment by some partners may reflect how issues were defined. Corporations identified the issues where they were under attack for bad practices. Issues which are relevant for NGOs are, among others: industry answerability beyond shareholder interests; fresh water, land, air; indices, impacts, indicators; climate; toxics.

Identifying relevant stakeholders The UN identified stakeholders through invitations to companies to take up the challenge. NGOs and trade unions were asked to join. Some companies are in the process of identifying further stakeholders in a cascading process. There is indirect involvement of others when the given agenda is worked through.

NGOs criticize that there is a lack of transparency about how stakeholders were identified, and that the most relevant stakeholders were not included. International NGOs that were identified are not necessarily the most relevant stakeholders; others criticize those NGOs which are involved for lending legitimacy to the process.

Identifying participants Various people are identified within the GC partners, participating NGOs and trade unions, for example to coordinate and represent sectors, and to be the GC focal point (usually high level).

Some NGOs say that companies that were under attack identified participants. More ethical companies were not involved.

Setting the goals The UN set the overarching goal of the GC: companies were to internalize the nine principles. Specific goals are set by GC partners. Agreed and joint activities develop over time through consultation with partners. The GC is designed as a flexible, evolutionary process. The overall process is starting from the set nine principles, then through consultations. When developments of goals occur, stakeholders can check with their constituencies (companies consult within). Regarding the annual issue dialogues, there is consultation and consensus decision-making to identify the issues.

The GC is perceived by business representatives as a very decentralized process. One approach, for example, would be to proceed as follows: if a Novartis supplier employs children, the supplier would have to explain to Novartis, who would have to communicate contentious issues such as the issue of child labour (including, for example, issues of the education provided for the children) on its website (and the progress report) as some kind of model case.

Some NGOs criticize that legitimization was given first; anything that happens afterwards is an add-on. Ideally, it should be the other way around. Membership should not imply that the company has achieved a standard just by having signed up to it. NGOs also criticize that the GC has only general goals (not time-specific, clear objectives;

indicators; monitoring mechanisms) which are not measurable as goals. Possible consultations upon issues and goals will finish with only a number of stakeholders agreeing on an issue.

Setting the agenda While the issue dialogue for 2001 has been identified (the role of the private sector in zones of conflict), the 2002 issue has yet to be identified. The identification of issues works via surveys and consultation.

Some companies state that they are committed to involve stakeholders to prove their credibility. Stakeholders can make suggestions and look into the process. Some NGOs are under the impression that industry is the driving force, and that NGOs and trade unions have little say in identifying the issues.

Setting the timetable There are:

- annual meetings of the learning forum;
- issue dialogues, eg 2001: dialogues on the role of the private sector in conflict zones with labour, business, NGOs; a series of meetings; the first meeting is to agree the process (March 2001), for example three to four meetings per year, including internet discussions; and
- maybe annual meetings of the GC.

Some companies have set up an annual implementation process. Some NGOs say they have not seen a timetable.

Preparatory process For example, issue dialogues: the first meeting on conflict zones is to plan the process for the year 2001. There was a series of meetings to agree the issue, and a survey by the UN of what issues would come into question. The UN then developed a package of material which went to all participants, asking them what the key issues and challenges are; then a ping-pong process occurred to agree the agenda for the initial meeting.

A checklist was given to GC partners by the UN for orientation purposes. It is perceived by some partners as a top-down approach, but they feel that new aspects can be integrated. No position papers or the like are prepared for meetings. Some NGOs perceive that this will not be a dynamic dialogue and that Southern NGOs have not been contacted.

Communication There is official political communication (face-to-face and in written format) between the UN and its partners. Within companies, internal communication involves meetings, followed up by email; externally, the website and press releases are used. Other stakeholders communicate through meetings and the email list server.

Companies tend not to perceive power gaps between the UN and themselves; rather, they perceive having different kinds of power (the UN holds the political power, while companies hold the economic power). Novartis, for example, characterized the GC as a 'good faith process'. There are, however, power gaps between companies and their suppliers (which can be used to create pressure). Power gaps also exist between companies and NGOs. One way of dealing with that is to focus on potential win–win situations and on common objectives.

Some NGOs criticize that involved international NGOs are not obliged to work with their Southern partners. NGOs perceive that there are power (and aspiration) gaps; there is no discussion to identify these clearly and no agenda to take account of power gaps.

There are no formal mechanisms of meta-communication during the process. This is rather happening in the media and via the internet. Media interest generates meta-communication.

Decision-making To identify the issues for the dialogues, there is a consensus-building process – partners must not just say 'no'. Experience has shown that involving professional facilitators can work, but an experienced, well-known and respected chair is better. The individual personalities are very important – more so than their professional background. Companies can make decisions within their range of power. They can negotiate with suppliers and define the process with suppliers on an ad hoc basis.

Some NGOs say that it is hard to define the decision-making process and feel too distant from it. Others say that as there is no specific objective, no decision-making is involved.

Implementation Compact partners say that implementation falls within the standard framework of the decision-making of the individual corporation. Some NGOs say that the GC is merely an informing, consultative process and is not about implementation.

Closure The GC has no time limit. The issue dialogues are time-bound (annual). Companies have to submit one case study per year. Some NGOs feel that the process timing is undefined, and that it needs renewal, or should be driven towards a conclusion in the near future.

Structural aspects

Institutional back-up UN Secretariat/Global Compact Unit. Within companies, there are steering or working groups (eg in Novartis there is the GC steering group (executive committee member), the GC working group (for planning and implementation) and the stakeholder's 'sounding' board ('challenging group')).

Facilitation UN Secretariat/Global Compact Unit, plus the participation of the UN Agencies involved (UNEP, the High Commissioner for Human Rights (HCHR), ILO). They facilitate between the UN and its partners; between partners, NGO and labour; and between the UN agencies, and thus include secretariat services. The full staff at the GC unit will be about six people (not all exclusively working on the GC); plus staff in the agencies – UNEP has created a new post for this. Within Novartis, for example, there is a working group to facilitate the process; its role is that of a central coordinating and implementation planning group. Some internal audits are in place and will be used for the GC (eg 'Health, Safety, Environment Audits').

Documentation The issue dialogues will be decided at the first meeting (March 2001). It is planned to start afresh on the issue dialogues every year, not to work with a firm model. GC partners publish information on a variety of corporate communication channels. Within GC partners, meetings are minuted; some plan to publish as soon as an implementation plan is developed and agreed on.

There is a lack of transparency as to how process developments are being published, other than the reports and statements on the GC website. Some NGOs perceive that the information flow is too low.

Relating to non-participating stakeholders With regard to India, for example, GC partners work on HIV, cities and basic education (on their own); they created these focus areas and work on them with other stakeholders. GC partners publish their involvement and activities through their means as they relate to the general public (or plan to do so). It is not clear if other stakeholders could feed into the process.

Relating to the general public The UN website, pages on GC partners' websites, folders, flyers and digi-card are all used. Interested journalists produce features for radio and newspapers (the UN is regularly approached). GC partners use various channels – websites, journals, press releases.

Some NGOs criticize that very little information is available, or is available only in 'UN speak' which is not accessible to the general public. Stakeholders could go out to businesses to challenge them more, but the dynamic of the process does not seem to lead to specific goals. There is no formalized method for criticism. On the other hand, there is too much emphasis on publicity but no tangible outcomes, which can only lead to cynicism.

Linkage into official decision-making From a UN perspective, the process is linked to official decision-making, which is the ultimate objective. The GC is aiming to create 'open learning action fora' instead of bureaucracy. The process is meant not to be institutionalized but creative; the GC staff are looking at the linkage question, making compact meetings part of UN agencies events (eg the UNEP Nairobi meeting), a conference at the Earth Summit 2002, with issue dialogues on zones of conflict in 2001 (the recommendations to go into the GA Second Committee upon request). On the UN side, there is hope that the GC will link into the Earth Summit 2002 process. There is the potential to link into CSD multi-stakeholder dialogues which would make the GC liable to organizations in the CSD process. Some GC partners and NGOs say that the GC is not a political decision-making process but that it supports global progress by providing good practice and creating transparency. Transparency depends on the effectiveness of the media and communication. The impact of stakeholders is not predefined and depends on the dynamics of the process. The branding of the term 'Global Compact' would increase the influence.

Companies perceive the increasing levels of compliance through the GC as other companies need to imitate its efforts. Those who lag behind or do not comply will eventually be sanctioned by their stockholders. Increasing compliance will create a more critical mass (for example awards in *Forbes* magazine).

Some NGOs perceive that stakeholders can impact the mechanism and that industry finds it very difficult to join the UN and dialogue process with NGOs. Industry also has difficulty in having a balanced dialogue as they are less accustomed to frustration and are less patient because they are used to a top-down decision-making process.

Funding UN budget: the GC is funded by governments and foundations; there is no funding from companies. Decentralized funding process: companies fund their own projects; there is little incremental costs at present, while costs for removing problem situations cannot be calculated in advance. Some perceive the process as driven by the funder.

Additional information In general, NGOs have been critical of the UN Global Compact Initiative, as have a number of governments. Discussions held at the UN General Assembly session in December 2000 led to a resolution that the Secretary-General is to prepare a report to the next GA session in 2001, addressing partnerships of the UN and civil society, particularly the private sector.

Some NGOs generally say that voluntary initiatives like the GC will be successful. Governments need to be involved and they need to regulate. Otherwise free riders can go ahead and won't be caught by the public eye if they are not one of the leading companies. The ethos of voluntary initiatives is useful in terms of making companies aware of the issues. Strategically, 'if companies are serious about the issues, there needs to be regulation' (a statement by Nike quoted by an interviewee). Some NGOs feel that overall, the process is not going well; that the objectives are not specific enough for people to raise the energy to engage; that it lacks accountability; that the outcome is ephemeral; and that the GC is threatening the UN mission and its integrity. Some NGOs say that the companies that they campaigned against now use the GC as a source of legitimization. Some NGO GC members have joined the process halfway through, as a result of which they did not feel really part of it. A number of civil society organizations have issued a 'Citizens Compact', with suggestions regarding some of the critical points raised by them.

MINING, MINERALS AND SUSTAINABLE DEVELOPMENT

World Business Council for Sustainable Development (WBCSD/International Institute for Environment and Development (IIED); Mining, Minerals and Sustainable Development Project (MMSD)

Issues International mining issues; stakeholder partnerships; sustainable development.

Objectives To identify how mining and minerals can best contribute to the global transition to sustainable development.

Participants Variable according to each MSP, wide scoping exercises being undertaken.

Scope International, regional and national, with some local processes and inputs.

Time lines April 2000–2002.

Contact URL IIED, London; www.iied.org/mmsd

Procedural aspects

Designing the MSP The MMSD is managed by the IIED in London, under contract to the WBCSD. The project was initiated by the WBCSD and is supported by the Global Mining Initiative (GMI). The process was started initially by an IIED scoping group, then included commercial parties, and eventually wider involvement occurred – a dynamic process.

In addition to the technical analysis and consultation, the stakeholder engagement element of the project is 'intended to promote an equitable, constructive, secure, and transparent set of processes for engagement of all interested stakeholders' at the global and local level. It has three elements:

1 To ensure that there is an adequate plan for stakeholder engagement both at the project level and in each of the individual project activities. This includes identifying and engaging with a diverse range of participants in workshops and other events.
2 Managing three large global stakeholder dialogues on key issues.
3 Producing a 'Principals of Engagement' document that embodies the mutually agreed values and principles that govern how the project approaches stakeholders.

Identifying the issues The process builds on IIED/WBCSD previous experience in carrying out an independent assessment of the world's paper industry and prospects for sustainability (see below). Regional processes use round-table structures and expert groups.

Identifying relevant stakeholders Through consultation, especially through the International Assurance Group.

Identifying participants The IIED, project staff among others identify participants through known contacts, networks, literature research, consultation, mass mailouts. Some key stakeholders may choose not to take part.

Setting the goals Goals outlined in the Scoping Report, prepared by the IIED for the WBCSD (1999), are:

- To assess global mining and mineral use in terms of the transition to sustainable development (track record, contribution to and detraction from economic prosperity, human well-being, ecosystem health and accountable decision-making will all impact on MSPs).
- To identify if, and how, services can be delivered in accordance with sustainable development.
- To propose key elements of an action plan for improvement.
- To build a platform for analysis and engagement for ongoing cooperation and networking between all stakeholders (which is crucial for long-term impact).

The MMSD is designed to produce concrete results during its two-year lifespan and to create structures that are capable of taking things forward thereafter. The MMSD does not exist to solve or address all the issues faced by the mining and minerals industry. It is a start in identifying different concerns and getting processes under way that in the long term will move issues towards solutions. Participants have opportunities to check back with their constituencies when changes are being proposed. The MMSD project aims to support the GMI.

Setting the agenda Various groups are involved since the process aims to use stakeholders to set the agenda. Other activities are spear-headed by IIED's London-based Work Group or directly contracted out to existing institutions with relevant expertise and networks. A large part of the work is decentralized to a series of regional centres in the principal mineral-producing and consuming regions of the world. An assurance group is charged with assuring adequate peer review of the project's outputs and so on.

Setting the timetable Set by the project's objectives and a time-frame for closure.

Preparatory process A multitude of MSPs, at different levels, is used within the project; each has its own characteristics. Three global stakeholder dialogues are planned: the role of financial institutions in funding mining programmes; information access; and the role of dialogue and Indigenous Peoples. The initial approach is via a small scoping group (there is no attempt at an MSP at this stage) which looks at certain issues and determines whether MMSD has anything to contribute. The MMSD will try to get hold of the best people (via known networks, and so on) to constitute a round-table brainstorming session to come up with ideas on how MMSD could inform issues and add value. Out of this falls the development of discrete areas of research around each project, an MSP networking process with regional partners on which groups to approach, who could input, who could critique and so on, plus interim research material. All this leads to an MSP work-shop of some kind to reflect on the work completed (40–60 people).

Communication All usual group work methods are used in addition to stakeholder techniques that ensure two-way communication. A 'very high degree of openness and transparency' underpins the project. All interim research will be released to stakeholders (participating and non-participating) as part of a broader engagement process (web-based). The communications process is meant to ensure 'that interested stakeholders, researchers and others have the means to communicate their ideas freely and effectively in ways that impact the project and its outcomes' (website).

Implementation Preparations for implementation are under way: the MMSD partner Stratos Inc produced a 'framework for the considerations of options' regarding planning the outcomes of the MMSD process. It outlines various categories of possible implementation mechanisms: norms and instruments (legal and policy, market-based, voluntary); processes (stakeholder processes, capacity development, technological improvement); institutional responses (new institutions, reformed institutions, knowledge management, financial mechanisms). The paper suggests the criteria for selecting desired outcomes and a number of factors to be used to guide selection. MMSD's work on 'planning for outcomes' will continue through reviewing implementation mechanisms, workshops to gather stakeholder and expert responses, and identifying concrete MMSD outcomes to be presented in the final report.

Closure The overall project is time-limited, ending in 2002. The expected results will be fed into Earth Summit, 2002. Individual MSPs have different time-frames.

Structural aspects

Institutional back-up MMSD Secretariat.

Facilitation Usually done by experienced facilitators. The MMSD Secretariat provides support services.

Documentation Participants receive all records of the process. The core of MMSD's work is directed towards the preparation of a draft report, due at the end of 2001, covering the broad scope of the issues investigated. Interim reports are to be released. The material will cover the network-building issue.

Relating to non-participating stakeholders MMSD regional staff and LA21 projects (overlaps in Indonesia). At the outset there was an idea that it might be possible to engage with local communities, but this cannot really be done by the MMSD London Work Group due to a lack of time and resources. However, it will happen to a smaller extent by regional contacts, and some groups, such as Indigenous Peoples, come as individuals, thus allowing the project to gain a particular perspective.

Relating to the general public This is a specialized issue, so there is no intentional public information. However, there is a clear, informative and open website, encouraging input and feedback.

Linkage into official decision-making MMSD will probably feed into various national and international decision-making processes (it is too early to detail). The final report is likely to contain three aspects:

- technical report with research;
- viewpoints (positive and negative); and
- stakeholder engagement – all the lessons learned and what dialogue developed.

Funding The overall budget for MMSD is US$9.5 million for all work globally (six regions), which is seen as constraining. Of the total, 60 per cent is from commercial sources.

Additional information The MMSD seems to exemplify a problem with all MSPs – a 'chicken-and-egg' situation. Do you start and then expose the work to a wider group of people, or do you start with a very open process and get pulled in 20 different directions immediately?

TOWARDS A SUSTAINABLE PAPER CYCLE

World Business Council for Sustainable Development (WBCSD)/International Institute for Environment and Development (IIED)

Issues The paper cycle; forestry practices, waste management.

Objectives The IIED in association with WBCSD undertook an independent assessment of the world's paper industry, examining the sector's life-cycle impacts and prospects for sustainability; to inform the debate, drawing on stakeholder consultations.

Participants WBCSD; IIED; private sector forestry and paper companies; environmental NGOs; academic sector, research institutions, government and international agencies.

Scope Global.

Time lines Research leading to the publication of the report 'Towards a Sustainable Paper Cycle', June 1996, and further activities.

Contact, URL IIED, London, and WBCSD, Geneva; www.iied.org and www.wbcsd.org

Procedural aspects

Designing the MSP Designed in a negotiation between IIED and WBCSD; multi-stakeholder advisory group (which proved to have relatively little input). A project sponsor task force was composed mainly of industry representatives and had more input to the study. Reports were distributed widely to a range of stakeholders for written comment. Also two regional multi-stakeholder workshops were held in Asia and Latin America during the study and one NGO consultation took place in London. Several multi-stakeholder workshops happened after the study was completed to discuss the findings.

Identifying the issues The issues were identified by IIED primarily but drew on suggestions from the WBCSD, the project task force, the advisory group, and information arising from regional workshops and

NGO consultations. At the Earth Summit, 1992, the WBCSD set out how industry might move into a more sensitive relationship with the environment. Later it was agreed that a sector example was required to show how the transition process might move the proceedings towards sustainability. The paper industry challenged the IIED to conduct a worldwide review of their social and environmental performance. The study demonstrates that the idea of finding global solutions to a set of diverse local problems will not work (there are different trade-offs, and so on).

Identifying relevant stakeholders Stakeholders were identified by the WBCSD and the IIED, but drew on suggestions made by organizations and individuals in different regions.

Setting the goals Goals were set by the WBCSD and the IIED but probably became less ambitious in the course of the study. The emphasis shifted from assessment to 'informing the debate' and 'providing raw material for dialogue'. 'The issues of sustainable forestry require open and transparent co-operation in new ways by all stakeholders. . . Therefore the primary aim of this project is to establish a factual base upon which to begin a constructive dialogue process with stakeholders in broader forest issues' (Bjorn Stigson, President, WBCSD, at www.wbcsd.org).

Setting the timetable Set by the WBCSD but an extension of the deadlines was negotiated by the IIED in view of the time taken for consultation and report delays.

Preparatory process There was a widespread consultation process with regional workshops, specialist meetings, task forces, numerous corresponding partners and an advisory group. The final study also drew on the findings of 20 substudies. An international group of senior advisers reviewed the research to ensure its independence.

Communication A mixture of communication channels was used – more than 500 stakeholder groups were contacted by IIED during the course of the study.

Closure There was no closure as such – the hope was that the report would facilitate and encourage further dialogue at different levels.

Structural aspects

Institutional back-up The IIED and WBCSD.

Documentation The WBCSD reported on the task force and advisory group meetings, but these were distributed only to participants. The

IIED reported on the regional workshops and NGO consultations. The main report was published by the IIED with the WBCSD. Numerous substudies were published by the IIED several months before and after the publication of the main report.

Relating to non-participating stakeholders There was no formal mechanism relating to non-participating stakeholders, but if they expressed interest in commenting on the report they were included on the distribution list.

Relating to the general public The final report was distributed widely and also marketed by the WBCSD and IIED. Otherwise, there was little opportunity for the general public to feed in or comment. The process attracted attention from environmentalists as it seemed to be used by some stakeholders to support incineration rather than paper recycling.

Linkage into official decision-making There was very little linkage.

Funding A mixture of donor (35–40 per cent) and industry funding (60–65 per cent) across five continents. Fund-raising was done jointly by the WBCSD and IIED, with the latter concentrating more on the donor funding but participating in presentations to potential industry sponsors. It is believed that the non-industry funding helped enormously in maintaining the credibility of the study as an independent objective analysis.

Additional information This initial project served as a model for the other WBCSD projects which are now underway (including MMSD, see above).

WORLD HEALTH ORGANIZATION (WHO), THIRD MINISTERIAL CONFERENCE ON ENVIRONMENT AND HEALTH FOR EUROPE – ACTION IN PARTNERSHIP, LONDON 1999

Issues Health and the environment.

Objectives A planning and informing process at European level. A complex process involving 11 working groups set up and run by the WHO, with substantial NGO input and with a parallel NGO forum, supported by the WHO and other UN agencies. The scope was health and the environment in its broadest sense; with the objective of furthering debate on a range of issues and helping to develop various protocols/agreements, including fresh water, transport and health, and a ministerial declaration on Environment and Health Priorities for Europe in the 21st century.

Participants NGOs; academics; health professionals.

Scope Regional.

Time lines 16–19 June 1999.

Contact, URL UNED Forum, London; www.unedforum.org/health/index.htm

Procedural aspects

Designing the MSP The process was designed by the WHO in consultation with UNED Forum who put together a multi-stakeholder advisory committee. There was some consultation with stakeholders on the process design facilitated by UNED. The European Environment and Health Committee (EEHC) helped to plan this with a relatively small group of professionals/representatives of different sectors and one or two NGOs, although NGO involvement increased markedly during the process.

Identifying the issues Largely set by the WHO European Regional Office as stakeholder involvement only began after the start of the process.

Identifying the relevant stakeholders NGOs and other stakeholders were invited into the process. The UNED facilitated the broadening out to stakeholders beyond that, although the WHO had their own links with stakeholders, too, with governments and health professionals being the most obvious groups. Local authorities also came into the process. Interestingly, the WHO did not use their own multi-stakeholder process (the Healthy Cities Initiative, see additional remarks, below) to any great extent. The reasons included the fact that this initiative has its own agenda and is a worldwide initiative in which the European part was not heavily involved. It was also possibly due to some internal matters within the WHO.

Identifying participants People have different perceptions as to how much outreach was done. The WHO did some in terms of identifying participants, but the perception was that it was rather 'hit and miss'. Most health professionals knew that it was happening. Bodies such as the Chartered Institute of Environmental Health Officers (CIEH) and the International Federation of Environmental Health (IFEH) who were already involved through the EEHC, did a lot to help involve a wider audience. Most of the other outreach was facilitated by UNED and the multi-stakeholder advisory group.

Setting the goals and agenda The main goal was to hold the event and second to come up with the relevant protocols, charters and so on. The remit also included setting up the working groups. Goals developed as the process progressed. As there had been two previous ministerial conferences, the dialogue-building process does go back a long way. The London process started immediately after the ratification of the previous meeting. It was pushed by EEHC, various governments, and international health and environment professionals. About 50 countries participated, with about 40 in the preparatory events. It was something of a consensus-building process. As with many of these international declarations, nothing would happen without a fairly substantial government consensus. Without this, members like the Vatican could block the aspects they disliked. But with this 3rd WHO conference of this type (after 1989 and 1994), hopefully the process has gone from a mere exchange of views through to the development of agreements, to implementation, although this last stage remains to be seen.

There was much serious checking back with constituencies at the governmental level. It is unclear (not documented) just how far other representatives checked back. There is the suggestion that people who go to these international processes tend to become sucked in and other attendees almost become their peer group, rather than those who sent them there in the first place. For example, the CIEH are still involved in the issues, but it is questionable, due to time constraints, how far they actually checked back with individual environmental health officers. It is also questionable whether the IFEH consulted back with bodies such as the UK CIEH.

Setting the timetable

This was set according to the conference date.

Preparatory process A preparatory process with a range of specialist working groups and NGOs consulted through various events. The Soesterberg conference was the main event, but by the time that NGOs became interested most of the agenda was set; the role then is mostly a working-out/lobbying role regarding 'What we will do about this or that?' as opposed to a 'What do we want to talk about?' But the increased NGO involvement and capacity building has already led to NGO involvement in the Budapest 2004 preparations (small groups format).

Communication Substantial use was made of electronic networks. The EEHC was the main coordinating body for various meetings both for the preparatory process and conference, and the working groups.

The UNED set up a list server, a quarterly newsletter and a website to keep stakeholders informed.

Power gaps Probably not much, partly because the WHO (an agency funded by governments) was 'desperately trying to get its staff to attend meetings' (one interviewee). They were extremely short of resources and reliant on national governments. Therefore it could be said that national governments probably had more power. NGOs also had a lot of power in terms of turning out to lobby at the right time and often after having done their homework much better than governments. A great deal depended on how strongly governments felt about something; if it was more open, then NGOs had quite a lot of power. Industry did not take the conference that seriously, so was not lobbying in the same way as NGOs.

Decision-making Agreement had to be sought in standard international process terms with governments able effectively to force a lowest common denominator.

Implementation Agreements go back to the working groups for implementation. Those that had funding are largely medical professionals run by a WHO senior professional.

Closure The process concluded with the London conference, but it has also impacted on the working groups and NGO process in the run-up to the Budapest conference in 2004. On all the main issues – fresh water, climate change, transport – far more is happening, but not necessarily as a result of the ministerial conference. On some of the other issues on the agenda – children's health, economics and health, local processes for environment and health – more might be expected to be happening than it actually is as a result of the London event.

Structural aspects

Institutional back-up and facilitation An international secretariat at the WHO, the EEHC, a NGO coordinating group which was close to being multi-sector. There is a question as to how far professional networks (IFEH) are included as NGOs. Business was not involved in NGO dialogues. They had more direct input through the WHO (a two-sided process).

Documentation All documentation is available via the WHO and UNED websites.

Relating to non-participating stakeholders Non-participating stakeholders had an opportunity to attend the meetings at the conference on the NGO process, and to feed in through their own agencies or to the WHO directly.

Relating to the general public Relatively little – a specialist process.

Linkage into official decision-making The conference was linked to an official decision-making process. Regarding transparency, at least people knew that a conference was happening. The Ministerial Declaration noted that it wished to 'encourage greater transparency in the work of the EEHC' and extended its membership by adding six representatives of Major Groups, including NGOs, local government, business, trade unions, and environment and health professionals, nominated by their appropriate organizations. The Declaration also noted the value of NGO input into the process, called for partnership to help with the implementation and in the 'regular and transparent reviews of progress'.

Funding The WHO provided some funding, while governments provided much of the key funding. The British Government funded the UK conference. But people like CIEH, Glaxo Welcome, the EU, and the UK and Dutch governments had to help fund NGO and other stakeholder involvement because insufficient money was available. The process as a whole was underfunded.

Additional remarks The WHO's Healthy Cities is a classic two-way partnership between the WHO and local authorities. Some of the individual Healthy Cities have been very effective in bringing other parties besides health professionals into the debate, such as business and voluntary sector groups.

WORLD BANK WORLD DEVELOPMENT REPORT ONLINE DISCUSSION, 2000

Issues Transparency, informing the dialogue, providing feedback.

Objectives To inform; to open up and inform the WB/WB Review process via an online e-conference and electronic exchange of moderated comments on the released draft of the World Development Report on Poverty.

Participants NGOs, academics, women's groups.

Scope International.

Time lines Six-week open process in 2000.

Contact, URL Bretton Woods Project, London; www.brettonwoods project.org

Procedural aspects

Designing the MSP Via an email exchange with 30 people deciding the pros and cons of trying the idea of an electronic exchange of comments and feedback on the first draft of the World Development Report on Poverty, 2000–2001. This process started the summer before the release of the draft report on the WB website. They solicited views on the idea and negotiated with the WB's lead author, Ravi Kanbur. This advance preparation eliminated the risks.

Identifying the issues The idea of an online conference was put forward by the Bretton Woods Project and the New Policy Institute. A formal steering group was appointed. They communicated mostly via conference calls and email to plan and review the documentation, and to communicate with the WB/WB Review.

Identifying relevant stakeholders An issue was how to recruit people to take part in the online conference who don't know how the WB works. This was tackled through fliers, mentions in relevant newsletters, fax alerts and electronically.

Identifying participants As above and by recruiting potential people through the Steering Groups' contacts. Effort was put into trying to get away from the 'usual suspects' and a purely EU/Northern emphasis. This meant a substantial amount of preparatory work. It was a very time-consuming process – three-and-a-half months' full-time input.

Setting the goals The online conference was an attempt to open the WB process. It was not a negotiating process, but it did have a charge to look at the final draft version of the World Development Report. There was informal input from the WB (by Ravi Kanbur) as to what its thinking was, but this was not constant feedback. However, even this level of contact had helped until the whole process became mired in the sudden departure of the report's author in late May 2000, following attempts by the WB and government officials to make him change his text before the final version was published (September, 2000).

NGO comment The WB Development Reports are written and marketed giving the impression that they convey broadly held views and contain objective research. But many civil society organizations feel that they are selective and biased. In recent years, WB teams have consulted NGOs on draft versions of reports, but groups have often commented that their responses have not been dealt with adequately. There is a need to make this process more credible.

Setting the agenda The debate was planned the summer before the report's release. Some benefits did arise, for example, participants were more in touch with each other outside the dialogue. Some even held meetings so they could prepare fully, as happened in Cameroon. The impetus for meeting and feeding back comments into the online conference was that feeling of being part of a global dialogue. There were also micro-spin-offs in terms of better developed relationships and credibility.

Setting the timetable This was set up to coincide with the WB process.

Preparatory process 1500 people participated, either as individuals or on behalf of an institution, plus there was academic involvement. All contributions were valid – it was not a prenegotiating body.

Communication Electronic exchange of views and comments. The Bretton Woods Project and New Policy Institute received a favourable response to their initiative.

Power gaps This was inevitable as the WB is still not an MSP. Processes are opaque. It was always known that the power gaps would be there, but that it was better to try to open up the dialogue to some degree. It did bring some pressure to bear on the WB.

The Bretton Woods Project did attempt some evaluation in the fifth week of the process. Issues included comments that some heavy-handed moderation was under way (people wanted their point put across even if it was not directly relevant to the process). As a result, another group was going to start an entirely open online debate, but this never happened and they conceded that the original process was acceptable. The idea of moderation (with topics set in advance at the start of each new week and a quick context-setting piece) was to prevent participants from being overloaded (the quickest way to reduce wide participation) and to keep matters focused.

Decision-making This project was about opening up perspectives. The project aimed only to bring different viewpoints into dialogue – it was not trying to reach a consensus.

Implementation It was too difficult to agree a meaningful level of consensus after only six weeks' exchange of views.

Closure A time-limited process – six weeks: 21 February–31 March 2000.

Structural aspects

Institutional back-up A Steering Group.

Facilitation A moderating team, all based in London. Their role included maintaining a list of conference participants, to answer queries, filter incoming messages and provide advice to people whose messages were not appropriate. A conference protocol was established as a guide to how the process worked: short messages, no self-promotion, and so on. Anyone who wished to submit a longer piece which did not fit the rules could send their message to the moderators for passing on to the WB author. The Bretton Woods Project and the New Policy Institute took it in turns.

Documentation The Bretton Woods Project did the summaries and so on, and translated them into French and Spanish as soon as they could (they paid for this service).

Relating to non-participating stakeholders It was an open process unless people had access to the technology. The main language of the conference was English. Submissions were accepted in French and Spanish but were not translated. The weekly and final summaries reflected all submissions and were available in the three languages.

Relating to the general public It was web-based only and is now closed as time was limited.

Linkage into official decision-making The MSP was linked to the WB as an intergovernmental body. Endless ramifications will exist for a long time as the inputs from the WB report are fed into aid packages etc.

NGO comment The endgame is not very transparent but the on-line conference did open this up a little. However, the real outcomes will always be made in 'smoke-filled rooms in Washington'. There was a two- to three-year campaign to get the WB to release a draft of the WDR, so this move is to be welcomed. But pressure must continue on the WB as this is not enough.

Funding MacArthur Foundation via Cornell University: £20,000. Funders had no direct contact or impact on the project.

GLOBAL ENVIRONMENT FACILITY (GEF), COUNTRY DIALOGUE WORKSHOP (CDW) PROGRAMME

Issues GEF issues, depending on the country; dialogue and capacity-building workshops for recipient countries; fostering an ongoing two-way dialogue between the GEF and member countries.

Objectives To inform stakeholders and GEF programmes. To facilitate a group dialogue among and between the workshop participants and the GEF; to inform a broad-based national audience about the GEF; to facilitate national stakeholder input to and information-sharing on the country's GEF programme to ensure that it reflects national priorities for GEF assistance; and to provide practical information on how to access GEF resources and how to propose, prepare and implement GEF-financed activities, including the dissemination of information on best practices and lessons learned; capacity-building; empowerment; to promote country ownership of GEF-financed activities.

Participants 23 recipient countries so far; target beneficiaries comprise a broad group of stakeholders from recipient countries identified through an initial needs assessment process. Beneficiaries include national and local governments, GEF national focal points and council members, GEF/SGP (Small Grants Programme) national coordinators or representatives from national steering committees, NGOs, the implementing agency and other donor country and regional staff, including regional development banks, academic institutions, (STAP) of the GEF, the private sector, the media and the populations they serve.

Scope National, regional (11 national and 2 regional workshops to date).

Time lines A three-year programme. Individual workshops are recommended to be four-day meetings. It is suggested that an additional day be added for a field trip to visit GEF projects.

Contact, URL www.undp.org/gef/workshop

Procedural aspects

Designing the MSP Each workshop is organized around a series of core 'Workshop Facilitation Materials' developed by the Programme. The Programme is guided by an Interagency Steering Committee which consists of representatives from the UNDP, UNEP, WB and the GEF Secretariat. The Programme is executed by the UNDP/GEF in New York on behalf of the GEF partners. The GEF Operational Focal Points (OFP) coordinate the workshop organization. The overall process should be a group effort to set in motion an effective dialogue. The organizers may wish at the outset to think about how best to establish a collaborative spirit, given their national circumstances (GEF Country Dialogue Workshop (CDW) Guidelines).

Identifying the issues The GEF OFP are responsible for ensuring that the workshop is tailored to meet specific national needs. In this regard, it is suggested in the GEF CDW guidelines that the OFP prepare a presentation for the workshop on national priorities as they relate to environment and development objectives.

  The OFP is invited to share a draft with the UNDP Country Office and UNDP/GEF for feedback in advance of the workshop. The OFP is also invited to request that others, such as the biodiversity and climate change focal points, make presentations during this session.

Identifying relevant stakeholders Countries are selected by an Interagency Steering Committee; the criteria include convention ratification, previous workshops in the pilot phase programme, cost-effectiveness, lack of strong GEF portfolio/pipeline, the significance of concerns in one or more of the focal areas, and the submission of the Biodiversity Strategy and Action Plan (BSAP) or National Communication on Climate Change. The GEF OFP takes the lead responsibility for organizing the workshop in close consultation with the GEF Political Focal Point, the implementing agencies and any other groups or institutions chosen by the OFP. It is recommended first that a tentative list of participants should be prepared and then that other stakeholders should be consulted to make the list more comprehensive, specific and accurate.

Identifying participants The OFP is responsible for seeing that all relevant GEF projects and other representatives working in the GEF focal areas are represented. It is recommended that the workshop participants comprise a broad group of stakeholders from the recipient country or countries identified through an initial survey carried out by the GEF OFP. Participants could include those from the stakeholder groups identified below that are involved in, or interested in becoming involved in the preparation and implementation of national and global environmental projects, strategies and action plans.

Setting the goals There are is preset by the GEF CDW Programme. The aim is to have a broad-based discussion and exchange of ideas to catalyse cooperation and capacity-building in the preparation of project proposals, project development and project implementation.

Setting the agenda The GEF OFP prepares and distributes the workshop agenda; it is suggested that the workshop should be based on the 'Workshop Facilitation Materials' prepared specifically for the GEF CDW by the GEF. The workshop structure should be adapted to match national priorities.

Setting the timetable The GEF OFP operates on the basis of the GEF CDW Programme, guidelines and material.

Preparatory process The GEF OFP is supposed to discuss a draft workshop agenda with the UNDP Country Office and the UNDP/GEF at least one month in advance of the scheduled workshop for their consideration and comments.

Communication process One of the key objectives of the workshops is to facilitate a group dialogue among and between the participants and the GEF. The materials allow for working group exercises and activities that aid in facilitating dialogue. A Facilitator's Kit provides information to the participants in support of the three Project Development working group exercises as outlined in the Facilitator's Notes. The kit contains ten handouts, including checklists to determine project eligibility, summaries of the operational programmes, a basic concept paper format, a list of strategic action programmes, a funding pathway table, a project brief format and a basic logical framework format. The workshop facilitators are invited to include additional handouts or to customize the existing handouts before distribution to the participants. Chairpersons should represent the various stakeholder groups attending the workshop. However, according to workshop reports (eg from Uzbekistan), speakers included only representatives of the GEF, WB, UNDP and so on, and there were no NGO speakers. The organizers are advised to choose a venue that accommodates all participants (people should live/eat together), and to ensure enough breaks as an essential opportunity for participants and facilitators to continue the dialogue in a less formal setting.

Decision-making The workshop participants formulate recommendations for the different stakeholders (for the national GEF, for the GEF, for ministries, agencies, private enterprises and NGOs). Recommendations focus on how stakeholders can better support GEF operational procedures, mechanism and operational programmes.

Closure The OFP should open and close the workshop with a defining message, and conduct the workshop evaluation using the form provided by the GEF CDW Programme.

Structural aspects

Institutional back-up and facilitation This GEF initiative is implemented by the UNDP/GEF. Country offices and OFPs are responsible for organizing and logistics. The chairpersons could represent the various groups attending the workshop. It is suggested that a different chairperson be appointed for each session to introduce the facilitators, presenters and experts. The chairpersons' task is to work with the facilitators to encourage dialogue and to keep the sessions focused on the most important issues. It is suggested that they are selected both for the stature they bring to the workshop and their ability to perform these tasks.

Documentation CDW materials (and individual GEF CDW reports) are available on the GEF website and CD-ROM. One or more rapporteurs are supposed to record the dialogue. The workshop organizers are encouraged to prepare a brief report outlining the key discussions, outcomes and recommendations of the workshop for distribution to the participants. It is recommended that the report should be prepared in an easy-to-read, action-oriented format that will generate interest and be produced immediately after the workshop to build on the momentum generated. A copy of the report should also be sent to the GEF Country Dialogue Workshops Programme, based at the UNDP/GEF in New York where it is posted on the internet so that countries can share experiences as the Programme develops.

Relating to non-participating stakeholders Countries are welcome to utilize materials in organizing workshops using other sources of financing (government, bilateral, UN agency, NGO, among others) in consultation with the GEF Implementing Agencies. The significance of the participation of many representatives of provincial organizations, which is an additional guarantee of experience dissemination all over the country, should also be specially noted.

Relating to the general public The media are supposed to be invited to the workshops. Workshop reports are available on the GEF CDW website.

Funding The UNDP Country Offices are disbursing workshop funds to the OFP based on an agreed budget. Costs are partly covered by the GEF and partly by the host country. As a first step, after initial consultation with the GEF CDW Programme, the GEF OFP will submit a workshop budget to the UNDP/GEF for consideration. Once the GEF OFP and UNDP/GEF have agreed on the workshop budget, arrangements will be made to disburse the funds through the UNDP Country Office according to UNDP administrative rules and regulations.

THE WORLD COMMISSION ON DAMS (WCD)

Issues The impacts of large dams around the world.

Objectives To conduct a rigorous independent review of the impact of large hydro-electrical and irrigation dams; to develop recommendations on future dam building and to propose practical guidelines for future decision-making; informing / advisory, not judicial.

Participants (Commission and Forum) Multilateral agencies; affected communities; international professional associations; international NGOs; government agencies; utility companies; research institutes; private-sector firms in the power and engineering sector; river basin authorities.

Scope International with regional inputs.

Time lines The WCD was launched in February 1998 and started work in May 1998 – November 2000 (publication of their report).

Contact, URL http://www.dams.org; complete report at http://www.damsreport.org/

Procedural aspects

Designing the MSP The WCD was established in February 1998 through a process of dialogue and negotiation involving representatives of the public, private and civil society sectors. It has attracted substantial interest because of the unique way in which the different sides of the debate were brought together and the belief that this may form a model for resolving other contentious development issues. It was set up and financed by aid agencies, industry, governments and NGOs. An Interim Working Group, composed of participants of a workshop facilitated by the WB and the IUCN in Gland, Switzerland was tasked with establishing the World Commission on Dams (WCD). The mandate for the work of the Commission is the result of agreements reached at the workshop in Gland, along with the subsequent preparatory work and consultation process that followed.

The WCD started as a debate within the WB. The WB used to fund large dams to a great extent (6–7 per cent of the WB's annual budget). This caused crises, for example with the Namada Dam, and the WB's involvement in dams building was looked at by an independent inspection panel (the WB's Operational and Evaluation Department's first evaluation of Bank financing of big dam projects). The Bank subsequently declined its lending, whereas coal-related lending increased. NGO campaigns called for comprehensive reviews of WB-funded dam projects. Companies were interested in finding a way forward on dam building, because of the criticism and the decrease in available loans by the WB and other funders.

The environmental advisers within the WB had discussed these issues critically all along – a debate took place to discuss the 'green position' of the Bank. The IUCN was then asked to create an external group to discuss the issue of large dams. The original idea of the WB and the IUCN was to set up a working group and to have a three-day conference which took place in Gland in April 1997. A wider group of stakeholders was then invited, including anti-dam groups. The IUCN contacted the International Rivers Network to obtain potential names and comments on the design of the event. It was important to have representation from people who were actually affected by these developments and therefore were strong critics, rather than what has been termed more 'establishment-type groups of NGOs', where the power gaps would have been less prominent and therefore the outcome would have been less progressive. The process of setting up the Commission was also supported by an NGO meeting in mid-March 1997 in Curitiba, Brazil, which had issued a Declaration calling for an international independent commission to conduct a comprehensive review of large dams. The Gland workshop brought together 39 participants representing governments, the private sector, international financial institutions, civil society organizations and affected people in a balance that later was mirrored in both the Commission and the Forum (World Commission on Dams, 2000, p27). One of the outcomes was the agreement reached on the last day of the meeting to continue the work, for example through a Commission. After the meeting, participants communicated via email.

In the view of some NGOs, the shape of any potential Commission – its scope and range – would have been narrower without the 'alternative stakeholder input' at Gland. A joint press statement issued by the WB and the IUCN noted that all stakeholders would collaborate on a study to review the effectiveness of large dams and of setting standards. Thus, all the stakeholders involved were established as central to the legitimacy of the process. The joint WB/IUCN press release read 'Dam-builders and some of their strongest critics agreed today. . .'. The IUCN and the WB noted how they had brought together the two sides of a highly contentious debate and forged consensus between them.

The workshop in Gland produced one recommendation: that people affected by dam building, particularly those that have to resettle, need to be (materially) better off after the building than before (a recommendation also put forward in the WCD report). The principles of transparency, consultation and independence were enshrined as key to the process.

Identifying the issues To ensure the independence of the Commission, the IUCN and the WB have maintained their roles as initiators, but neither institution interfered with the work programme of the Commission. Issues for the initial Gland meeting were identified by the WB and the IUCN. After that, issues were identified by participants, the Interim Working Group and subsequently the Commission and the Forum, and via input from regional hearings/meetings, and expert and stakeholder background papers.

Identifying relevant stakeholders Relevant stakeholders were identified before the initial conference in Gland by the WB and the IUCN. The issue of whether NGOs should participate was considered carefully, given the scarcity of their resources and time, and the issue that the usual power balance might happen and decisions would be favourable to the industry. Dam critics noted that there would be less chance of this happening if the Commissioners had integrity and the process was transparent.

Identifying participants Selecting the Commissioners was no easy process as some people felt that the suggested lists did not include adequate representation of people affected by dam building. The Commission was composed of a chair and 11 members, balanced by regional representation, expertise and stakeholders. Commissioners are members in their individual capacities, not representatives of organizations. Ensuring inclusiveness, independence and transparency were the goals of the process. 'As an international commission, our process has been unique in taking on board a range of interests and opinions previously held to be irreconcilable' (WCD, 2000). The WCD Forum is a consultative group consisting of 68 organizations, acting as a sounding board and advisory group for the WCD. It is a mix of participants at the initial Gland meeting, new stakeholders and interest groups. Selection criteria were relevance, balance and representation of a diversity of perspectives, interests and regions. The Forum is a mechanism for maintaining a dialogue between the WCD and the respective constituencies of the Forum members. Members of the Forum provide ongoing input into the Commission, play a key role in outreach and most likely in the follow-up work.

Setting the goals The Interim Working Group negotiated the form and mandate of the Commission. This group had been part of the Gland meeting and represented all stakeholders. The WCD addressed the conflicting viewpoints within the debate on large dams through:

- Undertaking a global review of the development effectiveness of large dams and assessments of alternatives.
- Developing a framework for assessing alternative option and decision-making processes for water and power development.
- Developing internationally acceptable criteria and guidelines for the planning, designing, construction, operation, monitoring and decommissioning of dams.

The goal was to undertake an independent review of large dams and their impacts as well as developing proposals for the future.

Setting the agenda This was identified at the Gland meeting and shaped at each and every consultation session. Ultimately the 12 Commissioners as representatives of all interested groups agreed the final agenda of the issues.

Setting the timetable After the Gland meeting communication took place between the participants, then by the Commission, including consultations with the Forum.

Preparatory process The process had a number of components:

- Commissioned research and submitted papers.
- A five-month preparatory phase (January–May 1998).
- Regional meetings; a thematic group which was increasingly important (a long list of stakeholders funded by themselves mostly); a Forum as a sounding board which also created commitment.
- Background papers were prepared to feed in expert and stakeholder views.

A large part of the Commission's work involved a broad and independent review of the experience with large dams. The resulting WCD Knowledge Base includes eight in-depth case studies of dams, several country reviews, briefing papers, thematic reviews and cross-check surveys, as well as the results of public (including regional) consultations, and 947 submissions made to the WCD.

Communication Meetings were held; otherwise there was huge email traffic. After the Gland meeting, NGOs were very thoughtful and business people too direct, which made the NGOs more powerful. Some business people have been 'converted' by this process and some NGOs changed their views too (comment from the WB and NGOs).

'The experience of the Commission demonstrates that common ground can be found without compromising individual values or losing a sense of purpose' (World Commission on Dams, 2000, Executive Summary). 'Those groups facing the greatest risk from the development have the greatest stake in the decisions, and therefore must have a corresponding place at the negotiating table' (ibid, 2000, p209). The WCD report aims to encourage 'improved decision-making processes that deliver improved outcomes for all stakeholders' (ibid, 2000, Executive Summary). The Commission grouped the core values that informed its understanding of the issues under five main headings: equity; efficiency; participatory decision-making; sustainability; and accountability. 'Only decision-making processes based on the pursuit of negotiated outcomes, conducted in an open and transparent manner and inclusive of all legitimate actors involved in the issue are likely to resolve the complex issues surrounding water, dams and development' (ibid, 2000, Executive Summary). Regarding gaining public acceptance, the report stated: 'Acceptance emerges from recognising rights, addressing risks, and safeguarding the entitlements of all groups of affected people. . . Decision-making processes and mechanisms are used that enable informed participation by all groups of people, and result in the demonstrable acceptance of key decisions' (ibid, 2000).

Bringing about change will require planners to identify stakeholders through a process that recognizes rights and risks.

Decision-making The WCD report is a consensus document by the Commissioners; the report includes a comment by one Commissioner concerning the overall approach and definition of development taken by the Commission, not individual conclusions or recommendations.

Implementation The Commission identified that they were not constituted to implement the recommendations and indeed did not have the mandate or authority to do so. One key aspect is development finance; the multi- and bilateral agencies have been tasked with responding to the recommendations. This may initiate some form of institutionalizing of the WCD process/recommendations. The WCD urged all groups to study their report and its recommendations, 'bearing in mind that it results from consultations that, in terms of inclusiveness and breadth of scope, are beyond the reach of any individual interest group' (ibid, 2000, p311). 'Capacity must be built if good outcomes are to be achieved, including strengthening civil society and particularly empowering women to make their voices heard' (ibid, p313). The report is being studied by individual governments, some of whom have adopted in some way or the other. Further steps are under discussion.

Closure The mandate of the Commission expired with the publication of the report in November 2000. Another WCD Forum meeting was held in February 2001 to assess and discuss follow-up, which might include a strategy of feeding the results into governmental decision-making, the establishment of regional commissions and establishing a follow-up group. The February 2001 Forum meeting was prepared by the Secretariat and a Forum Liaison Group (FLG) comprising representatives of the IUCN and WB, two of the civil society Forum members, and two of the industry, government and operators' Forum members. At the meeting, Forum members agreed 'to work through their diverse governmental, private-sector and civil society organizations and affiliations:

- To ensure widespread dissemination and understanding of the report, its findings and recommendations. . .
- To promote testing, refinement and adaptation in implementing the Commission's proposed guidelines in the varied practical contexts worldwide. . .
- To promote dialogue, information exchange and networking in working with the WCD report. . . (DAMS, No 9).

The meeting also mandated the FLG to take the lead in establishing new arrangements for follow-up, such as a 'Dams and Development

Forum', a 'Dams and Development Governance Group' and a 'Dams and Development Unit', a small office which may find its home at UNEP.

Structural aspects

Institutional back-up The WCD Secretariat; Capetown, South Africa.

Facilitation The WCD Secretariat.

Documentation Website at www.dams.org. A WCD report launched in November 2000 was described by Commissioners as a 'consensus document'. It 'sets out to distil more than two years intense study, dialogue and reflection by the Commission, the WCD secretariat, the WCD stakeholders' Forum and literally hundreds of individual experts and affected people on every aspect of the dams debate' (World Commission on Dams, 2000, Executive Summary). The WCD describe the report not as a blueprint but 'as the starting point for discussions, debates, internal reviews and reassessments of what may be established procedures and for an assessment of how these can evolve to address a changed reality'.

Relating to non-participating stakeholders The WCD has entered into partnerships with various organizations, networks and international agencies. These collaborations have led to exciting opportunities for sharing, reviewing and disseminating information of common interest. Some NGOs comment that a negative charge of elitism could be placed against the process – despite its claims of inclusiveness – as almost all WCD documents used the English language, and without internet access it would have been hard to obtain large amounts of the documentation (the reason given was the tight time-frame for their task).

Relating to the general public Website, publication, press releases, big public launch events in all regions (publicity involving celebrities like Nelson Mandela).

Linkage into official decision-making There are linkages via individual governments; many governments are currently reviewing the report. Government interest increased over the course of the Commission's work period. For example, Brazil decided to do its own WCD for Brazil (individual commission); Sweden decided to build no more dams (December 2000); Germany is reviewing the WCD report, and so on. Further linkages, for example into the Earth Summit 2002 process, are under discussion.

Funding The WB and the IUCN undertook to secure the initial core resources for the Commission to be created and to implement its work programme. The IUCN provided the initial administrative support system to facilitate the work of the Commission and the Secretariat. The Gland meeting was funded by the Swiss Development Corporation, with a contribution from the WB. The Commission then engaged in fund-raising activities, resulting in a large number of funders for the Secretariat and the Commission, including 17 governments and government agencies, 20 private-sector firms, 12 NGOs and foundations, and 4 multilateral agencies. The WCD has thereby implemented a new funding model involving all interest groups in the debate. Funding was sought from the public and private sectors as well as from civil society. Contributors had pledged funds equal to more than three-quarters of the Commission's total projected budget of about US$9.9 million.

Additional information The Global Public Policy Project, which is sponsored by the UN Foundation to explore the potential of public policy networks for increasing the effectiveness of the United Nations, recognized the value of the WCD as a trisectoral process (public, private, civil society). The process took on board all the different interests and moved the debate forward. The WCD report acknowledges that the conflict and 'stalemate' that was developing around the dams controversy benefited no one: 'A new way had to be found.' Understanding the WCD process is important because it is being hailed as a precedent for dealing with other controversial global policy issues (by the WB and others). Monitoring of the follow-up is necessaary – there is a need to learn from this experience. It is unclear as yet who could fulfil that monitoring role. The WCD report and the process received acclaim from dam critics such as the International Committee on Dams, Rivers and People (a coalition representing 13 countries). However, they have highlighted that 'it is one thing to get a good report and it will be quite another for the report actually to make a difference to real world practices' (McCully, 2001).

Some NGOs believe that among the many process-related factors that allowed such a welcome report is the fact that governments and international agencies were marginalized from the process, and the private-sector dam industry lacked a coordinated strategy. Some say that the whole process and report raises many more issues for countries than just dams – such as governance issues in general.

The World Resources Institute, the Lawyers' Environmental Action Team, and Lokayan are currently undertaking an independent assessment of the WCD. Preliminary findings as of April 2001 have been published at www.wcdassessment.org; the final report will be available in September 2001.

Part II

How to Do It

7

Designing MSPs: A Detailed Guide

Based on the building-blocks assembled in Part I, this chapter provides a detailed outline of the questions, issues and challenges which need to be addressed when designing a multi-stakeholder process. The aspects we discuss and the suggestions we make are addressed. We hope the considerations help to clarify a variety of options and point to the crucial aspects which can make an MSP work or fail.[1] The chapter begins with some general considerations and is then organized according to five possible phases of MSPs. A number of issues to be addressed throughout such processes are considered at the end.

Edward Sampson (1993, p98) said 'that the most important thing about people is not what is contained in them but what transpires between them'. Our suggestions on how to design and conduct MSPs are about how to set up a space that allows that what 'transpires between' people is a constructive contribution to sustainable development.

MSPs will have to be unique to their issue, scope, objectives, participants, resources, and so on. There is no 'one-size-fits-all' formula. Hence, we are not able to outline all possible options, and some of the points and suggestions below do not apply to all such processes.

What we are presenting here may sound ideal, but in 'real life' it will often not be possible to address all aspects sufficiently. However, we would recommend that conscious choices are made where and when it is possible, to go through the points raised and decide what to do with the limited resources at hand.

SOME GENERAL CONSIDERATIONS

The suggestions made here are addressed to institutions, organizations or groups that are considering designing a multi-stakeholder process.

Ideally, all stakeholders should be able and eligible to initiate MSPs. However, many stakeholder groups are not in a position to do so due to a lack of capacity and resources (see Funding).

It is crucial to invest sufficient time and resources in carefully designing MSPs in order to avoid failure. Failure can result in stakeholders walking away from dialogue, the inability of a group to make decisions or the lack of implementation of the decisions reached. After a failed attempt to carry out an MSP, the situation might be worse than before – entering the process raises stakeholders' expectations. Failure might increase conflict and distrust, confirm stereotypical views and diminish the ability and readiness to listen or collaborate. In other words, an unsatisfactory process can be a step back rather than forward.

Everybody who considers initiating an MSP should do so *in collaboration with other stakeholders*, namely representatives of those groups who should be involved. The idea is to make the design phase a multi-stakeholder effort itself. As early in the process as possible, initiating bodies should reach out and assemble a small group of representative stakeholders of high diversity. This group can become an initial coordinating group for the process, but the participants of the MSP itself need to decide if the group is to have a continuing role.

MSPs need precisely defined issues before them. The questions to be addressed and the goals of the process need to be very clear to all the participants and agreed by them. Possible changes over the course of an ongoing process also need to be agreed by the group, allowing for consultations within constituencies if necessary.

Every MSP is about learning. Every participant should be prepared to learn from and about others, and to learn how to work together as a team and come to creative, integrative solutions. The same applies to the process itself – every MSP should take a learning approach towards its procedures and, in some cases, the issues developing over time. Flexibility needs to be balanced by the process having clear objectives and cut-off points.

MSPs are about creating a space where dialogue can take place, 'a neutral, free and ordered space, where violence is replaced by verbal debate, shouting by listening, chaos by calm' (Asmal, 2000). An atmosphere that cultivates equity, respect, dignity, humility and hope will help to create a space where people can interact in such a way that their differences and their commonalities become clear so that they can begin to explore possible ways forward.

MSPs should not only publish their discussions and outcomes but also keep records of their design.[2] Information should be made available on who initiated the process and who was involved at a specific time, on the issues and questions, and on which mechanisms were employed to identify stakeholders, issues, objectives, rules and procedures, and so on.

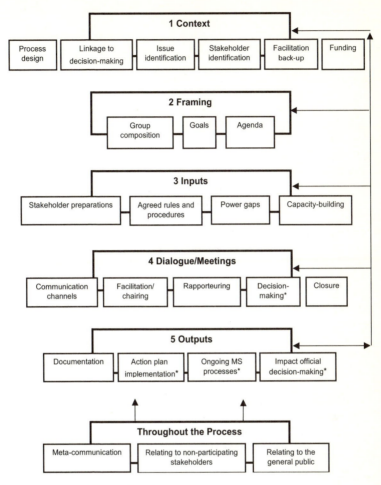

Arrows indicate reviewing/refining/repeating
*Optional

Figure 7.1 *Overview*

CONTEXT

Process design

Each situation or issue prompts the need for participants to design a process specifically suited to their abilities, circumstances and needs. Participants must be able not only to set out their individual goals and expectations, but also to establish a common agenda that addresses a mutually agreed problem.

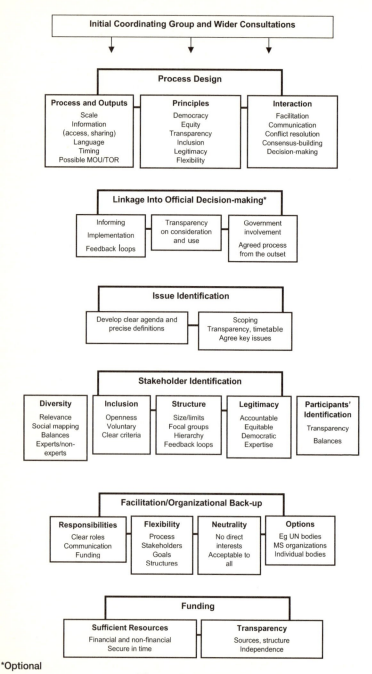

*Optional

Figure 7.2 *Context*

The most important mechanism to start building the necessary trust and ensure high quality from the outset is to design the process in a collaborative effort, not a unilateral one. This does not mean that there will be no conflicts on the issues, but it helps to avoid confusions on the process which tend to increase distrust.

Involving stakeholders in every aspect of the design process is crucial to achieve the best design, commitment to the process, credibility, legitimacy and trust. A core coordinating group may be required to manage the process, identify the issue to be addressed, approach possible independent facilitators and involve relevant stakeholders. Possible designs can be suggested by individual stakeholders but should be put to a multi-stakeholder group.

Procedures need to be agreed by the participants – the procedures of preparation, communication, the ground rules for the meeting, the issues around confidentiality, decision-making (if applicable), rapporteuring, documentation, relating to non-participants and the general politics, and fund-raising. As a rule, any changes in procedure throughout the process also need to be agreed – they should be suggested to the whole group and dealt with by them, including opportunities to check back with constituencies if participants choose to do so.

Procedures should be designed to ensure democracy, equity, mutual respect, transparency, legitimacy, accountability, and inclusiveness in order for the process to benefit from diversity; generate mutual understanding, creative outcomes and win–win solutions; and to encourage commitment.

An example which is not included in this study but offers insights on how to go about designing an MSP in a multi-stakeholder fashion is the development of the Urban Environmental Policy in Durban, South Africa. In stage one of the process, consultations with stakeholders lead to a 'public workshop' and an 'officials' workshop', out of which the facilitating agency developed a draft process agreement document. This was then put to review by the MSP founding meeting which involved all stakeholders (Commonground, 2000).

Allowing sufficient time for preparations and the process itself is another important point. Many of the examples have been conducted within a short time period which sometimes has created all sorts of problems. It can hinder groups participating in the preparations altogether or in checking back with their constituencies. The negative effects on the quality of the outcomes and the likelihood of agreement and implementation are easy to imagine. However, MSPs should have an agreed time-frame to keep participants focused and to avoid large ongoing expenses. Designing an MSP is about striking a balance between having enough time to learn, consult and develop, and having sufficient pressure to deliver. Caution should be exercised to ensure that MSPs are not used by some participants as a tactical device to delay or block decision-finding.

A process will be more difficult the greater the differences between participants' agendas and if the issue to be addressed lies in an area of existing or likely conflict. In that case, finding mechanisms to help overcome confrontational relationships and distrust will need to be in the centre of designing the process. The designing group should consider including conflict resolution techniques in the process: bargaining, third-party mediation or other dispute resolution techniques. In cases of stark conflict, however, it might be more appropriate to begin working with individual stakeholder groups first, before bringing the different groups together.

Finally, the MSP group can consider preparing and signing a Memorandum of Understanding (MOU) or Terms of Reference (TOR) that serves as the basis for cooperative work. The MOU can include the following components:

- Specific activities that are to be jointly undertaken.
- Respective roles and responsibilities of MSP group members.
- Responsibilities of facilitators and other positions within the MSP group.
- Types of information to be shared and standards for sharing of information, including agreements on confidentiality.
- Time-frame for completing each phase of the work.
- Methods for group decision-making and conflict resolution.
- How outcomes of the MSP will be integrated into the official decision-making processes.
- Resources to be provided by each member of the MSP group.

Linkage into official decision-making

A clear distinction needs to be made between a forum of stakeholder dialogue and collaboration and the deliberations of a democratically elected body or governing council that takes the responsibility for decisions.

Different types of MSPs provide different kinds of linkages into official decision-making bodies. Many of the dialogue-focused examples of informing processes have their weak point when it comes to identifying their linkage into official decision-making. Will delegates take up the points raised and recommendations made by the stakeholders? Will they put particular weight on aspects that the stakeholders agreed upon? There is a great need for transparency, ensuring that officials as well as stakeholders are very clear about what they are engaging in.

A chair's summary or another form of MSP outcome document can be produced and put into the decision-making process. In case the official body is to produce such a document, stakeholders should be consulted upon a draft to allow for input and clarification. The production and the status of such a document needs to be agreed within the decision-making body beforehand. For example, the input from the MSP will be more effective if officials receive the document as an official publication (such as a UN background paper) or a summary of the chair of dialogues and negotiations (as is practice at the CSD). It will put weight to the document and enable delegates to use it much as an official one.

In our view, the often purely informing role of stakeholder participation around (inter)governmental bodies should be expanded. This does not mean that democratically elected bodies should be disempowered. MSPs are meant effectively to give 'a voice, not a vote' (Edwards, 2000, p29), or rather voices, not votes. For example, stakeholders should be involved immediately in the steps towards implementation. They could be invited to study decisions and engage in action-oriented discussions on how to implement them. For example, the stakeholder dialogues at the beginning of CSD meetings could be complemented by sessions towards the end of the meeting. Stakeholders could be brought together again to work out how to implement the decisions, and which tools, strategies and partnerships would be needed. This would capture stakeholders' engagement and could generate more commitment, spark off partnerships and concrete pilot projects as outcomes, the results of which could be fed back into the policy-making process at an agreed time. 'Stakeholder implementation conferences', organized independently around official events, would be another option.

Such mechanisms could be taken one step further by consulting a multi-stakeholder forum on draft (inter)governmental decisions and resolutions. This would provide feedback to governments as to the practicability and likelihood of the implementation of policies. Such an approach implies some stakeholder involvement in official decision-making itself and would need political decisions to be taken by governments and the relevant intergovernmental bodies.[3]

Independent MSPs also need to be answerable to questions of democratic legitimacy and accountability. They cannot replace democratically elected bodies or governing councils to make decisions, but they can supplement and complement (inter)governmental decision-making processes. Wherever MSPs touch on areas where the involvement, guidance and/or control of governments are required, these bodies need to be part of the process from the beginning.

Issue identification

MSPs need a clear agenda and precise definitions of what issues they are going to address. Without a precise question before the MSP, participants will not be able to engage in productive dialogue. A crucial question is: Who can and who should identify an issue or problem area which needs to be addressed with an MSP? And how should that happen? Ideally, anyone who is a stakeholder should be able to suggest an MSP. As reported above, approaching a small group of stakeholders to begin consultations is a good first step.

Issue identification is therefore the first substantive stage of an MSP. It is helpful to have agreement on what it is that you are trying to do before deciding on the tools you will use. As a general rule, proper problem clarification saves time and reduces conflict later on. The various representations or understandings that stakeholders hold of the issue(s) at hand need to be clarified to arrive at a precise question before the MSP. The different understandings need to be clear for everybody involved to establish further what the group is addressing. Otherwise, the whole process will be hampered by ongoing battles about what to include or exclude from the discussions. It is highly unlikely that stakeholders will share a common understanding, hence the questions and subissues they will want to address will be different.[4]

In many cases, the issues to be addressed in an MSP are decided by the body which facilitates it and/or which has a vital interest in setting it up. Conducted in such a fashion, identifying the issues will result in a unilateral decision, with stakeholder groups being invited to participate in a process which has a preset agenda. This poses a dilemma for the invitees, since taking part in the process could mean agreeing to an agenda they might not approve of, whereas refusing to take part might lead to the MSP being conducted without them and their views not being included.

For the sake of ensuring the potential success of a process, appropriate measures need to be taken to avoid unilateral, non-transparent and inequitable identifying of the issues. These include:

- Carefully scoping the area of an issue of interest: those who consider initiating an MSP should aim to get a clear picture of the discussions in and around the area of interest before identifying a particular issue as the one to be addressed (see Eden and Ackermann, 1998).
- Involving stakeholders in discussions about potential issues and communicating to them all that that is being done.
- Based on initial consultations, setting a timetable for such identifying discussions and communicating it clearly.

- Supporting stakeholders to identify the issues of interest where necessary (eg by governments or foundations), including access to information and resources.

From the initial scoping and discussions, a group of people can emerge who are interested in actively pursuing the setting up of an MSP on a particular issue. This can be used as a starting point for creating a coordinating group of representatives from various stakeholder groups ensuring a diversity of views. Upon setting up the MSP, this group needs to be reviewed by all participants of the process and, if necessary, recomposed, so that it is acknowledged by all involved. An example of such a process is the GRI.

The initial scoping of an issue area might also lead to identifying research and knowledge gaps. In such cases, MSP design might involve commissioning such research.

It is important to create a mechanism for sharing information and a 'home' for a common knowledge base for the process, ensuring that all concerned have equal access to the relevant information from the outset. Such a base does not need to be in one place, but should be easily accessible to all. Everybody who might be involved in the process should be informed of this information base and how it is being assembled.

In the initial phase, agreement should also be reached on the language(s) to be used in the process. This will normally depend on the issues and groups who need to be involved. Using one language, such as English, can be exclusive. Many of the examples we looked at reportedly suffered from using one language only, mostly due to lack of time and money. Sufficient resources need to be available for translations where necessary.

Stakeholder identification

The main questions here concern issues, inclusiveness, diversity and size.

Open calls for participation should be the preferred mechanism. The motto could be 'Be as inclusive as necessary and possible', and deal creatively with the problems of numbers and diversity. As issues of sustainable development are very complex and affect a great number of stakeholders, a high degree of diversity of MSPs is desirable.

Principally, all who have a stake in a policy, process or project, should be part of a multi-stakeholder process relating to it. This requires careful analysis and consultation among those who are involved initially to identify all who need to be part of the process and to reach a necessary balance, for example of South and North or women and men. A great deal of power is involved in the decisions on participation. Each process needs to be clear and transparent on who identifies stakeholders, how that is being done, how stakeholders are being informed and invited. There is also a need for mechanisms to invite additional stakeholders into the process if gaps become clear. The criteria used and the processes employed to measure those criteria need to be made transparent and public.

In many cases, such decisions are not clear, and invitations are extended by the facilitating body without (visible) external communication. In other cases, those invited are picked from a set group of stakeholders, such as in the CSD dialogue process where the nine Major Groups identified in Agenda 21 define the 'sample' to choose from. Yet other stakeholders such as faith communities, parliamentarians, the media, the elderly, the education community, cyclists or others might be appropriate. Participation needs to be based on the same social groups as cultural and economic activities in communities, be they global, national or local, particularly when relevant to the respective issue. In other words, careful analysis of which are the 'high impact categories' is crucial.[5] With regard to many issues, for example, gender is such a category and policies affect women and men very differently. In other cases, gender might not have such a great impact. Careful 'social mapping' can be used to ensure the involvement of all parts of a community of stakeholders. Building on earlier experiences can be very useful, but developing 'traditions' too quickly is dangerous. Societies are dynamic and ever-evolving. New stakeholder groups or differentiations of previously rather homogeneous stakeholder groups might develop and need to be taken into account when 'mapping the scene' of relevant stakeholders. In short, thinking outside the box is required.

Increased diversity makes conflict more likely; therefore, one needs to consider the appropriate modes of communication, depending on the expected amount of conflict, including conflict resolution techniques and/or working with groups separately before commencing the MSP itself.

A crucial question is which bodies to approach to represent stakeholder groups. Criteria should include (see Chapter 5): the legitimacy and accountability of stakeholder representatives; equity within the represented stakeholder communities as regards their participation; the democratic processes of the election/appointment of representatives; expertise; commitment to the MSP approach. Well-established networks and caucuses of NGOs working on particular issues are in many cases a good starting point. Others are industry associations, trade union federations, local government associations, academic societies, and so on.

There needs to be sufficient stakeholder involvement to ensure that an MSP is going to have the desired legitimacy. For example, among NGOs, a split seems to be developing between those who are prepared to engage in multi-sectoral work and those who are not. If substantial parts of a sector are distancing themselves from a process, it will lack legitimacy. In such cases, it might be better to reconsider the setting up of an MSP and/or to work out carefully what kind of legitimacy it can claim, and conduct it clearly within those limitations. The question is, of course, what criteria should be employed to determine what a 'substantial part' of a sector would be?

Often, there are good intentions regarding involvement that are frustrated by the basic infrastructure of involvement. The issues of meeting time, meeting place, transport, childcare and handicapped accessibility, and so on, need to be considered. There will be some stakeholders who, for cultural, religious or other reasons, bring their own barriers. Special activities may be required if their input is to be included.

Principally, when decisions require government action, the appropriate policy and regulatory authorities should participate in an MSP. The involvement of governments and/or intergovernmental bodies is also an important strategy to deal with concerns that MSPs are intended to weaken or reduce their role. In contrast, government involvement in MSPs ensures that they fulfil an appropriate supplementary and complementary role to governments.[6]

Problems may arise from large numbers seeking to participate. There are limits to how many people can consult effectively in a meeting. However, this problem should not result in the exclusion of stakeholder groups but rather in finding creative and constructive ways for the inclusion of all, while keeping group(s) at manageable sizes. Unilateral decisions that limit the number of participants should be avoided. It is better for the process to put this challenge to the stakeholders involved, perhaps to an initial smaller coordinating group.

For example, MSPs do not have to be limited to one group or forum; they can comprise several strands or layers of work. This might involve core groups surrounded by a larger forum or parallel working groups on different aspects which feed into the plenary. Phases of enlargement and down-sizing also provide options to deal with large numbers and diversity. Larger groups will also be of help when it comes to the dissemination of MSP outcomes. Feedback loops between different levels (local, national, international) can help to inform dialogue and decision-making. If the process aims to develop concrete action plans, the involvement of groups involved in actual implementation, such as smaller NGOs and community-based organizations, is necessary.

The World Commission on Dams, for example, was a small group of 12 members but instituted a larger Forum of over 70 organizations around it and ensured a wider outreach into the various stakeholder networks. The WCD also engaged in regional hearings and commissioned case studies. The OECD / DAC process on National Strategies for Sustainable Development involved individual country analyses, and deliberations at the regional and global levels.

Another example, which was not included in our sample, is the Mediterranean Commission on Sustainable Development (MCSD) (UNEP, 2001). The MCSD, operating within a large web of partnerships, meets annually and allocates thematic groups, with task managers comprised of Commission members, to follow up specific issues. These groups receive technical support from MAP, involve experts from governmental bodies at local and regional levels, and conduct dialogues with stakeholders. Groups submit recommendations and proposals for action to MCSD.

Voluntary involvement is key. There is no point in trying to impose dialogue or partnerships upon stakeholders. It will create mistrust and can have a disempowering effect. The empowerment and confidence of stakeholders are not renewable resources.

Each stakeholder group needs to make its own decision about participation in an MSP. Stakeholders need to be informed sufficiently and early enough to make their decision, which includes the right to say 'No' to any arrangements. Such information should include what role the MSP group will play (advisory, decision-making), what kinds of commitments of time and resources will be involved, and what is expected from each participant.

Problems may arise because people may participate in a process with no intent to follow agreed ground rules and procedures. Participants may want to use the process as a stage to put forward their views without listening or integrating others' views. Or they might want to use it to stall decision-making. Based on the rules of procedure and any communication ground rules agreed beforehand, the facilitator should point out if and when a stakeholder does not play by those rules. Facilitators should not only rely on their own judgement but should take on the concerns that participants might raise (in private or in the meetings) about the seriousness of other participants. The group then needs to deal with the issue in a problem-solving manner, applying agreed rules of dialogue and decision-making.

Participants' identification

Having identified the participating stakeholder groups, decisions need to be made as to who should represent those groups at any given meeting. Stakeholder groups identify who should represent them. This is a very important point and stakeholders will need time to consult within constituencies. Representatives need to have the time to participate (taking part in MSPs is, for most stakeholders, not part of their job). The integrity and hence the effectiveness of a process can be compromised if the participating stakeholders are not given the opportunity to determine their representatives through their own processes and mechanisms. Bodies who initiate MSPs often invite certain people as representatives of their groups, employing unknown criteria of selection. However, when there is a lack of active associations and networks, or representativeness is not a key issue, special efforts to identify potential participants can be made by the organizing body. For example, for the hearings conducted in the UN Financing for Development process, the Secretariat actively sought out business representatives from developing countries.

Stakeholder groups should also be transparent to others about their elections or appointment criteria, and about the criteria being used to identify individuals with expertise on the respective issues at hand. The process of identifying individuals to represent groups is helped by regular election or appointment processes within stakeholder networks and associations – for example caucus coordinator elections among NGOs or the appointment of representatives to particular processes by stakeholder groups such as industry, trade unions, and so on. Other participants should be allowed to bring to the floor any problems they might have with criteria being used by other stakeholders. In some cases, such as local community participation, stakeholders should consider 'layered' participation to spread the burden of having to deal with unfamiliar norms and cultures (Hemmati, 2000d), or agree to 'share' representatives, as was done in the Lower Columbia River Basin process (see Chapter 7).

Another example is the Sustainable Agriculture and Food Systems (SAFS) caucus to the CSD who carried out an elaborate process to identify the NGO group of representatives to the CSD stakeholder dialogues on sustainable agriculture at CSD-8 (2000). Based on the agreed criteria of balancing by gender, region, age, expertise and background, the caucus developed a list of potential representatives which it then discussed and agreed.

It is important to balance the numbers of participants from each stakeholder group, and, in some cases, with regard to the views they are likely to represent. Stakeholder groups can be asked to meet certain balance criteria within their delegations, such as regional and gender balance.

Problems may arise if stakeholder representatives change and different individuals are involved on and off over time. This should be avoided whenever possible. If representatives have to be replaced, they need to be briefed carefully by the person whose part they are to take and be introduced to the group.

Where government involvement is required, it should be such that it ensures the buy-in from those capable of making the final decision. Where lower-level officials have to take an MSP outcome through the formal decision-making system, the necessary decisions might not be taken.

Facilitation/organizational back-up

MSPs need certain organizational or institutional back-up or facilitation. This is a very important aspect, as a failure of sufficient organizational support may cause the whole process to fail. Experiences have shown that responsibilities need to be marked clearly and be known to all participants, to avoid the diffusion of responsibilities, to ensure proper communication and in general to ensure a smooth running of the process. Yet flexibility is also very important. MSPs need to be supported by a flexible administrative structure which can be adapted as processes, participants and needs develop over time.

Again, organizational arrangements should be part of the planning phase and agreed by the group. Such arrangements are also closely related to the question of funding, as secretariat services can be expensive.

MSPs should be facilitated ideally by people who are not stake-holders and have no direct interest in the outcome of the process. In some cases, that might be possible, while in many others, it won't be, simply because of the complex and wide-ranging nature of sustainability issues. To ensure that there is a trustworthy 'honest broker' in place, organizations charged with facilitating an MSP need to be:

- explicit about their interests or possible interests;
- of diverse composition themselves – that is, made up of representatives of the various stakeholder groups; and
- acceptable to everybody involved.

At the international level, UN bodies might be appropriate resources for facilitation, particularly if the processes require or benefit from the involvement of intergovernmental organizations. UN bodies also have the benefit of relative neutrality towards various parties and regions. A problem might be that UN and other intergovernmental bodies only represent governments and have to operate on the basis of the rules of stakeholder involvement, which in most cases are fairly restrictive. These institutions are also often reluctant to take on additional administrative tasks, due to already overstretched budgetary and staff resources.

Another option are organizations which are multi-stakeholder themselves, governed and advised by representatives of all Major Groups and other stakeholders. Few such organizations exist at the various levels.[7]

Yet another option is to found a facilitating body for the sole purpose of facilitating the respective MSP. Some of the examples we looked at have either fully or partly employed this option, such as the World Commission on Dams with its own Secretariat or hybrid bodies of several organizations such as the WBCSD/IIED for the Mining, Minerals and Sustainable Development Project. Among the advantages are that the constitution of such a body can be tailor-made for the purposes of the MSP; that staff will be taken on for a specific task; that funding goes to the specific body and its purposes; and that a new body may be perceived as more neutral and having no accountability structure and responsibility other than to the process itself. The disadvantages include the necessary investments in time and resources to found an organization and provide a legal status which allows it to receive funds of various kinds, and the formality a process can develop once it has a formal structure and organizational basis. Indeed, some experiences have shown that the lack of formal legal status or constitution has created an informal and flexible framework which has benefited the process (see, for example, Hohnen, 2000c, p15).

The choice depends on a number of factors, the most important being the time lines and size of a process. For preparations of 'one-off' events, an MSP-initiator – or, preferably, a group of stakeholder representatives agreeing to design an MSP – may assign an appropriate organization to facilitate the process or simply choose to organize the event themselves. Such a procedure needs careful consideration of the possible consequences regarding legitimacy and credibility. However, problems can be addressed by ensuring maximum transparency about what is being done and why, and by checking with other stakeholders that they perceive the procedure as appropriate. Another strategy is for the facilitating organization to take a back-seat role explicitly on the subject matters throughout the preparations and at the event itself. For the processes of larger size and complexity, different requirements emerge.

Again, it seems advisable that dialogue about the appropriate organizational set-ups should be part of the designing process, and therefore should be conducted in a multi-stakeholder fashion. It is important to tell the relevant people what is being planned, to seek their advice on who else should be consulted, and to do so. Presenting a fixed and rigid structure and plan will not work. Rather, initiators of MSPs should demonstrate flexibility in response to the requirements and suggestions of potential participants. Otherwise, the process might lose out on the diversity of the participants which, in the end, will jeopardize the purpose of the whole exercise.

Funding

MSPs require funding for capacity-building and a range of operational aspects. If the appropriate resources are not available, the process will be in danger of failing due to, for example, lack of participation, facilitation, information dissemination and implementation options. It will also be in danger of being unbalanced or inequitable by putting better-resourced stakeholders in advantageous positions.

Participation requires resources for people to prepare for and attend meetings, to consult within their constituencies, and to build their capacities to input effectively. Larger and/or long-term processes need a stable funding base for their operations, including organizational and secretariat services.

Fund-raising targets and strategies beyond the initial start-up funding need to be agreed by the group; roles and responsibilities need to be assigned clearly. Participants should be fully informed about funding sources, budgets, etc. Keeping the process independent of individual funders is important; mixed funding sources are a way around that problem. Non-financial contributions such as printing, mailing and gifts of space can add value and should also be sought.

A lack of resources will undermine the capacities, effectiveness and possibly the entire potential of MSPs. The challenge is for society to find mechanisms which enable MSPs to be created around priority issues requiring urgent progress, and not just on those that are popular or enjoy the interest of resourceful parties. This will not be an easy matter to resolve.

One suggestion is that the UN, governments and/or independent foundations should set up a trust fund to support the creation of MSPs by providing financial resources and other assistance for stakeholder and public awareness and access to information (see, for example, Alexander, 2000). This should be invested, as a priority, in the participation and empowerment of groups who are most disadvantaged and under-represented, first and foremost the representatives from developing countries.

In principle, participants should not have a direct role in funding the process they are involved in. This could lead to further distortions in power relationships and compromise the integrity of the outcomes. It is necessary to define better the role and mechanisms of independent, purpose-built trusts and other arm's-length financial structures designed to ensure adequate funding for the process in question. Again, UN bodies may be well placed to take the lead in further work on this question.

In weighing up the costs of funding an MSP process, governments, business and other stakeholders should take into full account the high expense of operating current 'business as usual' systems, which often create an adversarial atmosphere. In many cases these do not produce decisions or produce decisions which are not going to be implemented. Given the high stakes surrounding many of the sustainability issues, for example climate change, it might be concluded readily that an investment in MSPs might prove to be cost-effective, particularly since they offer the possibility of more creative options and the virtual certainty of a strengthened network of stakeholders.

FRAMING

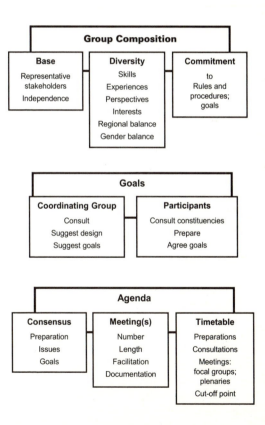

Figure 7.3 *Framing*

Group composition

It is important to ensure a rough symmetry of powers within MSPs. MSPs with equal participation from all stakeholder groups attempt to increase the equity between different sectors of civil society in their involvement and impact. They aim to level the playing-field between groups whose 'traditional' lobbying activities largely depend on their resources and are therefore grossly imbalanced.

There also needs to be sufficient diversity to make the largest possible number of resources available to the group. A mix of experts and novices is not harmful; indeed, it can be helpful. Within the MSP framework, we can consider all participants experts and novices at the same time – experts of their own views and knowledge, and novices to much of the others' views and knowledge.

An MSP should always include at least two representatives of each stakeholder group, and preferably in a gender-balanced manner. Research on minority influence has shown that a single member with a divergent view will be less heard and may become reluctant to contribute her or his divergent view. We also know that (power) minority representation needs to be above a certain critical level (research on gender has shown that the critical level lies at about 15–20 per cent). This needs to be kept in mind with regard to categories such as gender, region or ethnic group. Regional balance is particularly important for international processes; ensuring equitable participation from developing countries and countries in transition is the key.

However, in addition to such balances what matters is what and who is to be represented; gender balance, for instance, cannot by itself ensure that gender aspects will be addressed. It is the inclusion of participants with expertise on gender issues that is the crucial factor.

People should not be expected to represent more than one stakeholder group because individuals can only 'wear a limited number of hats' (at least in a balanced manner!). It also makes communicating difficult if a person keeps changing roles (even if it is done explicitly). For example, it makes no sense to count a woman from Zimbabwe who is working with an environmental NGO as representing the views of women, developing countries NGOs, and environmental NGOs. Expecting such representation and differentiation is, quite simply, ridiculous.

In some cases, initiating bodies have restricted the number of dialogue participants to a very small group of people. This has made it difficult to have all relevant high-impact categories represented and balanced. Again, problems with high numbers should be dealt with more creatively than by unilaterally limiting numbers, which can jeopardize the process.

To avoid 'groupthink' (extreme loyalty and lack of divergence – see Chapter 5), it should be checked that, within the group, not a significant number of participants is dependent on another member. This person or stakeholder group could otherwise quite easily assume leadership and dominate the process.

Again, problems may arise because people may participate in a process with no intent to follow the rules of discourse or to reach an agreement. Based on the rules of procedure and any communication ground rules agreed beforehand, this should be put to the whole group through the facilitator. The group then needs to deal with the issue in a problem-solving manner, applying agreed rules of discussion and decision-making.

Setting the goals

This question relates back to the different kinds of MSPs, which vary considerably as regards their specific goals and objectives: a frank exchange of views; agreeing upon disagreements; exploring possible common ground; achieving partial or full consensus; making decisions; implementing decisions; monitoring and evaluating implementation; revisiting them. It should be self-understood that goals need to be understandable and perceived as achievable. MSPs raise the expectations of the participants, and failure or delay may cause frustration. Furthermore, goals perceived as unachievable or unrealistic from the outside and/or relevant (inter)governmental bodies will decrease the MSPs' impact on official decision-making.

Agreeing a common goal (and agenda) will be more difficult when there are significant differences between participants' goals, even more so if the starting point is an area of existing or potential conflict. In these cases and before trying to agree common MSP goals, participants have first to overcome histories of distrustful and confrontational relationships. They need to try to build a minimum of trust through considerately sharing their views and listening (as opposed to 'hearing'). This might not always be possible, in which case an MSP is not a suitable way forward.

The first goal of an MSP needs to be to clarify the various representations that stakeholders have of the issue(s) at hand. There is a need for a phase that allows people to assess various understandings and possible common ground to work on, and to consider carefully how far they want their collaboration to go.

In many cases, however, goals are defined by an initiating body, through inviting stakeholders to take part in an MSP. Identifying the goals in a common design process is better. Suggested goals should then be reviewed by the whole group, or at least put to constituencies for comment, modified where necessary and adopted. Another option for identifying goals are 'common vision' exercises (see stakeholder preparations, below).

Time also needs to be allowed for stakeholders to consult anew with their constituencies when new proposals regarding MSP goals, for example concrete collaborations, are put forward.

This also depends on the scope of an MSP: international ones, no matter if they are dialogues or decision-making processes, allow for smaller scales of concrete action (specific development projects and the like) than those at national or local level. Whereas Local Agenda 21 processes might assemble the relevant actors to refurbish a city centre, for example, a global dialogue like the Global Mining Initiative attempts to return to local and national constituencies from an international perspective and help them implement possible decisions with a new group of partners at national and local levels.

Setting the agenda

Setting a concrete common agenda after agreeing issues and goals is a key MSP design issue. It can be suggested by an initial coordinating group but needs to be put to the group as a whole and to be agreed by all the participants.

This applies to logistical issues (how much of an exploratory phase is needed, how much time they need to prepare, how many meetings would be needed and what issues they should address in which order, how long meetings should be, how they should be facilitated, documented, and so on), as well as substantive issues (the key issues and the sequence for addressing them). The first substantive point on the agenda of an MSP needs to be to clarify the various representations that stakeholders hold of the issue(s) at hand (see above).

It will be necessary to agree which aspects of the MSP issue will be addressed and in which order. It is very important to keep a close check on power differences throughout this stage, otherwise more powerful and vocal stakeholders will succeed in dominating the agenda with their representation of a problem, and the subsequent exclusion of issues will not reflect the representations and requirements of marginalized groups. As MSPs should be designed indeed to give an equal voice to everybody, enough time and effort should go into this stage.

Setting the timetable

It is vital to meet the requirements of all stakeholders and their constituencies when designing a viable timetable for an MSP. Even a single event requires a preparatory phase; hence, all MSPs need a timetable. The best solution to such problems is to design the timetable through consultations and to agree it among the participants.

For example, when preparing for the Ministerial Dialogue at the 8th Informal Environment Ministers Meeting in Norway, 2000, NGOs insisted on including the contributions of women and Indigenous Peoples, working through their respective CSD caucuses. The Indigenous People's caucus had to decline as there was insufficient time to consult the draft NGO background papers within their constituencies. Instead, they sent a representative to speak at the dialogue, and the NGO background paper included contributions only by NGOs and the women's caucus.

INPUTS

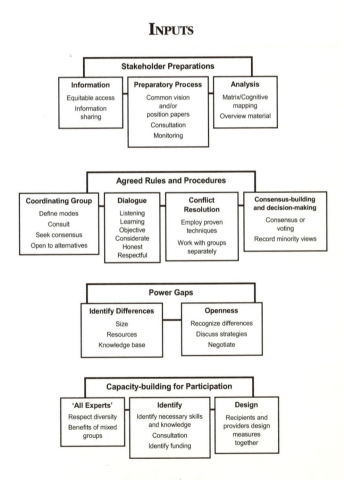

Figure 7.4 *Inputs*

Stakeholder preparations

All stakeholder groups need to have equitable access to all information. As a general rule, there needs to be sufficient communication among stakeholders before an actual meeting. Many processes use email list servers and telephone conferences. Participants need to agree on a preparatory process in a transparent manner, depending on the issues, goals, scope, resources, and so on. There are different options which should be discussed, as follows.

Experiences have shown that preparations in written format can be beneficial. Requiring all participating stakeholder groups to prepare initial position papers can be a viable tool. Preparatory documents should have an agreed, common format. As a minimum, they should be fully referenced and include background information. They also need to be submitted well in advance to allow others to study them.

The advantage is that in order to prepare such papers, stakeholders will engage in consultations. In addition, stakeholder groups can review all papers beforehand. This can speed up progress and it allows participants to speak for their constituencies even when reacting to positions of others.

Preparations can also include an analysis of initial background or position papers. The MSP coordinating group and/or the facilitating body can be charged with analysing the preparatory material in a manner that encourages dialogue at the MSP meeting(s). One option is to put all positions into a matrix format for comparison. Another option is 'cognitive mapping': via interviews or document analysis or a combination of the two, trains of thought, points and arguments are mapped out in a graphic structure which not only portrays the content of a paper but also the structure of causes and effects, values and proposed action, and other components of the views that a person or a group has of a particular subject. Such 'individual maps' can be combined into 'meta-maps' portraying the various arguments, thoughts and suggestions of a number of individuals or groups. Meta-maps can then also be put forward to a group for discussion. They help to identify commonalities and differences in understanding and priorities. Nowadays, software is available, making it relatively easy to develop such maps based on written material.[8] It will be worth experimenting with such techniques in MSPs, particularly in phases preparatory to actual meetings. Any such efforts need, of course to be agreed by the group. Any overview material produced should be made available to all participants well in advance of a meeting.

Preparation of the initial position papers, however, can run the risk of 'fixing' MSP group members into positions, creating a barrier towards finding common ground and agreement. Thus, the first step can also be to bring participants together to agree on a common vision of what they are trying to achieve or what their community (country or world) should ideally look like. After the vision exercise, the MSP group members can come to an agreement on their goals.[9] This provides a common framework for working together, which will be especially useful once different positions become clear.

Various options can be combined, of course; a first step of developing a common vision can be followed by preparing position papers by stakeholder groups. Such papers would then focus on outlining strategies to achieve the common vision.

An important question in this context is the representation of stakeholder groups by MSP participants who may want to design a process where participants can truly speak for a wider constituency. This will require consultations within constituencies, and communication within stakeholder groups becomes as important as communication between stakeholder groups. It might be appropriate to agree what are acceptable consultation processes within constituencies and even the mechanisms to monitor if and how that is being done. As a minimum requirement, participating stakeholder representatives need to make clear on whose behalf they are speaking and with what authority. Stakeholder groups need to be transparent about how they carry out the agreed preparatory process – that is, how they consult within their constituencies. Stakeholders may choose to conduct their preparations publicly, for example via open email list servers as some of the CSD NGO caucuses do.

With regard to any dialogue or consensus-building phases, which may include ideas and suggestions that have not been made available to all participants before the meeting, there needs to be a group decision on how to deal with the question of consultation with constituencies. Do people consult with their constituencies and reconvene? This will depend on the type of MSP. If it is a one-off event which starts and finishes over a day, such consultation will not be possible. If the dialogue goes on for a several of days, it might be possible to consult by email or telephone conferences. Again, equity needs to be ensured: not all stakeholder groups' constituencies have the same kind of access to communication technologies.

Preparations should also include information about the way that participants plan to communicate and interact. For example, it may be helpful to reproduce the ground rules developed here and offer them for discussion so that the group can adapt and adopt what seems to be most desirable.

Ground rules for stakeholder communication

The ground rules for the purpose of dialogue and/or consensus-building need to be agreed within the group. Participants in an MSP must assume that no one has all the answers. The purpose of an MSP is to try to assemble the collective wisdoms into a new vision of how to move ahead. One possibility to consider is for the preparatory team to develop a set of options on how to communicate and put it to the group for discussion and agreement.

The following rules have proved to be effective tools:

- A facilitator or a number of facilitators should be agreed on by the group (see below).
- During discussion, participants must make every effort to be as frank and candid as possible, while maintaining a respectful interest in the views of others. Participants need to refrain from personal attacks and avoid placating, blaming, preaching, dominating or passively resisting. Confrontation, blank ultimatums and prejudicial statements are not helpful. An atmosphere that cultivates directness, openness, objectivity and humility can be viewed as a prerequisite for successful dialogue and consensus-building.
- Participants need to be honest and trustworthy.
- A true dialogue cannot be entered into with the goal of 'getting one's way'. It must be entered into with the expectation of learning and change.
- All participants and their contributions need to be treated equally.
- Participants are asked to address the group as a whole, while showing concern for each point of view, rather than confronting and criticizing individuals.
- To help understanding and to clarify perceptions, participants and facilitators should be encouraged to restate one another's views in their own words ('active listening').
- Participants should refrain from presuming the motives of others and rather be encouraged to ask direct questions.
- Participants must argue on a logical basis and be prepared to back up their opinions with facts.
- Brain-storming can be helpful: conducting a session of putting forward ideas and collecting them without judgement for later discussion can create a larger pool of more creative ideas.
- When an idea it put forward, it becomes the property of the group. This sounds simple but it is a very profound principle: all ideas cease to be the property of any individual, subgroup or constituency. This can reduce the impact of personal pride and make it easier for others to adopt an idea.

- 'Learning exercises' that have been developed in Knowledge Management approaches, can be helpful to draw out the success factors of other processes and agreements.[10] This can be done by inviting others with such experience into the group and/or in separate meetings with experienced people. The group can use the outcomes to deepen the pool of ideas.
- Allow space and time for different modes of communication, both socio-emotional and strictly task-oriented. Humour – a good laugh – and space for informal encounters are legitimate tools and can go a long way to help the group to build trust and a sense of common ownership of the process, as well as release tension arising from differences.

Again, problems may arise because people may participate in a process with no intention of following the rules of communication. Based on the rules of procedure agreed beforehand, this should be put to the whole group through the facilitator. The group then needs to deal with the issue in a problem-solving manner, applying the agreed rules of discussion and decision-making.

Power gaps

MSPs need to provide the opportunity for participants to work together as equals to realize acceptable actions or outcomes without imposing the views or authority of one group over the other. Yet fundamental differences exist between stakeholders in such things as knowledge and information, size, nature and the amount of resources (such as money but also the 'high moral ground'), which define significant power gaps and unfair distribution of bargaining and negotiating power.

Constructive stakeholder communication between unlikely partners must be built slowly and carefully. Communication and trust must be established before engaging in consensus-building and decision-making. It is therefore essential to devote sufficient time to dialogue to develop mutual understanding. Crucial components of dialogue processes, such as honesty, openness and trustworthiness are indispensable, but it takes time and commitment for everybody to demonstrate these qualities.

The most important point is to be explicit about power gaps and not shy away from discussing their implications. This opens the door for dealing with the problem creatively. It needs to happen early in the process, often before trust has been built. Indeed, addressing this difficult question can help to build trust. Another important tool is to work on the basis of agreed formal procedures of communication.

If these conditions are not met, there will be a great risk that the powerless will have no real voice and no real involvement in the issues. No real partnerships will develop. This problem relates to questions of support and capacity-building for MSP participants in terms of access to information and resources, political experience, negotiating skills, and so on.

Providing sufficient resources for meaningful participation by disadvantaged groups is a means of empowerment. Adequate funding for MSPs is therefore a crucial component of dealing with power gaps within MSPs.

Capacity-building for participation

Ideally, participants should be well equipped to reflect their stakeholder groups' views and interests. But there will be areas where no stakeholder group has sufficient background or knowledge, or where there is an imbalance of knowledge and thus power.

If participants lack knowledge and/or the processes lack balance, then capacity-building measures should be considered. For example, in global processes, there can be a lack of knowledge, particularly with regard to often intricate cross-cutting issues such as of international institutional arrangements and agreements and trade relations. For the benefit of all parties planning to engage in MSPs, information about relevant agreements, policies and legislation needs to be shared widely. It also needs to be made available in an appropriate format, such as in local languages and non-expert vocabulary. If, for example, community-based organizations are to participate effectively in international processes, they need to be briefed about the context of their local experiences. This will help them to communicate their interests in a more effective manner.

National and local political processes may be even more difficult to understand than those at the international level, as national and local policy processes tend to be more opaque, involving uncertain interests and a mix of decisions. In order to achieve optimum results, providing information about such policy processes would therefore be desirable.

Capacities and skills which empower stakeholders to participate effectively in MSPs include:

- representatives: stakeholders are able to elect or appoint somebody who has the expertise and the time to participate;
- knowledge about other stakeholders, relevant policies, agreements, institutions;
- language skills;

- communication and negotiating skills: group decision-making skills, including effectively participating at meetings, team-building, conflict resolution; and
- capacities to consult within constituencies (time; financial resources).

It is important to note that capacity-building is to meet needs defined by the 'recipients', based on self-evaluations. Designing capacity-building measures therefore needs to be an interactive process of those receiving and those offering capacity-building. The MSP group needs to address those questions openly and to decide upon which capacities and skills are necessary and who should provide capacity-building for whom. Independent 'honest brokers' of the process and issue knowledge are required. The group needs to decide where to seek the funds for capacity-building measures if they are deemed necessary. As with the funding of MSPs in general, the independence of donors is important.

The question of capacity-building preparing for a particular MSP also relates to access to information and knowledge in general. Enabling equitable access therefore needs to be part of any framework policies on participation and MSPs.

Dialogue/Meetings

Communication channels

MSPs can use various channels of communication – face-to-face meetings, email, telephone, fax, letters, interactive websites. In the beginning of an MSP, face-to-face meetings certainly help to build trust. They provide direct interaction using more communication channels (body language). They offer more opportunities for informal contact and issue exploration. By contrast, electronic communication can provide a good basis for neutralizing differences in status and personality, as related to gender, age and ethnicity. Non-verbal characteristics will have little effect, which can benefit minorities. Research also suggests that electronic communication is more likely to reflect diversity. Written communication seems to focus people more effectively on the contents of the message. Yet without inflection or body language the tone and intention of electronic statements can be easily misconstrued. 'Communicate clearly, not cleverly' seems to be a good guiding line for electronic communication. Thus, the internet could be the ideal tool for collecting suggestions to a given problem in a brain-storming effort or for getting an overview of the diversity of opinions on a given subject

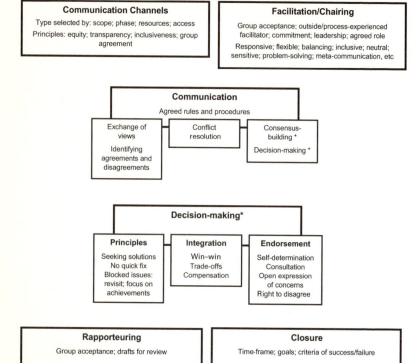

Figure 7.5 *Dialogue/Meetings*

matter, particularly with a larger group. However, for building or consensus, electronic communication is not the most useful tool.

When using electronic communication, the group needs to check if this is feasible for all participants. The same applies to the use of software tools which allow people to work collectively on a document (Lotus Notes, MS Word Track Changes, among others). Some participants may operate under tight constraints in terms of equipment and capacities.

The choice of communication channels, therefore, should be considered carefully, taking into account the respective stages of the process, numbers of participants, resources available to all participants and, not the least, cultural preferences. Choices can include a mix of communication channels and need to be guided by the principles of inclusiveness, equity and transparency. Such choices should be made by the group, and can be suggested by an initial coordinating group.

Facilitating/chairing

MSP meetings need facilitation and a facilitator needs to be accepted by all the participants as a suitable person without a direct stake in the process or the decisions to be taken. In several of the examples studied and in interviews with people involved in them, it is obvious that professional facilitators are seen as having a role to play – usually they can be accepted by everybody as impartial and are familiar with useful group work techniques and tools. For example, this has worked well in the Brent Spar process. Outside facilitators can also provide training on meeting facilitation to build the group's capacity to facilitate an ongoing process themselves. However, people also feel that a facilitator's commitment and integrity, high standing, political stature, experience in the political processes and expertise on the issues, charisma and other personal characteristics can be a crucial success factor. This has been asserted for the World Commission on Dams, the Global Compact meetings and the UN CSD dialogues, among others.

Using several facilitators, for example representatives from different stakeholder groups, to co-chair meetings or facilitate on a rotating basis, is another option that should be considered. The various options should be discussed in the group so that an agreement can be reached which everyone is satisfied with.

The following are important guidelines for the effective facilitation of MSPs:

- Facilitators should have been involved in the design process of the MSP to ensure their full understanding of it and their commitment to how the group decided to conduct it.
- Facilitating needs to be flexible and responsive to different situations – hence facilitators need considerable diagnostic skill to enable them to assess a given situation correctly.
- Facilitators have an essential role to play to ensure equity in discussions.[11] Chairing in a way that capitalizes on diversity needs to stress the benefits of diversity. The modes of communication and decision-making suggested here largely depend on a facilitator encouraging and guiding the group to put them into practice.
- Facilitators need to be sensitive to the different cultural backgrounds of participants and not impose a 'way of doing things' based on their own culture.
- Facilitators should encourage people to speak freely and invite everybody to take the floor, including drawing out quieter participants.
- Facilitators need to help create an open and positive atmosphere which will encourage respectful listening and possibly learning and

changing of views among the participants. Facilitators should help the participants and the group to surface 'what is hidden', allowing time for each participant to share concerns, thoughts and feelings. At the same time, facilitators need to help the group to stay focused.

- Facilitators should help to ensure that all participants feel recognized and part of the group.
- Facilitators should keep to agreed timetables and speaking times, which need to be the same for everybody (with obvious exceptions for participants operating in another language, and the like).
- Facilitators need to keep track of everybody's contributions to draw together aspects of common ground and to summarize at regular intervals what has been said. They also need to keep track of which points might be missing in the discussion and to encourage the group to address aspects that have not arisen.
- When exploring differences, facilitators should ask problem-solving questions, not judgemental ones, and encourage all participants to do so.
- In cases of conflict, the facilitator should encourage participants to focus on the 'positive intent' or 'grain of fact' in their opponent's position. This can be done by encouraging participants to restate opposing views in their own words (known as 'active listening' or 'mirroring').
- When summarizing, differences should be stated clearly and there should be no pressure to conform. Stating and restating common ground and agreements along the way can help to build confidence and momentum.
- Facilitators need to be sensitive regarding issues on which participants will need to consult with their constituencies.
- The group needs to agree on how to deal with possible substantive contributions from the facilitator. Alternating the role of the facilitator is an option.
- In some cases, it might be worth considering to work with special facilitators as the link into particular stakeholder groups. For example, at the local level, it might be advisable to work with local facilitators to develop the appropriate meeting styles.
- Suggestions regarding how to deal with participants who do not 'play by the rules' have been outlined above and facilitators have a key responsibility to deal with such behaviour and/or concerns appropriately.
- Using flip-charts, meta-plans or other facilitation techniques is recommended in order to transparently keep track of what is being said, enable summarizing and help decision-making. Such techniques also allow for the same pieces of information to be displayed in various modes (oral or written), which helps participants to follow discussions and actively contribute. This can also relieve participants

from taking notes themselves, allowing people to look at each other rather than at their notepads, which helps to create trust. Other group work techniques are worth considering and experimenting with. These include scenario, or future, workshops, citizens' juries (depending on the situation, the issue, the cultural context and the group).

Rapporteuring

Rapporteurs (or persons responsible for reporting on the group's activities) need to be assigned beforehand and agreed by the group, as the documentation process itself. Rapporteuring needs to be done in the most neutral fashion possible, reflecting the full breadth and depth of discussions. If summaries and reports are not perceived as truly representative of what happened, the whole process will suffer with regard to credibility, the participants' commitment and the quality of decisions. The coordinating group (or facilitating body) should suggest rapporteurs and a documentation process and put that to the group for decision.

In the example of the Lower Columbia River Basin process, the group worked with different stakeholders, providing rapporteurs on a rotating basis. This will help not only to spread the workload more equally, but also will increase the sense of ownership on all sides.

Decision-making

Participants need to agree in the beginning of the process on what kind of decision-making process will be used.[12] Consensus is the preferred method of decision-making because it will generate better solutions and commitment by all. Seeking consensus will urge participants to find an agreement that incorporates all points of view. Consensus can take different shapes, for example:

- unanimity, ie total agreement; or
- a willingness to step aside and live with the 'whole package', not blocking an agreement because of disagreement with one or another point. This is the willingness to compromise and support the compromise and agree with it as the group consensus.

Groups should decide explicitly if and when they want to enter into decision-making. They need to be clear at which point they want to test consensus or seek a majority vote. When going for a decision by vote, the group needs to decide what constitutes a majority. We suggest the following: the group should strive for consensus as this fosters patience, exploring possible common ground, but a majority vote should be introduced to bring about a conclusion and make the decision, if necessary. The group should make the decision about the appropriate time of voting. A decision can be reached when the respective majorities of the stakeholder groups represented are in favour of it. Minority viewpoints should be recorded in final decisions when consensus cannot be achieved.

Entering into decision-making should not happen too early. Groups of high diversity can have a tendency towards depolarizing and compromising too quickly for truly integrative solutions to emerge. As long as the dialogue process is not exhausted and not all the ideas have been put forth and scrutinized, the group should refrain from entering into decision-making. Groups need to be challenged to deliver maximum creativity, which can be helped by the facilitator. Premature consensus or majority rule tends to lead to decreased commitment and will therefore be an obstacle to implementation. There are a number of possible procedures that will help groups to agree without compromising prematurely:

- Participants should avoid arguing for favourite proposals but make innovative suggestions. They should be challenged to be creative and integrating, to seek the best ideas, not to win support for their own ideas.
- Participants should avoid 'against-them' statements.
- Participants should avoid agreeing just to avoid conflict.
- Participants should view differences as helpful.
- When a decision is stalled, the facilitator should state the points of agreement on which to build.
- When no agreement can be reached on an issue, the group can agree to revisit it at the next meeting.

Other techniques that aim to counter premature agreement involve using 'devil's advocates', working parallel in different small groups on the same task and avoiding public voting.

Acceptable decisions are those which integrate the needs and requirements of everybody. Sometimes this will not be possible and trade-offs or compensations might be sought, if all parties agree.

The fundamental right of communities to self-determination needs to be respected. In cases where a potential agreement affects the future lives of a stakeholder group, they need to have the right to say 'No'. For example, if all stakeholders except the affected local community agree to a tourism development plan, the plan should not be carried out. Discussions on the question if a 'No' is being based on sufficient information should be allowed. However, placating participants by declaring that they are making uninformed or incompetent decisions is destructive and needs to be avoided.

Again, based on the rules of procedure agreed beforehand, the facilitator should point out if and when a stakeholder does not play by them and address concerns that participants might raise (in private or in the meetings) about the seriousness of other participants. The group then needs to deal with the issue in a problem-solving manner, applying agreed rules of dialogue and decision-making.

Another question concerns possible secondary or tertiary consequences of policies, such as agreements within a local community which might affect adjacent communities. If possible, such potential consequences should be addressed and the question of involving representatives of those affected needs to be considered.

Closure

MSPs need to agree a time-frame and a clear goal. They need to agree cut-off points and criteria of closure, for failure and success alike. Participants need to develop a sense of ownership not only of the process but also of an output that they feel comfortable promoting – a document outlining the different positions, a concrete set of suggestions, toolkits or agreed actions. Once the group agrees that this point is reached, the process should be brought to an end.

OUTPUTS

Documentation

Depending on the type of process and the timing vis-à-vis official decision-making processes, there are various conditions that will define the type of documentation process required. For example, it is always preferable to have draft minutes and reports put to the group for review before they are published. If there is enough time, these can be sent out to participants, giving a clear deadline for comments. Unless otherwise stated, no comment should count as agreement (one of the rare cases where silence can be taken to mean assent!). If there is insufficient time, drafts should be discussed with the participants directly after the meeting. For example, at the CSD in 1999, stakeholders were invited to comment on the Secretariat's draft summary of the dialogue sessions overnight; at the Bergen ministerial meeting,

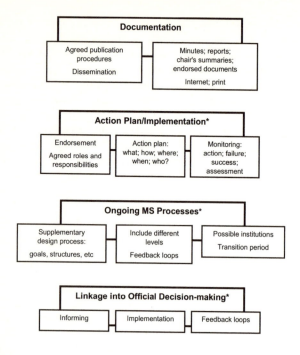

*Optional

Figure 7.6 *Outputs*

stakeholders met late in the evening to discuss a draft of the chair's summary.

Often, a facilitator's summary, rather than a document formally endorsed by the group, is the best choice, particularly if there is insufficient time for participants to check back with their constituencies. Endorsements by stakeholders will require various procedures of constituency agreement and will be a necessary component in decision-making and implementation processes. They will not be required in dialogue processes where the group has been able to discuss a chair's summary and which is clearly labelled as such.

All documentation should be forwarded to other stakeholder groups and made publicly available.

Implementation

Once a decision has been reached, all of those involved need to make sure that it is implemented and to engage their constituencies' support. Without solid support from the represented stakeholder groups, decisions will not be implemented successfully.

Implementation is the crucial test for the quality of the group's decision-making. In cases of (premature?) agreement reached by majority vote, it is a common problem that not everybody will support it with their actions. Often, minority members who lost the vote will not engage in implementation but keep to their views, and sometimes will even work to undermine successful implementation. Upon failure of implementation, they will be able to point out that they were 'right all along'. If consensus was achieved, everybody involved will support a decision and do their part in implementing it. Then, a decision can be properly evaluated against reality and it can be changed if genuine deficiencies are detected. Therefore, action-oriented MSPs should aim to produce a consensus about a way forward that those involved will be committed to implemention. Given trustworthy, transparent, continuous monitoring and evaluation the mechanisms, likelihood of successful implementation is highest. If the decision was wrong, common learning will lead to revisiting it.

However, this should not lead to a 'tyranny of consensus' which can easily be a tyranny of the majority. That is why avoiding premature decision-making is so important and why the group should consider carefully which kind of decision-making it is going to use.

But no matter how elaborate the dialogue and decision-making processes will be, MSP participants will not always be able to reach consensus, even in the form of a compromise as in 'agreeing with the whole package'. Everybody should always have the right to speak out against a decision even if they participated in a process. Participation does not mean that people give up their right to oppose a decision down the road that they do not agree with.

Any implementation needs to be based on agreed roles and responsibilities. It needs a clear plan outlining who is to do what, when, where and with whom. In short, an action plan needs to be agreed by the group. It could be developed by an assigned person or small group and put to the whole group for discussion. Otherwise, the so-called 'diffusion of responsibilities' – when everybody believes somebody else but themselves is responsible for carrying out a task – is likely to take place, and nothing will happen.

The group should also decide how to monitor and evaluate implementation. Monitoring and evaluation activities and time lines can be assigned to a group made up of different participating stakeholders to ensure neutrality and balance. Third party, 'independent' monitoring and evaluation should only be an option when all participants truly agree with it. Otherwise, such monitoring and evaluation can be perceived as an imposition, and will be questioned for its independence and credibility.

Monitoring and evaluation also involve the question of how to deal with non-compliance. MSPs which involve implementation activities need to agree what to do if stakeholders don't do what they said they would do.

Impacting official decision-making

Processes that are linked to official decision-making are designed to impact them. As was said before, most of those processes are meant to inform decision-makers and, by means of a wider input, improve decision-making. It will be important to ensure that any MSP outcome documents have a high status in the official process and receive the desired attention.

We have discussed above that the current, mostly informing role of stakeholder participation should be expanded. We have also outlined some possible mechanisms for immediately involving stakeholders in implementation. Such steps towards increased involvement of stakeholders would, on the one hand, make clear to governments where stakeholders stand, ready to implement, if agreements are reached. On the other hand, they would enable stakeholders to develop a better understanding of political processes and what is politically possible at a given point.

Ongoing MSPs

Arriving at the agreed cut-off point, groups may decide to move into a new phase. For example, dialogue processes need to provide the space possibly to develop into action-oriented MSPs – if groups want to move from talking to joint action, for example promoting the outcomes together or engaging in implementation. In some cases, follow-up will involve some kind of institutionalizing, which needs to be worked out by the group. This may include finding a new 'home' for a process, engage in new fund-raising activities, and so on. As some examples such as the Global Reporting Initiative and the World Commission on Dams have shown, transitions need to be prepared and managed carefully. Principally, in such cases groups need to engage in a supplementary MSP design process.

Documentation, implementation, impacting official decision-making and possibly ongoing MSPs are the more tenable outputs of MSPs. However, there are other, less tenable but equally important outcomes: when MSPs go well they will lead to more trust and better relations between participating stakeholder groups, and to improved communication and networks, which may in turn lead to further collaboration. These are the more long-term effects of MSPs which are clearly benefits for the whole of society.

THROUGHOUT THE PROCESS

Meta-communication	**Relating to Non-participating Stakeholders**	**Relating to the General Public**
Reflection Reassessment Feedback procedures	Openness Transparency on use of input Creative solutions on numbers	Inform throughout the process Who and how Agreed vs individual

Figure 7.7 *Throughout the Process*

Mechanisms of meta-communication

Multi-stakeholder processes need to include mechanisms which allow participants to reflect on the process they are participating in (meta-communication). Even if issues such as agenda, participants, ground rules of communication and decision-making, necessary structures, resources, capacity-building, and so on have been agreed by participants at the outset, there needs to be space for reflection upon that same process and how it is working. How this is best done will depend on the length of the process, the scope and size of the group involved, and the structural and organizational arrangements. For example, meta-communication can be ensured by facilitators asking for reflections on the process at certain points in meetings or through feedback loops being coordinated by a process secretariat. It is important that such feedback exercises are suggested to the group to discuss in a transparent and inclusive manner and that *all* participants are included in the exercise. Some level of formality for meta-communication is therefore desirable.

As has been underlined before, groups increase their effectiveness if they work on the basis of an agreed set of rules – hence they need to communicate about the way they communicate. Meta-communication also creates space for dealing with problems which arise when members feel that other members are not playing by the rules.

Many MSPs take place in culturally mixed contexts. Meta-communication allows participants to discover what are indeed cultural differences, which are more common than we generally tend to believe.

For the process of meta-communication and agreeing procedures, it is helpful if the group is aware of the general effects of high diversity, so that they can deal creatively with potential problems.

Relating to non-participating stakeholders

MSPs should be kept open for input from non-participating stake-holders. This can be done via a frequently updated interactive website, which is an easy but also problematic strategy because of access divides. Participating stakeholder groups should also consider calling for inputs from non-participating groups, particularly in cases where the number of participants has been limited. For example, the NGO group called for input from the women's caucus and the Indigenous Peoples caucus when they were preparing for the Bergen Ministerial Dialogues. Another option was demonstrated by the World Commission on Dams process, which consisted of the Commission itself, with 12 members, plus a larger Forum of around 70 organizations. The Forum served as a sounding board for all process considerations and draft material, and allowed the inclusion of a larger number of groups and a larger variety of stakeholder views.

Such calls for input need to provide clear information on how it will be considered and used. Similar to hearings and consultations that (inter)governmental bodies often use to obtain stakeholders' views, those who invest time and resources in providing such input need to be able to make an informed decision on whether they feel it is worth the effort. Experience has shown that people will not participate (or participate again) if they don't see where their inputs are going. That does not mean that an MSP has to take every input on board, but it should be clear how such inputs are being processed.

Problems arising from non-participating stakeholder groups that aim to disrupt and hinder the multi-stakeholder process should be addressed within the group if possible in order to develop a common strategy.

Many of the other issues raised with regard to relating to the general public also apply here.

Relating to the general public

Relating to the general public is very important. MSPs in sustainable development are new developments in decision-finding and govern-ance, and touch on issues which, eventually, will be of concern to everybody. Since they are, in some senses, self-appointing, it is crucial that they are open and transparent to the wider public as to their objectives, structure and processes.

Even though sustainability questions relate directly to people's everyday lives, many involved in sustainable development debates often find it very difficult to explain what they are doing in a language free of jargon. This observation applies equally to Local Agenda 21 processes as to those around the UN. Other processes are very specialist, addressing issues which are highly technical and require a professional or quasi-professional knowledge base. However, even then, relating to the general public should be a priority. The group should face the challenge and aim to make the process and its issues understandable to the general public. A useful motto for all participants can be: 'Communicate as if people mattered'.

Within the MSP, it will be crucial to agree on who will relate to the public – through agreed statements, website contents, and so on – and how. In general, every participant should be able to share information with the public and present it from their perspective. To avoid public confusion, however, the communication from the process or group as a whole should be agreed and coordinated. To facilitate external communication, the group should consider engaging people (and 'experts'!) from outside the process to convey the message to the general media.[13] This is a question of resources and prioritization, and should not be forgotten when fund-raising for an MSP.

A good information strategy includes identifying target audiences; developing partnerships with key information sources; identifying appropriate methods and channels; creating effective messages; and evaluating strategies.[14] It will be important also to release information progressively throughout all stages of a process and not only to present a finished product. This should be the norm and not just when one wants to open the process for input and comments from the public.

Discussions should also include the choice of media. Especially in the case of global processes, an MSP might need a mix of channels, as different media are accessible in different parts of the world. Television, in connection with internet sites, might be suitable in industrialized countries, particularly the US, while radio could be more appropriate in developing countries. The reality is that huge numbers of people are not consulted or readily accessible to decision-making processes. In structuring an MSP, decisions need to be made about how close to the affected communities the process shall take place. In some cases, it might be appropriate to take the MSP to the people, rather than locate it, say, at UN Headquarters in New York.

Hohnen (2000a, p7) notes that one of the main challenges 'for the designers of multi-stakeholder processes' will be to 'enable and encourage inputs from parties both within and without the process', saying that the internet offers an 'ideal tool for facilitating transparency and cost-effective input from civil society throughout any dialogue'.

The advent of the internet indeed enables wide public communication and consultation. Websites can be updated regularly, are relatively cheap to maintain once they are set up and running, and are hardly restricted with regard to the amount of information which can be set up. They can be interactive and include message boards, chat rooms, list servers, and so on. They can also allow web-casting of meetings, the provision of video-streaming and radio broadcasts.

For this to be effective, however, several concerns need to be addressed. As noted above, these include communication with disadvantaged groups (victims of the 'digital divide'), and the need to summarize materials and key questions in a manner that encourages and enables public interest and input. The internet is a means rather than an end. Placing information on the web should not be regarded as 'communication' or 'consultation', but as a means of enhancing it. The greater the focus of the MSP and the extent to which it can be concrete about the choices to be made and their implications, the greater the chance will be that the public will engage.

8

The Short-cut

PRINCIPLES OF STAKEHOLDER PARTICIPATION AND PARTNERSHIP

The following are suggested as key principles and strategies of multi-stakeholder processes:

PRINCIPLES	STRATEGIES
Accountability	Employing agreed, transparent, democratic mechanisms of engagement, position-finding, decision-making, implementation, monitoring, evaluation; making these mechanisms transparent to non-participating stakeholders and the general public
Effectiveness	Providing a tool for addressing urgent sustainability issues; promoting better decisions by means of wider input; generating recommendations that have broad support; creating commitment through participants identifying with the outcome and thus increasing the likelihood of successful implementation
Equity	Levelling the playing-field between all relevant stakeholder groups by creating dialogue (and consensus-building) based on equally valued contributions from all; providing support for meaningful participation; applying principles of

	gender, regional, ethnic and other balance; providing equitable access to information
Flexibility	Covering a wide spectrum of structures and levels of engagement, depending on issues, participants, linkage into decision-making, time-frame, and so on; remaining flexible over time while agreed issues and agenda provide for foreseeable engagement
Good governance	Further developing the role of stakeholder participation and collaboration in (inter) governmental systems as supplementary and complementary vis-à-vis the roles and responsibilities of governments, based on clear norms and standards; providing space for stakeholders to act independently where appropriate
Inclusiveness	Providing for all views to be represented, thus increasing the legitimacy and credibility of a participatory process
Learning	Requiring participants to learn from each other; taking a learning approach throughout the process and its design
Legitimacy	Requiring democratic, transparent, accountable, equitable processes in their design; requiring participants to adhere to those principles
Ownership	People-centred processes of meaningful participation, allowing ownership for decisions and thus increasing the chances of successful implementation
Participation and engagement	Bringing together the principal actors; supporting and challenging all stakeholders to be actively engaged
Partnership/ cooperative management	Developing partnerships and strengthening the networks between stakeholders; addressing conflictual issues; integrating diverse views; creating mutual benefits (win–win rather than win–lose situations); developing shared power and responsibilities; creating feedback loops between local, national or international levels and into decision-making

Societal gains	Creating trust through honouring each participant as contributing a necessary component of the bigger picture; helping participants to overcome stereotypical perceptions and prejudice
Strengthening of (inter)governmental institutions	Developing advanced mechanisms of transparent, equitable, and legitimate stakeholder participation strengthens institutions in terms of democratic governance and increased ability to address global challenges
Transparency	Bringing all relevant stakeholders together in one forum and within an agreed process; publicizing activities in an understandable manner to non-participating stakeholders and the general public
Voices, not votes	Making voices of various stakeholders effectively heard, without disempowering democratically elected bodies

A CHECKLIST FOR MSP DESIGNERS

Summarizing the considerations and recommendations discussed in Chapter 7, the following is a brief list of key points which need to be addressed when designing MSPs. 'Addressing' does not mean that all processes have to include all respective components – in fact, this will hardly ever be the case – but you may find it useful to consider them.

General points

	Yes	No
Are you prepared to learn and change? (Ask yourself why/why not)		
Are you in danger of imposing your ideas, eg agenda, time lines, issues, participants, goals?		
Could others perceive you as imposing? With whom should you communicate, and how, to address that?		
Are you sure you are keeping records of all that you are doing, including how the process was developed?		

	Yes	No
Are you making sure that all procedures are designed to ensure the core principles of MSPs?		

Context

Process Design

	Yes	No
Have you found all the best people to design the process together?		
Have you got a core coordinating group of representatives of all relevant stakeholders? (Reflect on the criteria you are using)		
Are those you are working with formally representing their groups; are they well connected within their groups?		
Have you consulted with stakeholders who else should be involved?		
Is the coordinating group developing suggestions regarding issues, objectives, scope, time lines, procedures of preparation, dialogue, decision-making, rapporteuring, documentation, relating to the wider public, fund-raising?		
Have you dealt with issues around confidentiality?		
Is there conflict over the issue you have in mind or is it likely to develop in the process?		
Do you know how to resolve possible conflict?		
Have you considered abandoning the MSP idea for the time being due to too much conflict?		
Have you considered developing a Memorandum of Understanding (MOU) or Terms of Reference (TOR) for the MSP?		
Have you decided on the language(s) of your process?		
Have you considered translation services?		
Are you keeping the process flexible?		

Linkage Into Official Decision-making

	Yes	No
Is your process linked with any official decision-making?		
If yes, have you established continuous communication links with officials?		
Has the institution issued a document that clearly states the purpose, the expected outcomes, deadlines, and status of the outcome in the official process?		
Do you have an MOU with the institution? (If not, consider suggesting it)		
Have you considered suggesting more than an informing role for your process? (eg implementation; monitoring; reporting back)		
If not, do you know how officials will perceive your process		
Do you want to include officials somehow? Or try to keep them out?		

Issue Identification

	Yes	No
Are you making decisions on issues and agenda in a coordinating group of stakeholder representatives?		
Are you deciding upon issues in a transparent manner?		
Are you conducting the process of issue identification to an agreed timetable?		
Are you sure that those you talk to are consulting within their groups?		
Is support available for stakeholders to engage in the process of issue identification?		
Are you scoping the area of interest carefully?		
Have come across information gaps? If yes, how can you fill them?		
At the end of issue identification, have you developed a clear agenda and precise definitions of the issues?		

	Yes	No
Are agenda and issues understood and agreed by everybody?		

Information base

	Yes	No
Have you established mechanisms for sharing information and a common knowledge base within the process?		
Do all participants have equitable access to it?		

Stakeholder Identification

	Yes	No
Have you issued an open call for participation?		
Are you dealing creatively with problems of numbers and diversity?		
Have you identified all high-impact groups? (Scoping the issue area and consulting with stakeholders will tell you. Think outside the box)		
Are all those who have a stake in the issues involved? (If substantial parts of a sector don't want to participate, reconsider your MSP idea)		
Do you know how to approach them?		
Do you think all participants need to be 'experts'?		
Have you assembled a diverse group?		
Are you keeping the group open in case the need arises for other stakeholders to be involved?		
Do stakeholders need support to be able to participate effectively?		
Do suggested goals, time lines, preparations, communication channels, etc, meet their needs and interests?		
Could people feel coerced into participation?		
Does your process require government action? (Then involve officials)		

	Yes	No
Have you made decisions through consultation?		

Identification of Participants

	Yes	No
Are stakeholder groups themselves selecting their representatives?		
Do you know how they do that? (Aim to make this known to everybody)		
Have you ensured that there is an equal number of participants from each stakeholder group?		
Do you want them to meet balance criteria within their delegations? (gender, region, age?)		
Have you ensured that representatives will remain the same persons over the course of the process?		
Do you have a briefing mechanism for newcomers?		
Are governments or intergovernmental institutions involved? (Then make sure it is high level)		

Facilitation/Organizational Back-up

	Yes	No
Is it clear who is providing organizational back-up, and is that acceptable to all participants (eg a UN agency; a multi-stakeholder organization)		
Do you need to create a facilitating body?		
If yes, have you considered bylaws and other legal requirements? Have you considered the necessary time lines and funding?		
Are logistics and infrastructure agreed and funded?		

Funding

	Yes	No
Have you developed a realistic budget for the process?		

	Yes	No
Have you included external communications, translations, capacity-building, and follow-up activities?		
Have you agreed to fund-raising targets and strategies within the coordinating group?		
Have you informed all participants about the funding situation, sources, etc?		
Is the process independent, eg through mixed funding and donors who will not try to impact on the process?		

Framing

Group Composition

	Yes	No
Is your group diverse enough?		
Are all the high-impact categories involved?		
Are all groups equally represented?		
Do you have at least two representatives of each group?		
Do you expect anybody to represent more than one stakeholder group?		
Do you have overall gender and regional balance in your group?		

Goals Setting

	Yes	No
Is the goal of your process clear?		
Is it: a frank exchange of views; agreeing upon disagreements; exploring common ground; achieving consensus; making decisions; joint action; joint monitoring and evaluating; impacting official decision-making?		
Are your goals understandable and achievable?		
Does everybody agree with them?		

	Yes	No
Have you made sure that the first goal and issue on the agenda will be for participants to clarify their respective understanding of the issue(s)?		

Agenda Setting

	Yes	No
Have you developed a concrete agenda?		
Have you ensured that participants agree upon logistical and substantive aspects of the process?		

Setting the timetable

	Yes	No
Have you developed a precise timetable for your process?		
Does it meet the needs of all participants?		

Inputs

Stakeholder Preparations

	Yes	No
How shall stakeholders prepare for the process/meetings?		
Have you considered the various options within the coordinating group (eg initial position papers; developing a common vision first; preparing strategy papers based on a common vision, etc?)		
Have you ensured that preparatory papers are disseminated well in advance?		
Have you considered analysing them to point out common-alities and differences, and disseminate that as well?		
Have you ensured that all have equitable access to all information?		
Does everybody agree with the preparatory process?		

	Yes	No
How will participants relate to the stakeholder groups they represent (if they are not there in their individual capacity)?		
Do they have enough time for consultations within their constituencies during preparations?		
Are you providing support for such consultations?		
Are participants informing each other on how they consult within their constituencies?		

Communication Ground Rules

	Yes	No
Have you agreed a set of ground rules for communication?		
Do these rules foster dialogue?		
Do they encourage people to listen, learn, be open, honest and considerate?		
Have you agreed on a facilitator (or several facilitators)?		
Does s/he enjoy the trust of all participants?		
Will s/he be competent to enhance the creativity of the group, deal with potential conflict, avoid premature decision-making?		
Do you know what to do when people don't play by the rules?		
Have you agreed that this will be brought to the group through the facilitator and in a constructive manner?		

Power Gaps

	Yes	No
Are there any power gaps within the group?		
Do you know how you want to deal with them?		
Has the group talked about power gaps?		
Have they talked about what constitutes power in this setting? (eg money; decision-making; moral ground)		

Capacity-Building For Participation

	Yes	No
Have you identified the capacities, skills and knowledge that are necessary to participate effectively in your process?		
Do all participants have them?		
Has the group talked about capacity-building?		
Have potential capacity-building measures been designed by those receiving and those offering them?		

Dialogue/meetings

Communication channels

	Yes	No
Have you considered the various options of communication channels (eg face-to-face meetings, email, telephone, fax, letters, interactive websites)?		
Has the group talked about this question?		
Have you decided which ones you want to use at which stage?		
Are they easily accessible for all participants?		

Facilitating/Chairing

	Yes	No
Have you decided if you want an outside professional or an insider?		
Have you involved the facilitator in the design process?		
Are your facilitators committed, flexible, responsive, balancing, inclusive, encouraging, respectful, neutral, problem-solving oriented, disciplined, culturally sensitive, capable of meta-communication and comfortable with their role?		
Have you decided which kind of facilitation techniques you want to use (eg flip-charts, meta-plan, brain storming, scenario workshops, future labs, and so on)?		

	Yes	No
Have you talked with the coordinating group and the facilitator which would be best and when?		

Rapporteuring

	Yes	No
Have you identified rapporteurs to take minutes?		
Have you identified who is to draft outcome documents?		
Are they acceptable to everybody?		
Are minutes and reporting done in a neutral fashion?		
Do they reflect the breadth and depth of discussions?		

Decision-making

	Yes	No
Do you have agreement on what constitutes a good decision?		
Will a decision be based on consensus?		
Does consensus mean unanimity?		
Does consensus mean compromise ('being content with the whole package')		
Will a decision be taken by majority vote?		
Are you recording minority voting?		
Do the decisions on your MSP have consequences outside the space covered by participants?		
Are you involving those affected?		
Is it clear that everybody has the right to walk away or to say 'No'?		
Are you taking enough time before making decisions?		
Could the group be more creative and integrating before making a decision? (How?)		

Closure

	Yes	*No*
Does the process have a clear, agreed cut-off point (for success or failure)?		

Outputs

Documentation

	Yes	*No*
Are you putting draft minutes and reports to the group for review?		
Have you built time for reviewing into your schedule?		
Have you clarified the status of your documents: minutes by rapporteurs; facilitators' summaries; endorsed consensus documents? (They require different consultation procedures and time)		
Are you disseminating the outcome documents to other stakeholder groups and the public?		

Action Plan/Implementation

	Yes	*No*
Have you agreed a precise, concrete action plan: who will do what, when, and with whom?		
Have you considered how to monitor implementation and how to deal with non-compliance?		
You planned a dialogue, now they want to continue and explore possible joint action: Is the group engaging in an MSP design process, agreeing objectives, scope, structures, time lines, funding, etc?		
Are you managing such a transition carefully?		

Throughout the process

Mechanisms of meta-communication

	Yes	No
Do participants have space to reflect upon the process?		
Do you have regular feedback mechanisms so that everybody can raise concerns and suggestions?		
Is the facilitator bringing this up?		

Relating to Non-participating Stakeholders

	Yes	No
Have you kept the process open for input from non-participating stakeholders?		
Are you sure the arrangements for that will work?		
Have you made clear how any input from outside will be used?		
In case of opposition to the process from the outside, are you addressing this in the MSP group as a whole?		

Relating to the General Public

	Yes	No
Does the public know about your process?		
Are you effectively communicating its objectives and outcomes? Have you found the right language and media?		
Are you releasing information throughout the process?		
Should members of the general public be able to contribute? (How?)		
Are you using professionals to relate to the public? (Why/why not?)		
Are you relying solely on the internet? If yes, can you do more?		
Have you discussed these questions in the MSP group?		

9

Conclusion: More Than One Step Beyond – What Next?

To develop MSPs further as a tool for sustainable development, two main steps need to be taken.

First there is a need for common learning on MSPs. Despite a great number of processes which have been carried out over the last few years and those which are ongoing at the moment, it is remarkable that there is little communication between them. One reason appears to be that people are typically working within specific sectors, such as environment, poverty, gender equity, and so on. Concentrating on their respective goals, they have built networks within their sectors but rarely across the sectors and issues. Also, many people are focusing their work on a particular level (international, regional, national, local) and there is a chronic problem of missing links between those levels, which again leads to limited networks.

As our work has shown, what is potentially emerging is a large amount of expertise and experience which seems at the moment to be rather scattered and unconnected. People carrying that expertise, however, form a rich and resourceful 'community of practice'. This knowledge management term describes a group of people who do similar work but do not necessarily work in the same organizations or sectors. They share many interests and concerns, and find solutions to similar problems in very different environments. It seems that as regards MSPs, there is a community of practice, or even a movement, 'out there' which needs to connect much more and begin to define itself.

As we move ahead in developing MSPs, it will be important to enable this community to come together, to share their experiences and create opportunities to learn from each other. MSP practitioners would benefit from 'learning exercises', drawing out the common factors of success and failure, the results of which could be made available for people who are designing new or adapted multi-stakeholder processes.

Developing the network would also help to promote the MSP ideas more powerfully. It would also be an important basis for developing monitoring and evaluation mechanisms for MSPs. In order to establish the effectiveness of MSPs and their components, it will be necessary to develop shared sets of indicators and standardized tools for evaluation to determine their impact in 'real life' terms. The question of measuring the effectiveness of participatory mechanisms in sustainable development has not been addressed sufficiently, and again, work that has been done needs to be shared much more widely to avoid duplication and the reinvention of wheels. This will be an important component of further learning on MSPs; it will help to develop the concept and to promote those features and components which have indeed proved to work.

It would be very useful to set up a unit or mechanism for information exchange and overall coordination or advice on matters of multi-stakeholder participation and collaboration, which would provide a stakeholder hub for learning, networking, indicators' development and promotion. This should be set up as a multi-stakeholder effort.

What we say here about MSPs and learning concerns the need to do this correctly and thoroughly, otherwise there is a danger that MSPs will turn out to be just another fashionable buzz-word and activity, which will soon fade to make way for the next one. We need to be careful not to waste such an important concept.

Experimenting with a common framework such as the one we propose here will help to promote MSPs. We will find out more about what they can deliver and how best we use their potential – as independent processes as well as ones designed around official decision-making.

Second, for MSPs to contribute their potential more effectively, governments and intergovernmental institutions will need to develop more consistent policies as regards stakeholder participation. At the moment, different bodies are experimenting with different structures and mechanisms. And it is indeed difficult for stakeholders to understand what is expected of them, what they are being invited to do and how reliable that role will be. In addition, governments should involve stakeholders more effectively, for example by challenging them to discuss the implementation of policies and decisions in multi-stakeholder settings. This would alert stakeholders to their responsibilities, generate their commitment and forge partnerships, thus helping to make things happen.

The UN has a key role to play in developing appropriate mechanisms and making suggestions to its members. Agreeing advanced mechanisms of transparent, equitable and legitimate stakeholder participation will ultimately strengthen (inter)governmental institutions, in terms of democratic governance as well as of adequately addressing global challenges. Reinicke et al (2000) have suggested a clearing house that would act as an information hub. One could imagine a unit within the UN Secretary-General's office, governed 50–50 by the UN and stakeholders, with staff being seconded from the UN and various stakeholder groups. It could produce material for member states, laying out the various options and experiences as well as suggestions on how to move forward.

The increase of corporate power and the rise of influential NGO movements presents a great challenge for democratic systems. By addressing the challenge proactively rather than reacting to pressures from powerful stakeholders or engaging in various, rather unconnected individual initiatives, governments and intergovernmental bodies will also avoid their own disempowerment. Multi-stakeholder processes offer a tool by which governments and intergovernmental institutions can channel their relationships with stakeholders.

MSPs are being created not only because we need to develop new tools beyond 'business as usual, government as usual and protest as usual' (Hohnen, 2001). They are emerging because the solutions are often as complex as the problems, and all stakeholders have ideas about possible solutions and need to be part of them. The challenge is to provide them with the fora to bring their wisdom to the table effectively and equitably.

Appendix I

Methodology of the Project

This book is the result of a UNED Forum project, undertaken between October 2000 and June 2001. Gathering some of the necessary building-blocks of a methodological framework for multi-stakeholder processes (Part I), we aimed to distil a step-by-step guide which allows for transparent, equitable, democratic and gender-balanced processes of stakeholder involvement and collaboration. The goal was to develop a framework that is agreeable to stakeholders and can be adapted to various situations and issues (Part II).

We produced a draft report on the project website (www.earth summit2002.org/msp) and asked for comments from a variety of stakeholder representatives, including UNED Forum's International Advisory Board, representatives of the processes studied, government representatives and researchers. Over 30 people provided us with comments, questions, amendments and literature, some of them in the form of general guidance, some in great detail. On the basis of these comments, we redrafted the text, developed a set of principles and send it to participants prior to a two-day workshop, held in New York on 28–29 April 2001. The presentations and discussions at the workshop were again incorporated into the work, which resulted in this book.

METHODOLOGY OF THE REVIEW OF SCIENTIFIC LITERATURE

We conducted searches in social sciences libraries and via the PsycInfo database of psychological research, theoretical and empirical work on communication, consensus-building, conflict resolution, power relationships, and decision-making in groups; group composition, leadership, and so on. We also contacted experts in social and organizational psychology to obtain their suggestions on relevant research material. They provided further pointers to relevant literature. Analysing the material, we focused particularly on review and applied literature. We received comments on a first draft from a number of experts and incorporated them into the final version of Chapter 6.

METHODOLOGY OF ANALYSING MSP EXAMPLES

From the large number of existing examples, we picked a variety regarding their issues, objectives, scope, time lines, participants and linkage to official decision-making. We obtained information about the examples in print and via the internet. Much of the process design-related information which we were looking for was publicly available. We also interviewed people who are/were involved in the examples, either in person, by telephone or email. Almost every example presentation in this book is based on a combination of literature research and interviewing.

Studying the examples was not aimed at giving an assessment or evaluation via a representative group of people being interviewed. Of course, people do make judgements and that shines through in some cases (marked 'comment'). The goal was to obtain a descriptive analysis of the respective MSPs. All people who have contributed to obtaining that information are listed in Appendix II, along with other people who commented on drafts, gave guidance on the draft documents or parts thereof, and so on.

The following is the list of questions we used.

General information

Name:

Issues:

Objectives:

Participants:

Scope:

Time lines:

Contact details/URL:

Procedural aspects

Designing the MSP How was the process designed? And by whom? Were there consultations with stakeholders on the design?

Identifying the issues Who identifies the issues? And how?

Identifying relevant stakeholders Who identifies relevant stakeholders? And how?

Identifying participants Who identifies the participants? And how? Possibly different for the various participating stakeholder groups.

Setting the goals Who sets the goals? And how? Can goals develop over the course of the MSP – eg from an informing process into a dialogue/consensus-building process; from mere exchange of views to implementation? Do participants have opportunities to check back with their constituencies when changes are being proposed?

Setting the agenda Who sets the agenda? And how? Do participants have opportunities to check back with their constituencies when changes are being proposed?

Setting the timetable Who sets the timetable? And how?

Preparatory process How is the dialogue prepared (consultations within constituencies; papers; initial positions; and so on)? Are the preparations within stakeholder groups being monitored somehow?

Communication How is the communication conducted (face-to-face/telephone/email, etc; chairing/facilitation; atmosphere; summarizing)?

Dealing with power gaps Are there power gaps between participating stakeholder groups? How are they addressed/dealt with?

Are there mechanisms of meta-communication during the process? What kind?

Decision-making/procedures of agreement Depending on the type of MSP, is agreement being sought? If so, how is that conducted? And by whom?

Implementation How is implementation decided/planned/conducted? By whom?

Closure How and when does the process conclude? Who makes the decision and how?

Structural aspects

Institutional back-up Is there a secretariat, facilitating body, board, forum?

Facilitation Who facilitates the MSP? What is the exact role of a facilitating body? How does the facilitating organization work with stakeholders? Does that include secretariat services?

Documentation Rapporteuring from meetings; summarizing outcomes; publication of documentation – by whom, when and how?

Relating to non-participating stakeholders Do other stakeholders know about the process? Can they feed into the process? And how?

Relating to the general public What kind of information about the MSP is available to the public? Via which channels? Who provides that information? Can the public comment/ask questions/feed in? And how?

Linkage into official decision-making Is the MSP linked to an official decision-making process? Of governments, intergovernmental bodies, other stakeholders? Via which mechanisms? How transparent and predictable are these mechanisms? Can stakeholders impact the mechanisms? And how?

Funding Is the process being funded? By whom? Who fundraises? How much does it cost? What impact do funders have on process, structures and outcomes?

Appendix II

Contributors, Commentators and Interviewees

We thank everybody who has contributed to this book.

The people listed below have contributed to various parts of the document, providing information about the examples studied, input into the review of scientific research, the discussions on values and ideology, the recommendations on designing MSPs, and so on. The list does not imply any kind of endorsement of our work, neither by the individuals nor their organizations.

Amina Adam, UN Division for the Advancement of Women; Marc Bacon, UK Government Department of Environment, Transport and the Regions; Jeffrey Barber, Integrated Strategies Forum/SPAC Caucus/TOBI, Washington, US; Sue Barber, School of Social Science, Middlesex University, UK; Dieter Beck, Public Administration Research Institute, Speyer, Germany; Norma Bubier, Durrell Institute of Conservation and Ecology, UK; Simon Burall, One World Trust, UK; Chris Church, The Northern Alliance for Sustainability/ANPED, the Netherlands; Paul Clements-Hunt, United Nations Environment Programme, Geneva, Switzerland; Barry Coates, World Development Movement, London, UK; Nigel Cross, International Institute for Environment and Development, London, UK; Alison Crowther, The Environment Council, London, UK; Barry Dalal-Clayton, International Institute for Environment and Development, London, UK; Navroz Dubash, World Resources Institute, Washington, US; Kevin Dunion, Friends of the Earth Scotland; Michael Edwards, The Ford Foundation, New York, US; Kaspar Eigenmann, Novartis, Switzerland; Nader Farahwaschy, Free University of Berlin, Germany; Ahmad Fawzi, Director, UN Information Centre, London, UK; Thomas Forster, CSD NGO Sustainable Agriculture and

Food Systems Caucus; Ulrich Gebhard, University of Hamburg, Germany; Bill Gellermann, Communication Coordination Committee for the UN, New York, US; Nazila Ghanea-Hercock, Institute of Commonwealth Studies, University of London, UK; Robert Goodland, World Bank, Washington, US; Rob Graff, Global Reporting Initiative, US; Maryanne Grieg-Gran, International Institute for Environment and Development, London, UK; Stephanie Hanford, World Business Council for Sustainable Development, Geneva, Switzerland; Navid Hanif, UN Division for Sustainable Development, New York, US; Malcolm Harper, United Nations Association of Great Britain and Northern Ireland, London, UK; John Hill, TXU-Europe; Paul Hohnen, former Director of Greenpeace International and adviser to international NGOs, organizations and corporations, Amsterdam, the Netherlands; Megan Howell, Department of Planning, University of Auckland, New Zealand; Steve Hyde, TXU-Europe; Harsh Jaitli, Society For Participatory Research in Asia, New Delhi, India; Klaus Jonas, Technical University Chemnitz, Germany; Peter Kearns, Organisation for Economic Co-operation and Development, Paris, France; Mike Kelly, KPMG, UK; Suzannah Lansdell, The Environment Council, London, UK; J Gary Lawrence, Sustainable Strategies and Solutions Inc, Seattle, US; Maria Lourdes (Malou) Lesquite, Novartis, Switzerland; Juliette Majot, International Rivers Network, US; Paul Markowitz, Institute for Sustainable Communities, US; Robert Massie, Global Reporting Initiative, US; Patrick McCully, International Rivers Network, US; Frank McShane, International Institute for Environment and Development, London, UK; Rosemarie Mielke, University of Hamburg, Germany; John Mitchell, World Bank, Washington, US; Oswald Neuberger, University of Augsburg, Germany; Antares Numi*On, Magick River, Malaysia; Nicky Nzioki, Cohort For Research on Environment, Urban Management and Human Settlements, Nairobi, Kenya; Denise O'Brien, UN Global Compact Unit; Philippine Institute of Alternative Futures (Secretariat to the Philippine Council for Sustainable Development); Federica Pietracci, UN DESA Finance for Development Secretariat, New York, US; Josephine Pradella, WI Sustainable Futures Network; Peter Sanders, UNA-UK, London, UK; Lorena San Roman, Latin America and Caribbean Programme Coordinator, The Earth Council, Costa Rica; Lucien Royer, International Confederation of Free Trade Unions, Paris, France; Marie Samuel, Yachay Wasi, New York, US and Cuzco, Peru; Richard Sandbrook, Mining, Minerals and Sustainable Development, London, UK; Kai Sassenberg, Friedrich Schiller University Jena, Germany; Miguel Schloss, Transparency International, Washington, US; Andreas Seiter, Novartis, Basel, Switzerland; Kishore Shah, independent consultant, Cambridge, UK; Gordon Shepherd, WWF International, Gland, Switzerland; Mara Silina, European Environment Bureau, Brussels, Belgium; David Smith, One World Trust, London, UK; Jan-Gustav Strandenaes, Chair, GEF NGO Network, Oslo,

Norway; David Taylor, New Zealand Government; Gino Van-Begin, International Council for Local Environment Initiatives Europe; Jeremy Wates, United Nations Economic Commission for Europe, Geneva, Switzerland; Jack Wheelan, International Chamber of Commerce, Paris, France; Paul Whiffen, Tearfund, London, UK; Daniel Wiener, ecos.ch ag, Switzerland; Alex Wilks, Bretton Woods Project, London, UK; Erich Witte, University of Hamburg, Germany; James Workman, World Commission on Dams, Capetown, South Africa; June Zeitlin, Women's Environment and Development Organization, New York, US.

From UNED Forum: Beth Hiblin, Danielle Morley, Derek Osborn, Margret Brusasco-Mackenzie, Rosalie Gardiner, Toby Middleton.

Appendix III

UNED Forum

From 1 January 2002 UNED Forum will be known as Stakeholder Forum for Our Common Future. We are an international multi-stakeholder organization committed to the promotion of global sustainable development. Based in London, UNED's activities support the work of the UNEP, the UNDP, the CSD and other UN bodies committed to sustainable development.

Since 1998 the UNED Forum has been building its work in preparation for Earth Summit 2002 in Johannesburg. Within this remit, the UNED Forum is engaged in the following activities:

- Promoting multi-stakeholder partnerships.
- Researching and influencing policy.
- Providing and spreading information.
- Training and building capacity.

UNED Forum operates both internationally and within the UK, where it operates as UNED-UK Committee.

Members of UNED Forum's International Advisory Board and its UK-based Executive Committee include representatives from local government, trade unions, industry, NGOs, women, youth, academics, faith community, education community and the media.

UNED Forum's work on multi-stakeholder processes is a key activity, linked to most of our activities. We are building on our experiences, increasing the network and promoting the approach, experimenting, aiming to create a learning hub for stakeholders.

UNED Forum
3 Whitehall Court
London
SW1A 2EL
UK

Tel: (+44) 207 930 2931
Fax: (+44) 207 930 5893
E-mail: info@earthsummit2002.org
Websites: www.unedforum.org &
www.earthsummit2002.org

References

Dates given for publications on the internet indicate when a document was last accessed

Abbot, J (1996) *Sharing the City*, Earthscan, London

Acland, Andrew (2000) 'Uncovering the Roots of Stakeholder Dialogue', The Environment Council', *Elements for Environmental Decisions*, vol, 1, no 1

Adams, Barbara (1999) 'ECOSOC and NGOs: A Review of the Review', in Montreal International Forum (ed) *Civil Society Engaging Multilateral Institutions: At the Crossroads*, pp8–12, FIM, Montreal, Canada

Adorno, Theodor W (1991) *Minima Moralia*, Suhrkamp Frankfurt, (orig 1951)

Agarwal, Anil, Nairain, Sunita and Sharma, Anju (eds) (1999) *Green Politics: Global Environmental Negotiations*, 1, Centre for Science and Environment, New Delhi, India

Alexander, Titus (2000) 'Global Accountability: How to Improve International Decision-Making', a discussion paper in two parts, Charter 99, London, UK

Allison, Stuart T and Messick, David M (1985) 'The Group Attribution Error', *Journal of Experimental Social Psychology*, no 21, pp563–579

Altman, Dennis (1999) 'UNAIDS: NGO on Board and on the Board' in Montreal International Forum (ed) *Civil Society Engaging Multilateral Institutions: At the Crossroads*, pp19–23, FIM, Montreal, Canada

Annan, Kofi (1997) Inaugural Address to the International Conference on Governance for Sustainable Growth and Equity in UNDP, *Conference Report*, pp19–21, UNDP, New York

Annan, Kofi (1999) Address to the World Economic Forum Davos, Switzerland, www.globalpolicy.net/UNandGPP.htm

Annan, Kofi (2000a) *UN Secretary-General's Millennium Report*, United Nations, New York

Annan, Kofi (2000b) 'Africans Know That Democracy Is for Them, Too', *International Herald Tribune*, 5 December, p8

Arts, Bas (1998) *The Political Influence of Global NGOs: Case Studies on the Climate and Biodiversity Conventions*, International Books, Utrecht

Asch, Solomon E (1951) 'Effects of Group Pressure Upon the Modification and Distortion of Judgements' in H Guetzkow (ed) *Groups, Leadership and Men*, Pittsburg, PA, Carnegie Press

Asch, Solomon E (1956) 'Status of Independence and Conformity: A Minority of One Against a Unanimous Majority', *Psychological Monographs*, vol 70, no 9

Ashmore, D Richard and DelBoca, Frances K (1986) 'Gender Stereotypes', in D Ashmore and T DelBoca (eds) *The Social Psychology of Female–Male*

Relations: A Critical Analysis of Central Conceptions, Academic Press, New York

Asmal, Kader (2000) 'First World Chaos, Third World Calm: A Multi Stakeholder Process to "Part the Waters" in the Debate over Dams', *Le Monde*, 15 November 2000

Bahá'í Community of the United States (2001) 'Introductions', www.us.bahai. org/community/index.html

Bahá'í Community of Canada (1993) 'Issues of Concern to the World's Aboriginal Peoples', submission by the Bahá'í Community of Canada to the Royal Commission on Aboriginal Peoples in November 1993, www.bahai.org/ article-1-9-1-8.html

Bahá'í International Community (2000) 'Consultation', www.bahai.org/article-1-3-6-3.html

Bahá'í International Community (2001) 'Sustainable Development: The Spiritual Dimension', a statement by the Bahá'í International Community to the first session of the Preparatory Committee of the World Summit on Sustainable Development, 30 April–2 May, New York

Bartlett, Christopher A and Ghosal, Sumantra (1987) *Managing Across Borders: The Transnational Solution*, Harvard Business School Press, Boston, MA

Bassett, Libby, Brinkmann, John T and Pedersen, Kusumita P (eds) (2000) *Earth and Faith: A Book of Reflection for Action.* United Nations Environment Programme/Interfaith Partnership for the Environment, New York

Baughman, Mike (1995) 'Mediation' in O Renn, T Webler and P Wiedemann (eds) *Fairness and Competence in Citizen Participation: Evaluating Models for Environmental Discourse*, Kluwer, Dordrecht, Boston, London

Beck, Dieter et al (1999) 'Zur Funktion unterschiedlicher Gruppenrollen fuer die Zusammenarbeit in Gruppen' ['The Function of Diverse Group Roles for Cooperation in Groups']. *Gruppendynamik*, vol 30, no 1, pp175–190

Becker, Egon, Jahn, Thomas, Stiess, Immanuel and Wehling, Peter (1997) Sustainability: A Cross-Disciplinary Concept for Social Transformations. Report on the first phase of the MOST Project: 'Towards Sustainable Development Paradigms and Policies', UNESCO, Paris and ISOE (Institute for Social-Ecological Research), Frankfurt, Management of Social Transformation (MOST) Project, Policy Papers No 6 UNESCO, Paris

Beijing+5 Global Forum (2000) Online Discussions, Archives, www.un.org/ womenwatch/forums/beijing5

Belbin, R Meredith (1993) *Team Roles at Work. A Strategy for Human Resource Management*, Butterworth-Heinemann, Oxford

Bendell, Jem (ed) (2000a) *Terms for Endearment. Business, NGOs and Sustainable Development*, Greenleaf, Sheffield, UK

Bendell, Jem (2000b) 'Talking for Change? Reflections on Effective Stakeholder Dialogue', paper for the New Academy of Business Innovation Network, October

Berger, Joseph and Zelditch, Morris Jr (eds) (1985) *Status, Rewards and Influence* Jossey-Bass, San Francisco

Bernstein, Johannah (2000) Tracking the Global Governance Reform Agenda in World Business Council for Sustainable Development (ed) *Designing Better Governance. An Issue in Dialogue*, WBCSD, Geneva

Bertelsmann Stiftung/Forschungsgruppe Jugend and Europa (1998) *Eine Welt der Vielfalt. Ein Traningsprogramme des 'A World of Difference-Institute' der Anti-Defamation League, New York. Praxishandbuch fuer Lehrerinnen und Lehrer (A World of Diversity. A Training Programme of the World of Difference-Institute of the Anti-Defamation League, New York. A Practical Handbook for Teachers)* Bertelsmann Verlag Stiftung, Guetersloh

Bieberstein Koch-Weser, Maritta von (2000) Innovative Kooperationsformen fuer nachhaltige Entwicklung Innovative Forms of Collaboration for Sustainable Development in *innovartis, Sonderdruck zum Heft*, no 1, pp3–6, Novartis Pharma, Nuremberg, Germany

Bingham, Gail (1987) 'Resolving Environmental Disputes: A Decade of Experience' in R Lake (ed) *Resolving Locational Conflict*, Center for Urban Policy Research, The State University of New Jersey

Birch, David (Corporate Citizenship Research Unit, Deakan University, Melbourne, Australia) (2000) Broadening the Stakeholder Base: Rio Tinto's Business With Communities Programme, presentation at the WBCSD 2000 Conference 'Euro Environment 2000. Conference on Industry & Environmental Performance', Aalborg, Denmark, October

Bjerke, Siri (2000) Informal Environment Ministers Meeting, Bergen, Norway, 15–17 September, Chairman's Summary, Ministry of the Environment, Oslo, Norway

Blackburn, James, Chambers, Robert and Gaventa, John (August 1999) 'Learning to Take Time and Go Slow: Mainstreaming Participation in Development and the Comprehensive Development Framework (CDF)', prepared for Operations Evaluation Department, World Bank

Blakar, Rolv M (1984a) Communication: A Social Perspective on Clinical Issues. Universitetsforlaget, Oslo

Blakar, Rolv M (1984b) 'Towards a Theory of Communication in Terms of Preconditions: A Conceptual Framework and Some Empirical Explorations' in H Giles and R Clair (eds) *Recent advances in language, communication, and social psychology*, pp10–41, Lawrence Erlbaum Associates, London

Blumer, Herbert (1969) *Symbolic Interaction*, Prentice Hall, Englewood Cliffs, NJ

Boos, Margarete (1996) Entscheidungsfindung in Gruppen. Eine Prozeßanalyse (Decision-making in Groups. A Process Analysis), Huber, Bern

Boyles, Ann (1996–97) 'The Meaning of Community. The Bahá'í World', pp197–219, www.bahai.org/article-1-9-1-1.html

Boyles, Ann (1995–96) 'Consumers, Citizens, Values, and Governance. The Bahá'í World', pp223–240, www.bahai.org/article-1-9-1-2.html

Brehm, Vicky (2000) 'NGO Partnerships: Balancing the Scales', *ontrac* – the newsletter of the International NGO Training and Research Centre (INTRAC), Oxford, no 15, May 2000

Bretton Woods Project (2000) 'Major Bank Plans Under Fire', *Bretton Woods Update*, June

Bretton Woods Project (2000) 'WDR Resignation Embarrasses Bank', *Bretton Woods Update*, August

Brown Mallock, Mark (1999) Foreword, in 'The Human Development Report', UNDP, New York

Brown, Rupert (1995) *Prejudice. It's Social Psychology*, Blackwell, Oxford

Brown, Rupert (2000) *Group Processes* (2nd edition). Blackwell, Oxford

Browne, Sir John (2001) 'Time to Engage With Pressure Groups', *Financial Times*, 2 April

Brundtland, Gro Harlem (1987) Chairman's Foreword in *The World Commission on Environment and Development: Our Common Future*, Oxford University Press, Oxford

Bruno, Kenny and Karliner, Joshua (2000) 'Tangled Up In Blue. Corporate Partnerships at the United Nations. CorpWatch – Holding Corporations Accountable', www.corpwatch.org/un/reports/tangled.html

Canadian Round Tables (1993) Building Consensus for a Sustainable Future. Guiding Principles. An Initiative Undertaken by the Canadian Round Tables, August

Chalmers, Robert (1999) Relaxed and Participatory Appraisal. Notes on Practical Approaches and Methods. Notes for Participants in PRA Familiarisation Workshops in the Second Half of 1999, UK/Participation Group, Institute for Development Studies (IDS), Sussex

Charon, Joel M (1998) *Symbolic Interactionism*, Prentice-Hall, Upper Saddle River

Chiriboga, Manuel (1999) 'NGOs and the World Bank: Lessons and Challenges', paper prepared for the international conference 'Civil Society and the Multilateral Institutions: At the Crossroads', Montreal International Foum, www.fim civilsociety.org

Chomsky, Noam (2000) 'Summits. At Coalition for Global Solidarity and Social Development', www.globalsolidarity.org/articles/chomsky_summits.html

Christie, Ian (1999) 'LA21 and Modernising Local Government', *EG Local Government News*, October

Church, Chris and McHarry, Jan (1999) 'One Small Step – A Guide to Action on Sustainable Development in the UK', Community Development Foundation, London

Church, Chris (1997) *The Local Agenda 21 Process in the UK: Lessons for Policy and Practice in Stakeholder Participation. The Challenge of Environmental Management in Urban Areas*, Ashgate Publishing, London

Church, Chris (2001) personal communication

Citizens Compact on the United Nations and Corporations (2000) document and endorsements at www.corpwatch.org/trac/globalization/un/citizenscom pact.htm

Commission on Global Governance (1995) *Our Global Neighbourhood*, Oxford University Press, Oxford

Commission on Global Governance (1995) *Our Global Neighbourhood. The Basic Vision*, Commission on Global Governance, Geneva

Commonground, South Africa (2000) 'The Development of the Durban Urban Environmental Policy', paper presented at the Sustainable Cities Programme & Urban Environment Forum Meeting in Capetown, South Africa, September

CSD NGO Steering Committee/Sustainable Agriculture and Food Systems (SAFS) Caucus (2000) 'Priority Concerns of NGOs and Indigenous Peoples to CSD-8 Intersessional', drawn from NGO Major Groups papers presented for CSD-8 Multi-stakeholder Dialogues, draft, 15 April

CSD NGO Steering Committee (2000) 'Rules for Caucuses', www.csdngo.org/ csdngo

CSD NGO Women's Caucus (2000) 'Women & Sustainable Development 2000–2002. Recommendations in Agenda 21 and Related Documents and Suggestions for a Review of Implementation', paper drafted by Minu Hemmati for discussion at the UN CSD sessions

DAMS, the WCD Newsletter (2001) 'Gone... But Not Forgotten. A New Initiative is Born at Final WCD Forum', no 9, March

Delbecq, André L, Van de Ven, Andrew H and Gustafson, David H (1975) 'Group Techniques for Program Planning', *Human Communication Research*, no 10, pp557–574

Department of the Environment, Transport and the Regions (2001) *DETR Departmental Annual Report 2001*, The Stationery Office, London

Desai, Nitin (1999) Promoting Sustainable Development Through the UN Commission on Sustainable Development. The CSD 7th Session: 'Anatomy of an International Negotiation – Focus on Sustainable Tourism', prepared for presentation at the LEAD International Session, April, www.lead.org/lead/training/international/usa/1999/docs/papers/promosd.htm

Deutsch, Morton (1973) *The Resolution of Conflict*, Yale University Press

Dewey, John (1910) *How We Think*, Heath, Boston

Dick, Petra (1993) 'Mikropolitik in Organisationen', *Zeitschrift für Personalforschung* ('Micro-Politics in Organisation', *Journal of Personnel Research*), no 7, pp440–467

Dietz, Thomas (1995) 'Democracy and Science' in O Renn, T Webler and P Wiedemann (eds) *Fairness and Competence in Citizen Participation. Evaluating Models for Environmental Discourse*, ppxvii–xix, Kluwer, Dordrecht, Boston, London

Dietz, Thomas (2001) 'Thinking about Environmental Conflicts' in L Kadous (ed) *Celebrating Scholarship*, College of Arts and Sciences, George Mason University, Fairfax, Virginia

Dion, Kenneth L (1985) 'Sex, Gender, and Groups: Selected Issues' in V O'Leary, R Kesler Unger and B Strudler Wallston (eds) *Women, Gender, and Social Psychology*, Erlbaum, Hillsdale, NJ

Dodds, Felix (ed) (1997) *The Way Forward – Beyond Agenda 21*, Earthscan, London

Dodds, Felix (ed) (2000) *Earth Summit 2002 – A New Deal*, Earthscan, London

Dodds, Felix (1996) 'Indicators for Citizens' in U Kirdar (ed) *Cities Fit for People*, pp415–421, UNDP/United Nations Publications

Dodgson, Mark (1993) 'Organisational Learning: A Review of Some Literature', *Organisation Studies*, no 14, pp175–194

Doise, Willem (1978) *Groups and Individuals*, Cambridge University Press, Cambridge

Donald, James and Rattansi, Ali (eds) (1992) *'Race', Culture and Difference*, Sage and Open University Press, London

Drucker, Peter (1967) *The Effective Executive*, Pan, London

Earth Summit '92, Agenda 21, Chapter 1, Preamble, United Nations, New York

Edelman News (2000) Non-Government Organizations More Trusted than the Media. Survey One Year After Seattle WTO Meeting Finds NGOs More Credible Source for Information, More Likely to Act on Public's Behalf, New York, 1 December www.edelman.com/edelman_newsroom/releases/4652.htm

Eden, Colin and Ackermann, Fran (1998) *Making Strategy. The Journey of Strategic Management*, Sage, London

Edman, Jan (2000) 'Information Use and Decision-Making in Groups', The Economic Research Institute, Stockholm School of Economics

Edwards, Michael (1999) *Future Positive. International Co-operation in the 21st Century*, Earthscan, London

Edwards, Michael (2000) 'NGO Rights and Responsibilities. A New Deal for Global Governance', The Foreign Policy Centre in association with NCVO/ Voice of the Voluntary Sector, London

Ellis, B Aubrey and Fisher, Donald G (1994) *Small Group Decision-Making* (4th edn) McGraw-Hill, New York

Elsass, Priscilla and Graves, Laura (1997) 'Demographic diversity in decision-making groups: the experiences of women and people of color', *Academy of Management Review*, vol 22, pp946–997

Environics International (1997) 'The Environmental Monitor. Global Public Opinion on the Environment. 1999 International Report, Environics International, Toronto

Environics International (1998) The Coming Green Wave. Global Public Opinion on the Environment. The 1998 International Environmental Monitor Survey', presentation at the World Bank, Environics International, Toronto

Environics International (1999) 'The Environmental Monitor. Global Public Opinion on the Environment. 1999 Intenational Report', Environics International, Toronto

Environics International and The Prince of Wales Business Leaders Forum (1999) 'The Millennium Poll on Corporate Social Responsibility. Executive Briefing', Environics International, Toronto

Estrella, Marisol (ed) (2000) *Learning From Change. Issues and Experiences in Participatory Monitoring and Evaluation*. Intermediate Technology Publications & International Development Research Centre, London and Ottawa

Esty, Daniel C (2000) 'The Value of Creating a Global Environmental Organization', *Environment Matters*, pp13–14

European ECO-Forum News (2000) Aarhus Convention: Review of Compliance/ Compliance Mechanisms of the Aarhus Convention, ECO-Forum, Moscow, 21 November

Festinger, Leon (1954) 'A Theory of Social Comparison Processes', *Human Relations*, no 7, pp117–140

Festinger, Leon, Schachter, Stanley and Back, Kurt (1950) *Social Pressures in Informal Groups*, Harper, New York

Fiedler, Fred E (1958) *Leader Attitudes and Group Effectiveness*, McGraw-Hill, New York

Fisch, Rudolf, Beck, Dieter and Englich, Birte (eds) (2001) *Projektgruppen in Organisationen – Praktische Erfahrungen und Ertraege der Forschung (Project Groups in Organisations – Practical Experiences and Research Results)* Verlag fuer Angewandte Psychologie, Goettingen

Fisher, Ronald J (1997) *Interactive Conflict Resolution*, Syracuse University Press, Syracuse, NY

Floers, Betty Sue (2000) 'Global Governance. Scenario Platforms for Discussion' in World Business Council for Sustainable Development (ed) *Designing Better Governance. An Issue in Dialogue*, WBCSD, Geneva

Florini, Ann M (1999) 'Does the Invisible Hand Need a Transparent Glove? The Politics of Transparency', paper prepared for the Annual World Bank Conference on Development Economics, Washington, DC, 28–30 April

Forsyth, Don R (1999) *Group Dynamics* (3rd edn), Brooks/Cole, Pacific Grove, CA

Fowler, Alan (2000) 'Civil Society, NGDOs and Social Development: Changing the Rules of the Game', United Nations Research Institute for Social Development, occasional paper no 1

Frankel, Carl (1998) *In Earth's Company – Business, Environment and the Challenge of Sustainability*, Canada New Society Publishers, Gabriola Island, BC

Franklin, Michael (1999) Message No 16, December, DEVFORUM: Partnering with Civil Society, a World Bank email list server

French, Hilary (1996) The Role of Non-State Actors in J Werksman (ed) *Greening International Institutions*, pp251–258. Earthscan, London

Friedel-Howe, H (1990) 'Ergebnisse und offene Fragen der geschlechtsvergleich-enden Führungsforschung', *Zeitschrift für Arbeits- und Organisationspsychologie* ('Results and Open Questions of Gender Comparative Research on Leadership, *Journal of Labour and Organisational Psychology*), no 34, pp3–16

Fussler, Claude (2000) Governance and Business, in World Business Council for Sustainable Development (ed) *Designing Better Governance. An Issue in Dialogue*, WBCSD, Geneva

Gergen, Kenneth and Gergen, Mary M (1988) Narrative and the Self as Relationship, in L Berkowitz (ed) *Advances in Experimental Social Psychology*, no 21, pp17–56, Academic Press, San Diego, CA

Geser, Hans (1996) 'Auf dem Weg zur 'Cyberdemocracy'? Auswirkungen der Computernetze auf die oeffentliche politische Kommunikation' ('Towards 'Cyberdemocracy'? Effects of the Internet on Public Political Communication'), www.unizh.ch/~geserweb/komoef/ftezt.html

Global Public Policy 'Connecting Coalitions for Change, 2000', The United Nations and Global Public Policy Networks, www.globalpublicpolicy.net/UNandGPP.htm

Gotanco, Christopher (1999) 'Civil Society and Private Sector Partnership: A Philippine Experience', *Cooperation South* (UNDP), no 2, pp134–139, December

Gribben, Chris, Pinnington, Kate and Wilson, Andrew (2001) 'Government as Partners. The Role of Central Government in Developing New Social Partnerships. The Findings from Seven European Countries', The Copenhagen Centre & Ashridge Centre for Business and Society, Copenhagen

Guimico Dagron, Alfonso (2001) 'Making Waves. Stories of Participatory Communication for Social Change', a report to the Rockefeller Foundation, Rockefeller Foundation, New York

Habermas, Juergen (1984) *Theory of Communicative Action. 1: Reason and Rationalization of Society*, Beacon, Boston

Habermas, Juergen (1987) *Theory of Communicative Action. 2: System and Lifeworld*, Beacon, Boston

Hain, Peter (2001) *The End of Foreign Policy? British Interests, Global Linkages and Natural Limits*, The Fabian Society/Green Alliance/The Royal Institute of Foreign Affairs, London

Hambrick, Donald C (1994) 'Top Management Groups: A Conceptual Integration and Reconsideration of the 'Team' Label', *Research in Organizational Behaviour*, no16, pp171–213

Hare, A Paul (1976) *Handbook of Small Group Research* (2nd edn), The Free Press, New York

Hare, A Paul (1982) *Creativity in Small Groups*, Sage, Beverly Hills, CA

Hare, A Paul (1992) *Group, Teams and Social Interaction. Theories and Applications*, Praeger, New York, Westport, London

Hart, Paul, Stern, Eric, K and Sundelius, Bengt (eds) (1997) *Beyond Groupthink. Political Group Dynamics and Foreign Policy-making*, The University of Michigan Press, Ann Arbor

Haslam, S Alexander (2001) *Psychology in Organizations: The Social Identity Approach*, Sage, London

Heertz, Noreena (2001) *The Silent Takeover. Global Capitalism and the Death of Democracy*, Heinemann, London

Heinrich, D (1995) A UN Parliamentary Assembly in United Nations Reform in E Fawcett and H Newcombe (eds) *United Nations Reform. Looking Ahead After Fifty Years*, pp95–99, Canada Science for Peace, Toronto

Hemmati, Minu (2000a) Gender-Specific Patterns of Poverty and (Over-)Consumption in Developing and Developed Countries, in E Jochem, J Sathaye and D Biulle (eds) 'Society, Behaviour, and Climate Change Mitigation', proceedings of IPCC Expert Group Meeting on Social Scientific Approaches to Climate Change Mitigation, Kluwer, Dordrecht, Boston, London, pp169–190

Hemmati, Minu (2000b) 'Informal Networking: Barriers and Opportunities for Women', paper presented at the 2nd European Conference on Gender Equality in Higher Education, Zurich, September

Hemmati, Minu (2000c) 'Access and Benefit-Sharing: Relevant International Agreements and Issues for Dialogue Between Stakeholders', background paper for the UNED Forum and Novartis International panel discussion at the United Nations Commission on Sustainable Development 8th Session, 'Access and Benefit-Sharing: Building Equitable Partnerships Between Local Communities and International Corporations?', UNED Forum/Novartis International, London/Basel, www.unedforum.org/publi/abs/abs background.htm

Hemmati, Minu (2000d) 'Access and Benefit-Sharing: Building Equitable Partnerships Between Local Communities and International Corporations?', summary of the discussions at a UNED Forum and Novartis International AG panel discussion at the United Nations Commission on Sustainable Development 8th Session, www.unedforum.org/publi/abs/abs discussion.htm

Hemmati, Minu (2000e) Women and Sustainable Development: From 2000 to 2002, in F Dodds (ed) *Earth Summit 2002 – A New Deal*, Earthscan, London, pp65–83

Hemmati, Minu (2000f) Future Workshops – From Vision Into Action: Women's Role in City Planning in Heidelberg, Germany, in *Sustainable Cities Programme (UNEP/UNCHS): Integrating Gender Responsiveness in Environmental Planning and Management*, The Environmental Planning and Management Source Book Series, UNEP/Habitat, Nairobi, pp83–87

Hemmati, Minu (2001) 'Multi-Stakeholder Processes. A Methodological Framework', paper presented at the UNED Forum Workshop 'Examples, Principles, Strategies, New York, April, www.earthsummit2002.org/msp/workshop.htm

Hemmati, Minu, Wintermantel, Margaret and Paul, Markus (1999) Wie wirken ausländerfeindliche Ereignisse auf die Betroffenen? Empirische Untersuchungen kognitiver, emotionaler und handlungsbezogener Konsequenzen, in R Dollase et al (eds) *Politische Psychologie der Fremdenfeindlichkeit, Opfer – Taeter – Mittaeter* (What are the Impacts of Xenophobic Events on Foreigners? Empirical Studies of Cognitive, Emotional and Behavioural Consequences in R Dollase et al (eds) *Political Psychology of Xenophobia: Victims - Actors – Collaborators)* Juventa, Munich

Hill, John (TXU Europe) (2000) 'Stakeholders & Systems – Our Approach to Creating a More Sustainable Business', presentation at the WBCSD Conference 'Euro Environment 2000, Conference on Industry and Environmental Performance', Aalborg, Denmark, October

Hiltz, Starr R and Turoff, Murray (1993) *The Network Nation: Human Communication Via Computer*, MIT Press, Cambridge Mass

Hinsz, Verlin B, Tindale, R Scott and Vollrath, David A (1997) 'The Emerging Conceptualization of Groups as Information Processors', *Psychological Bulletin*, vol 121, no 1, pp43–64

Hofstede, Geert (1980) *Culture's Consequences: International Differences in Work-Related Values*, Sage, Beverly Hills, CA

Hofstede, Geert (1991) *Cultures and Organizations: Software of the Mind*, McGraw Hill, London

Hohnen, Paul (2000a) 'NGO Engagement: How Close is Too Close?', paper presented at the Conference on 'Challenges & Opportunities for Civil Society in the Emerging World Order', Valencia, Spain, 27–28 November

Hohnen, Paul (2000b) 'Global Reporting Initiative in 2010: A Vision', paper presented at the Global Reporting Initiative (GRI) Symposium, Washington, DC, 13–15 November

Hohnen, Paul (2000c) 'Greenpeace & the Financial Sector – The Possibility of Profitable Relationships Between Not-For-Profits and For-Profits', Greenpeace International, case study for the UN Vision Project on Global Public Policy Networks, www.globalpublicpolicy.net/CaseStudyAuthors.htm

Hohnen, Paul (2001) 'NGOs. Challenges and Opportunities', presentation to the UNEP Multi-stakeholder Workshop on 'UNEP Today and Tomorrow', Nairobi, 1–2 February

Hohnen, Paul (2001) 'Multi-Stakeholder Processes: Why, and Where Next?', paper presented at the UNED Forum Workshop 'Examples, Principles, Strategies', New York, April, www.earthsummit2002.org/msp/workshop.htm

Holliday, Chad and Pepper, John (2001) *Sustainability Through the Market. Seven Keys to Success*, World Business Council for Sustainable Development, Geneva

Horkheimer, Max and Adorno, Theodor W (1988) (orig 1944) *Dialektik der Aufklaerung (Dialectis of Enlightenment) Philosophische Fragemente*, Fischer, Frankfurt

Howell, Megan (1999) The NGO Steering Committee and Multi-Stakeholder Participation at the UN Commission on Sustainable Development, in Montreal International Forum (ed), *Civil Society Engaging Multilateral Institutions: At the Crossroads*, pp33–38, FIM, Montreal, Canada

Humphreys, Patrick C (1998) 'Discourses Underpinning Decision Support', in D Berkeley et al (eds) *Context Sensitive Decision Support Systems*, Chapman & Hall, London

Hussain, Saneeya (2001) 'The World Commission on Dams', paper presented at the UNED Forum Workshop 'Examples, Principles, Strategies', New York, April, www.earthsummit2002.org/msp/workshop.htm

Institute for Development Studies (IDS), Sussex, UK/Participation Group, 2000, 'Poverty Reduction Strategies: A Part for the Poor?', *IDS Policy Briefing Issue*, no 13, April

Institute of Social and Ethical Accountability/The Copenhagen Centre/Novo Nordisk A/S/Copenhagen Business School and The House of Mandag Morgen (1999) 'Building Stakeholder Relations', Third International Conference on Social and Ethical Accounting, Copenhagen, Denmark, 14–16 November

International Council for Local Environmental Initiatives (ICLEI in cooperation with UN DESA), (1997) Local Agenda 21 Survey: A Study of Responses by Local Authorities and Their National and International Associations to Agenda 21, in The Earth Council, *Rio+5. Implementing Sustainable Development*, summaries of Special Focus Reports prepared for the Rio+5 Forum, The Earth Council, San José, Costa Rica, pp35–37

Jackson, Susan E (1996) The Consequences of Diversity in Multidisciplinary Work Teams, in M West (ed) *Handbook of Work Group Psychology*, John Wiley & Sons, Chichester, NY

Janis, Irving (1972) *Victims of Groupthink*, Houghton Mifflin, Boston

Janis, Irving (1982) *Groupthink. Psychological Studies of Policy Decisions and Fiascos* (2nd edn), Houghton Mifflin, Boston

Juma, Calestous (2000) 'The UN's Role in the New Diplomacy', *Issues in Science and Technology*, vol XVII, no 1, pp37–38. United States National Academy of Sciences, www.nap.edu/issues/17.1/stalk.htm

Jungk, Robert and Muellert, Norbert (1989) *Zukunftswerkstaetten (Future Laboratories)*. Heyne, Munich

Kaul, Inge, Grunberg, Isabelle and Stern, Marc A (eds) (1999) *Global Public Goods. International Cooperation in the 21st Century*, Oxford University Press, New York, Oxford

Kaul, Inge (2000) Bereitstellung oeffentlicher Gueter als Ziel von Global Governance. Beitrag zu den Beratungen der Enquete-Kommission des Deutschen Bundestags 'Globalisierung der Weltwirtschaft' (Providing Global Public Goods as a Goal of Global Governance. Contribution to Consultations of the Commission 'Globalisation of the Global Economy' of the German Federal Parliament), www.bundestag.de/gremien/welt/weltfr2.html

Kelman, Herbert C (2000) 'The Components of a Principled Compromise', *The Boston Globe*, 18 July

Kerr, Elaine B and Hiltz, Starr R (1982) *Computer-Mediated Communication Systems: Status and Evaluation*, Academic Press, New York, London

Khagram, Sanjeev (2000) 'Beyond Temples and Tombs: Toward Effective Governance for Sustainable Development Through the World Commission on Dams', case study for the UN Vision Project on Global Public Policy Networks, www.globalpublicpolicy.net/CaseStudyAuthors.htm

Khor, Martin (1999) Civil Society Interaction with the WTO, in Montreal International Forum (ed) *Civil Society Engaging Multilateral Institutions: At the Crossroads*, FIM, Montreal, Canada, pp39–47

Khosla, Ashok (1999) 'Who Sets the Global Agenda?', paper prepared for the LEAD International Session, April, www.lead.org/lead/training/international/usa/1999/docs/papers/ashok.htm

Kiesler, Sarah, Siegel, Jane and McGuire, Timothy W (1988) 'Social Psychological Aspects of Computer-Mediated Communication' in I Greif (ed) *Computer-Supported Cooperative Work: A Book of Readings*, Morgan Kaufman, San Matei, CA

Kirchmeyer, Catherine and Cohen, Aaron (1992) 'Multicultural Groups: Their Performance and Reactions With Constructive Conflict', *Group and Organization Management* vol 17, no 2, pp153–170

Kjaer, Louise, Abrahamson, Peter and Raynard, Peter (2001) 'Local Partnerships in Europe. An Action Research Project', first phase summary report, The Copenhagen Centre, Copenhagen

Klein, Naomi (2000) *No Logo*, Flamingo, London

Knowledge Transform (2001) 'Frequently Asked Questions about Knowledge Management', www.ktransform.com/faq2.htm

Knox, Paul (1997) 'Environmental Issues Heating Up, Poll Shows', *The Globe and Mail*, 10 November

Kolb, Deborah M (1992) 'Women's Work: Peacemaking in Organizations' in D Kolb and J Bartunek (eds) *Hidden Conflicts in Organizations: Uncovering Behind-the-Scenes Disputes*, Newbury Park, CA

Krell, Georg and Ruggie, John (1999) 'Global Markets and Social Legitimacy: The Case of the "Global Compact"', paper presented at an international conference 'Governing the Public Domain Beyond the Era of the Washington Consensus? Redrawing the Line Between the State and the Market', York University, Toronto, Canada, 4–6 November

Kuepper, G (1994) 'Personalentwicklung für weibliche Führungskräfte? Verdeckte Barrieren beim beruflichen Aufstieg von Frauen – eine sekundär-analytische Studie', *Zeitschrift für Personalforschung* ('Career Development for Female Leaders? Hidden Barriers Towards Women's Careers – a Seconday Analysis, *Journal of Personnel Research*), no 8, pp107–123

Kunugi, Tasturo and Schweitz, Martha (eds) (1999) 'Codes of Conduct for Partnership in Governance: Texts and Commentaries', provisional version presented to the World Civil Society Conference 'Building Global Governance Partnerships', United Nations University, Montreal, Tokyo, 7–11 December

Lansdell, Suzannah (The Environment Council) (2000) '"Just Because You Can, Doesn't Mean You Should!" Responding to the Challenges of Business Sustainability Through Stakeholder Dialogue', presentation at the WBCSD 2000 Conference 'Euro Environment 2000, Conference on Industry & Environmental Performance', Aalborg, Denmark, October

Larson, James R and Christensen, Caryn (1993) 'Groups as Problem-Solving Units: Toward a New Meaning of Social Cognition', *British Journal of Social Psychology*, no 32, pp 5–30

Latane, Bibb, Williams, Kipling and Harkins, Stephen (1979) 'Many Hands Make Light the Work: The Causes and Consequences of Social Loafing', *Journal of Personality and Social Psychology*, no 37, pp822–832

Leadership for Environment and Development (LEAD) (2001) 'Reflections on International Institutions for Environment and Development', prepared by Lee A Kimball, LEAD, London

Lerner, Steve (1991) *Earth Summit. Conversations with Architects of Ecologically Sustainable Future*, published by Commonwealth and Friends of the Earth US, Common Knowledge Press, Blinas, CA

Lewin, Kurt (1958) 'Group Decision and Social Change', in E Maccoby, T Newcomb and E Hartley (eds) *Readings in Social Psychology*, Holt & Co, New York

Lintner, Stephen (2000) 'Corporate Citizenship in a Globalized Economy – the International Finance Corporation's Role in Promoting Sustainable Private Sector Investment', *Environment Matters*, pp16–21

Mackie, Diane M and Hamilton, DL (eds) (1993) *Affect, Cognition, and Stereotyping: Interactive Processes in Group Perception*, Academic Press, San Diego

Maier, Norman R F (1970) Leadership Principles for Problem Solving Conferences, in N Maier (ed) *Problem Solving and Creativity*, Brooks/Cole, Monterey, CA

Markowitz, Paul (2000) *Guide to Implementing Local Environmental Action Programs in Central and Eastern Europe*, Institute for Sustainable Communities, USA, and Regional Environmental Center for Central and Eastern Europe, Hungary

Markus, Hazel Rose and Kitayama, Shinobu (1991) 'Culture and the Self: Implications for Cognition, Emotion, and Motivation', *Psychological Review*, no 98, pp224–253

Martens, Jens (2000) Muehsamer Start zur UN-Finanzkonferenz (Cumbersome Start for the UN Financing for Development Conference) Forum Umwelt & Entwicklung Rundbrief, no 4, pp16–17, Projektstelle Umwelt & Entwicklung, Bonn

Maznevski, Martha FL (1994) 'Understanding Our Differences: Performance in Decision-Making Groups with Diverse Members', *Human Relations*, vol 47, no 5

McAlpine, Peter (2000) *A Vision of World Citizenship is Essential for the Effectiveness of Sustainable Development and Environmental Protection: A Wake-up Call for the World's Travel and Tourism Industry*, Mahodil University International College, Bangkok, Thailand

McCully, Patrick (2001) 'How to Use a Trilateral Network: An Activist's Perspective on the World Commission on Dams', paper prepared for Agrarian Studies Program Colloquium, Yale University, 19 January (Campaigns Director, International Rivers Network)

McGarty, Craig and Haslam, S. Alexander (eds) (1997) *The Message of Social Psychology*, Blackwell Publishers, Oxford

McGee, Rosemary and Norton, Andrew (2000) 'Participation in Poverty Reduction Strategies: A Synthesis of Experiences with Participatory Approaches to Policy Design, Implementation and Monitoring', IDS Working Paper no 109, Institute for Development Studies (IDS), Sussex, UK/Participation Group

McGrath, James E (1984) *Groups, Interaction and Performance*, Prentice-Hall, Englewood Cliffs, NJ

McLaughlin, Corinne (1996) 'The Multi-stakeholder Dialogue Approach to Consensus-building', www.visionarylead.org/multis.htm

Mensah, Chris (1996) 'The United Nations Commission on Sustainable Development' in J Werksman (ed) *Greening International Institutions*, Earthscan, London, pp21–37

Merriam-Webster's Collegiate Dictionary and Thesaurus (2001) www.m-w.com/cgi-bin/dictionary

Mining, Minerals, and Sustainable Development (MMSD) & International Institute for Environmental Development (IIED) (2001) Reports, draft reports, charters, calls, guidelines, etc. www.iied.org/mmsd

Moghaddam, Fathali M, Taylor, Donald M and Wright, Stephen C (1993) *Social Psychology in Cross-Cultural Perspective*, Freeman, New York

Mohiddin, Ahmed (1998) 'Partnership: A New Buzz-Word or Realistic Relationship?', *Journal of the Society for International Development*, vol 41, no 4, December, sidint.org/publications/development/vol41/no4/41-4b.htm

Montreal International Forum/Forum International Montreal (FIM) (1999) 'The Globalisation of Civil Society?' in Montreal International Forum (ed) *Civil Society Engaging Multilateral Institutions: At the Crossroads*, FIM, Montreal, Canada, pp5-7

Moreland, Richard L and Levine, Joseph M (1992) 'The Composition of Small Groups', *Advances in Group Processes*, no 9, pp237-280

Moscovici, Serge and Lage, Elisabeth (1976) 'Studies in Social Influence, III: Majority Versus Minority Influence in a Group', *European Journal of Social Psychology*, no 6, pp149-174

Moscovici, Serge and Zavalloni, Marisa (1969) 'The Group as a Polarizer of Attitudes', *Journal of Personality and Social Psychology*, no 12, pp125-135

Moscovici, Serge (1980) 'Toward a Theory of Conversion Behaviour' in L Berkowitz (ed) *Advances in Experimental Social Psychology*, no 13, Academic Press, New York, pp209-239

Mummendey, Amelie and Simon, Bernd (eds) (1997) *Identitaet und Verschiedenheit. Zur Sozialpsychologie der Identitaet in komplexen Gesellschaften (Identity and Difference: The Social Psychology of Identity in Complex Societies)*, Huber, Berne

Murphy, David F, Coleman, Gill (2000) 'Thinking Partners. Business, NGOs and the Partnership Concept' in J Bendell (ed) (2000a) *Terms for Endearment. Business, NGOs and Sustainable Development*, Greenleaf, Sheffield, UK, pp207-215

National Spiritual Assembly of the Baha'is of the United States (1994) 'Unity and Consultation: Foundations of Sustainable Development', www.bcca.org/~glittle/docs/unity.html

National Spiritual Assembly of the Baha'ís of South Africa (1997) 'Statement to the Truth and Reconciliation Commission', www.bahai.org/article-1-9-1-7.html

Nelson, Jane and Zadek, Simon (2001) *Partnership Alchemy. New Social Partnerships in Europe*, The Copenhagen Centre, Copenhagen

Nemeth, Charlan J and Staw, Barry M (1989) 'The Tradeoffs of Social Control and Innovation in Groups and Organizations', *Advances in Experimental Social Psychology*, no 22, pp175-210

Neuberger, Oswald (1981) *Miteinander arbeiten - miteinander reden! (Working Together - Talking to Each Other!)*, Bayerisches Staatministerium für Arbeit und Sozialordnung, Munich

Neuberger, Oswald (1985) *Individuelles Handeln und sozialer Einfluß. Eine problemorientierte Einführung in die Sozialpsychologie, (Individual Behaviour and Social Influence. A Problem-Oriented Introduction)* Westdeutscher Verlag, Opladen

Neuberger, Oswald (1990) *Führen und geführt werden (Leading and Being Led)* Enke, Stuttgart

Neuberger, Oswald (1991) Symbolisierung in Organisationen (Symbolisation in Organisations), in Kastner, M and Gerstenberg, B (Hrsgn) *Denken und Handeln in Systemen*, Quintessenz, Munich, pp163–170

Neuberger, Oswald (1995a) Die Probleme selbst in die Hand nehmen. Möglichkeiten der Beratung in einem eskalierten Konflikt (Taking the Problems in Your Own Hands. Options of Consultation in an Escalated Conflict), in Volmerg, B, Leithäuser, Th, Neuberger, O, Ortmann, G and Sievers, B (Hrsgn) *Nach allen Regeln der Kunst*, Kore, Freiberg, pp270–314

Neuberger, Oswald (1995b) *Mikropolitik. Der alltägliche Aufbau und Einsatz von Macht in Organisationen, (Micro-Politics. Every-Day Building and Use of Power in Organisations)* Enke, Stuttgart

Neuberger, Oswald (1996) Gaukler, Hofnarren und Komödianten. Rückwärtsgewandte Überlegungen zur Gegenwart des Vergangenen im Rollenverständnis von PersonalentwicklerInnen (Jesters and Comedians. Backward-Looking Considerations on the Presence of the Past in the Self-Understanding of Personnel Developers), in Sattelberger, T (Hrsgn) (1996) *Human Resource Management im Umbruch*, Gabler, Wiesbaden, pp157–184

New Economic Foundation/Centre for Participation (2000) 'Tools for Participation', NEF, London

New Webster's Illustrated Dictionary & Thesaurus (1992) Ferguson, Chicago

Novartis Germany (2000) 'Drittes Novartis Forum, Biotechnologie und Nachhaltige Landwirtschaft', Third Novartis Forum (Biotechnology and Sustainable Agriculture) in innovartis, no 1

Ohmae, Kenichi (1990) *The Borderless World*, Harper Business, New York

Olsson, Micael (2001) Multi-Stakeholder Processes Used at Education Development Center's Multichannel Learning Center, personal communication, 7 March

Organisation for Economic Co-operation and Development (OECD) (2000) 'Genetically Modified Foods. Widening the Debate on Health and Safety', The OECD Edinburgh Conference on the Scientific and Health Aspects of Genetically Modified Foods. OECD Consultation with Non-Governmental Organizations on Biotechnology and Other Aspects of Food Safety, 1999, Paris, France

Organisation for Economic Co-operation and Development (OECD) (2000) 'The OECD Guidelines for Multinational Enterprises', OECD, Paris, www.oecd.org/daf/investment/guidelines/mnetext.htm

Organisation for Economic Co-operation and Development (OECD) (2001) 'Strategies for Sustainable Development', statement by the DAC high-level meeting upon endorsement of the 'Strategies for Sustainable Development: Practical Guidance for Development Co-operation', www.nnsd.net

Organisation for Economic Co-operation and Development/Development Assistance Committee (OECD/DAC) (2001), 'Strategies for Sustainable Development: Practical Guidance for Development Cooperation', note by Secretariat, submitted for REVIEW and APPROVAL at the DAC meeting, 3 April, DCD/DAC (2001) www.nnsd.net

Osborn, Derek and Bigg, Tom (eds) (1997) *Earth Summit II. Outcome and Analysis*, Earthscan, London

Oudenhoven, Jan Pieter van and Willemsen, Tineke M (eds) (1989) *Ethnic Minorities. Social Psychological Perspectives*, Swets & Zeitlinger, Amsterdam

Parks, Craig D and Sanna, Lawrence J (1999) *Group Performance and Interaction*, Westview Press, Boulder, Oxford

Patel, Sheela (2000) 'When Can Communities Begin to Drive Development Really?', presentation made in Prague at the World Bank Meeting on Community Driven Development, 22 September

Pavitt, Charles (1993) 'What (Little) We Know About Formal Group Discussion Procedures. A Review of Relevant Research', *Small Group Research*, no 24, pp 217–235

Pentikäinen, Antti (2000) 'Creating Global Governance.The Role of Non-Governmental Organizations in the United Nations', Finnish UN Association, Helsinki

People First, (2000) 'Universal Charter of Good Governance. For Global Sustainability', June, www.peoplefirstindia.org/5universial.htm

People First (2001) 'Democracy for Sustainability. The Earth Charter Initiative/ Resource Material', www.peoplefirstindia.org

Petkova, Elena and Veit, Peter (2000) 'Environmental Accountability Beyond the Nation-State: The Implications of the Aarhus Convention', World Resources Institute, Institutions and Governance Program, *Environmental Governance Notes*, April

Pettigrew, Thomas (1989) 'Intergroup Contact Theory', *Annual Reviews of Psychology*, no 49, pp65–85

Phillips, Gerald M and Wood, Julia T. (eds) (1984) *Emergent Issues in Human Decision-making*, Southern Illinois University Press, Carbondale

Presas, Teresa (Tetra Pak) (2000) 'Interdependence and Partnership'?, presentation at the WBCSD 2000 Conference 'Euro Environment 2000, Conference on Industry and Environmental Performance', Aalborg, Denmark, October

Prince of Wales Business Leaders Forum (1996) 'Learning From Experience Programme: Final Report and Outcomes', PWBLF, London

Purcell, Randall (2000) (draft) 'Good Practice in Global and Regional Programs. Resource Mobilization and Cofinancing', The World Bank Development Grant Facility (DGF), Washington

Regelbrugge, Laurie (ed) (1999) 'Promoting Corporate Citizenship: Opportunities for Business and Civil Society Engagement', CIVICUS/World Alliance for Citizen Participation, Washington

Reinicke, Wolfgang and Deng, Francis, with Witte, Jan Martin, Benner, Thorsten, Withaker, Beth and Gershman, John (2000) *Critical Choices – The United Nations, Networks & the Future of Global Governance*, IDRC, Ottawa

Reinicke, Wolfgang (2000) 'The GRI in 2010 – A Global Public Policy Perspective', paper presented at the Global reporting Initiative (GRI) 2nd Symposium, Washington, DC, November, http://globalreporting.org/Events/November 2000/Proceedings/ReinickeDay3.pdf

Renn, Ortwin, Webler, Thomas and Wiedemann, Peter (eds) (1995) *Fairness and Competence in Citizen Participation. Evaluating Models for Environmental Discourse*, Kluwer, Dordrecht, Boston, London

Richman, Roger et al (1986) *Intergovernmental Mediation. Negotiations in Local Government Disputes*, Westview Press, Boulder, London

Ridgeway, Cecilia L (1987) 'Nonverbal Behaviour, Dominance, and the Basis of Status in Task Groups', *American Sociological Review*, vol 52, no 2, pp682–694

Ropers, Norbert and Schlotter, Peter (1993) 'Multilateral Conflict Management in a Transforming World Order. Future Perspectives and New Impulses for Regional Peace Strategies', Foundation Development and Peace, Bonn, in cooperation with the Institute for Development and Peace of the University-GH-Duesburg, SEF, Bonn

Rukato, Hesphina and Osborn, Derek (2001) 'Count Us In. Count On Us', Co-chair's Summary, 'UNED Forum. Multi-stakeholder Processes: Examples, Principles, Strategies', International Workshop, New York, 28–29 April, Workshop report, prepared by Jasmin Enayati and Minu Hemmati, www. earthsummit2002.org/msp/workshop.htm

Rustemeyer, Regina (1988) 'Geschlechtsstereotype und ihre Auswirkungen auf das Sozial- und Leistungsverhalten' ('Gender stereotypes and their effects on social and competitive behaviour'), *Zeitschrift für Sozialisationsforschung und Erziehungssoziologie*, no 8, pp115–129

Sampson, Edward E (1993) *Celebrating the Other. A Dialogic Account of Human Nature*, Harvester Wheatsheaf, New York

Schmackpfeffer, Ralf and Bork, Jette (KPMG Deutsche Treuhand Gesellschaft) (2000) 'Sustainability Management. A Key to Successful Management', presentation at the WBCSD 2000 Conference 'Euro Environment 2000, Conference on Industry and Environmental Performance,' Aalborg, Denmark, October

Seibold, David R (1999) 'The Impact of Formal Procedures on Group Processes, Members, and Task Outcomes' in L Frey (ed) *The Handbook of Group Communication Theory and Research*, Sage, Thousand Oaks, CA

Seiter, Andreas (1999) 'Industry's Role In Public Policy Networking – A European View', paper presented at the Global Public Policy Project Workshop, Washington, DC, November

Seiter, Andreas (2001) 'Bio-Society Issues and Related Processes', paper presented at the UNED Forum Workshop 'Examples, Principles, Strategies', New York, April www.earthsummit2002.org/msp/workshop.htm

Sharman, James (1999) Message, 20 May, CDF (Comprehensive Development Framework), email list server. A discussion forum sponsored by the World Bank

Shaw, Marvin E (1981) *Group Dynamics: The Psychology of Small Group Behaviour*, McGraw-Hill, New York

Shell Report (2000) www.shell.com/royal-en/content

Sherif, Muzafer and Sherif, Carolin W (1953) *Groups in Harmony and Tension*, Harper, New York

Sherman, Richard (2001) 'You Have Been Consulted! Climate Change Multi-Stakeholder Processes', paper presented at the UNED Forum Workshop 'Examples, Principles, Strategies', New York, April, www.earthsummit2002. org/msp/workshop.htm

Simon, Bernd (1993) 'On the Asymmetry in the Cognitive Construal of Ingroup and Outgroup: A Model of Egocentric Social Categorization', *European Journal of Social Psychology*, no 23, pp131–147

Smadja, Claude (2001) 'The Dangers of a Divided World: With Slower Economic Growth in Sight, the Need for Effective Global Governance Has Never Been More Pressing', *Financial Times*, 25 January

Smith, Eliot and Mackie, Diane M (1995) *Social Psychology*, Norton, New York

Smith, Eliot R and Mackie, Diane M (2000) *Social Psychology* (2nd edn), Psychology Press, Sussex, Philadelphia

Smith, Peter B and Noakes, Julia (1996) Cultural Differences in Group Processes, in M West (ed) *Handbook of Work Group Psychology*, John Wiley & Sons, Chichester, New York

Soerensen, Preben J (2001) 'Governance and Partnership – with Business Towards Sustainability', *Sustainable Development International. Strategies and Technologies for Agenda 21 Implementation,* no 4, pp37–39

Sommer, J (1987) 'Dialogische Forschungsmethoden' (Dialogical Research Methods), Weinheim

South Centre (1996) *For a Strong and Democratic United Nations. A Southern Perspective on UN Reform*, South Centre, Geneva, Switzerland

Sproull, Lee and Kiesler, Sara (1993) 'Computers, Networks and Work' in L Harasim (ed) *Global Networks. Computers and International Communication*, MIT Press, Cambridge, MA

Starbuck, William H (1983) 'Organisations As Action Generators', *American Sociological Review*, no 48, pp91–102

Strandenaes, Jan-Gustav (2000) 'A Review With the Aim to Involve Major Groups in the Works of UNEP to help Promote the Environment Agenda, Relevant Environmental Conventions, a Global Environment Compact and to Further the Involvement of UNEP in the Rio+10 Process for 2002 and Beyond', unpublished manuscript

Streck, Charlotte (2000) 'The Network Structure of the Global Environment Facility (GEF)', case study for the UN Vision Project on Global Public Policy Networks, www.globalpublicpolicy.net/CaseStudyAuthors.htm

Stroebe, Wolfgang, Kruglanski, Arie W, Bar-Tal, Daniel and Hewstone, Miles (eds) (1988) *The Social Psychology of Intergroup Conflict, Theory, Research and Applications*, Springer, Berlin

Strong, Maurice (1999) 'Global Governance for Sustainability', prepared for presentation at the LEAD International Session, April, www.lead.org/lead/training/international/usa/1999/docs/papers/global.htm

Swiss State Secretariat for Economic Affairs, Swiss Federal Institute of Intellectual Property and Swiss Agency for the Environment, Forests and Landscape (2000), 'Draft Guidelines on Access and Benefit Sharing Regarding the Utilisation of Genetic Resources', paper submitted to the 5th Conference of the Parties to the Convention on Biological Diversity, 15–26 May

Tajfel, Henri and Turner, John C (1979) 'An Integrative Theory of Intergroup Conflict', in W Austin, and S Worchel (eds) *The Social Psychology of Intergroup Relations*, Brooks/Cole, Monterey, CA

Tannen, Deborah (1998) *The Argument Culture. Changing the Way We Argue*, Virago, London

Taylor, Marilyn (1995) *Unleashing the Potential*, Joseph Rowntree Foundation, York

'The Copenhagen Charter, A Management Guide to Stakeholder Reporting', published by the House of Mandag Morgen (1999), www.stakeholder.dk/download/thecopenhagencharter.pdf

The Earth Council (1997) 'Rio+5. Implementing Sustainable Development', summaries of Special Focus reports prepared for the Rio+5 Forum, San José, Costa Rica

The Earth Council (2000) 'Multi-Stakeholder Paths to Peace', www.ecouncil.ac.cr (Developing Ideas Digest)

The Environment Council/Case Study Series, 'Stakeholder Dialogue in Action' (1998), The Environment Council, London

The Environment Council (1999) 'Clarification on GMO Stakeholder Dialogue', press release. www.the-environment-council.org.uk

The Environment Council 'Beyond the Twilight Zone. Defining and Managing Key Survival Issues for Corporate Environmental Sustainability', Steve Robinson, London

The Environment Council (2001) 'Environmental Resolve', an environmental mediation service in the UK, www.the-environment-council.org.uk/er.htm

The Green Alliance (1997) 'How Can Biotechnology Benefit the Environment?', report of A European Federation of Biotechnology Task Group on Public Perceptions of Biotechnology/The Green Alliance Workshop, 13 January, London/Amsterdam

The International NGO Training and Research Centre (INTRAC), 'Strengthening NGOs for the 21st Century', Oxford, UK

The Royal Institute of International Affairs/Energy and Environmental Programme (2000) 'Global Environmental Institutions. Analysis and Options for Change', report prepared for Department of the Environment, Transport and the Regions (UK) by Joy Hyvarinen, Associate Fellow, and Duncan Brack, Head of Programme

The World Bank/Global Environment Facility (GEF)/Country Dialogue Workshops Program (2000) Status on the GEF Country Dialogue Workshops Programme, October, briefing note

The World Bank/Poverty Group/Poverty Reduction and Economic Management Network (1999) 'Consultations with the Poor: Methodology Guide for the 20 Country Study for the World Development Report 2000/01', February, www.worldbank.org/wbp/voices/reports/method/method.pdf

The World Bank/Social Development Department/NGO and Civil Society Unit (2000) 'Consultations With Civil Society Organisations, General Guidelines for World Bank Staff', www.worldbank.org/ngos

The World Bank (1998) 'Working With Us', Consultative Meeting with NGOs and Civil Society, I. Introductions/Welcome and Introductions of Resource People, II. Equitable, Sustainable, and Effective Partnership, May, www.world bank.org/ngos

The World Bank (2000) 'World Development Report 2000/2001: Attacking Poverty', WB, Washington

The World Commission on Dams (2000) *Dams and Development. A New Framework for Decision-Making*, Earthscan, London

The World Commission on Dams (2001) Work programme, meeting reports, press releases, www.dams.org

Triandis, Harry C (1989) 'The Self and Social Behaviour in Different Cultural Contexts', *Psychological Review*, no 96, pp506–520

Triandis, Harry C (1995) *Individualism and Collectivism*, Westview Press, Boulder, San Francisco, Oxford

Triandis, Harry C, Hall, E R and Ewen, Robert B (1965) 'Member Heterogeneity and Dyadic Creativity', *Human Relations*, no 18, pp33–55

Tubiana, Laurence (2001) 'Peut-on Organiser la Mondialisation de la Planète?', *Le Monde Economie*, 22 January

Turkle, S (1995) *Life on the Screen*, Simon & Schuster, New York

Turner, John C et al (eds) (1987) *Rediscovering the Social Group: A Self-Categorization Theory*, Blackwell, Oxford

UK Coalition Against Poverty (UKCAP)/UK Commission on Poverty, Participation and Power (2000) 'Listen Hear – The Right to be Heard', UKCAP, London

UK Government Department for Environment, Transport and the Regions (DETR) (2000) 'Achieving a Better Quality of Life: Review of Progress Towards Sustainable Development. Government Annual Report 2000', The Stationery Office, January

United Nations Economic Commission for Europe (UNECE) (2001) 'Introducing the Aarhus Convention', www.unece.org/env/pp

UNED Forum (2000) Dialogue Sessions: 'Water for Basic Needs. Energy for a Sustainable Future', 8th Informal Environment Ministers Meeting, Bergen, Norway, September, edited by Danielle Morley, UNED Forum, London

UNED Forum (2000) 'Global Internet Connectivity. Status, Indicators, and Use in Developing and Developed Countries', by Markus Paul, UNED Forum, London www.unedforum.org/publi/connectivity/connreport.htm

UNED Forum (2000) 'History of the Dialogues at the UN Commission for Sustainable Development (CSD)', www.unedforum.org/publi/dialoguehistory.pdf

UNED Forum (2001) 'Multi-Stakeholder Processes: Examples, Principles, Strategies', International Workshop, New York, 28–29 April. Workshop report by Jasmin Enayati and Minu Hemmati, www.earthsummit2002.org/msp/workshop.htm

UNED-UK and Novartis (1999) 'Bio-Prospecting and Benefit Sharing', report of a UNED-UK/Novartis Workshop, hosted by the Rockefeller Foundation, New York, April 22, edited by Minu Hemmati, Rosalie Gardiner, Dieter Brauer and Andreas Seiter, UNED-UK/Novartis, London, Basel

UNEP Task Force on Environment and Human Settlements (1998) Task Force Report, United Nations, Nairobi

UNEP Mediterranean Action Plan (2001) The Mediterranean Commission on Sustainable Development (MCSD), UNEP/MAP, Athens, Greece www.unepmap.org

United Nations/Financing for Development (FfD) (2000) Civil Society Hearings, www.un.org/esa/ffd/NGO/1100hear/panel_list1.htm

United Nations/Financing for Development (FfD) (2000) Private Sector Hearings, www.un.org/esa/ffd/1200hear/panel_list2.htm

United Nations Commission on Human Rights/Sub-Commission on the Promotion and Protection of Human Rights (2000) Intellectual Property Rights and Human Rights, 52nd Session, Agenda item 4, The Realization of Economic, Social and Cultural Rights, E/CN.4/Sub.2/2000/7

United Nations Commission on the Status of Women Acting as the Preparatory Committee for the Special Session of the General Assembly Entitled 'Women 2000: Gender Equality, Development and Peace for the Twenty-First Century'. Third Session, 3–17 March 2000. Summary of the WomenWatch Online Working Groups on the 12 Critical Areas of Concern of the Beijing Platform for Action. Note by the Secretary-General. Item 2 of the Provisional Agenda, United Nations, New York

United Nations Department of Economic and Social Affairs (DESA)/NGO Section (2001) Guidelines. Association Between the United Nations and Non-Governmental Organizations (NGOs), www.un.org/esa/coordination/ngo/pdf/guidelines.pdf

United Nations Department on Economic and Social Affairs/Division for Sustainable Development (2001) Multi-Stakeholder Dialogue Segments, www.un.org/esa/sustdev

United Nations Department on Economic and Social Affairs/Division for Sustainable Development/CSD Secretariat and the Consensus Building Institute (2001) Analytic Study of the CSD's Experience with the Multi-stakeholder Dialogues. Project Information, www.johannesburgsummit.org/web_pages/study_of_multi-stakeholder_dialogue.htm

United Nations Development Programme (UNDP) Civil Society Organizations and Participation Programme (CSOPP) (2000) 'Empowering People – A Guide to Participation', www.undp.org/csopp/CSO/NewFiles/documents.html

United Nations Development Programme (1996) 'Governance for Sustainable Human Development', UNDP, New York

United Nations Development Programme (1997) 'Governance for Sustainable Growth and Equity', report of an International Conference held at the United Nations, New York, 28–30 July, UNDP, New York

United Nations Development Programme (1999) 'Human Development Report', UNDP, New York

United Nations Economic and Social Council (1993) Resolution 1993/207, United Nations, New York

United Nations Economic Commission for Europe (2000) 'The Aarhus Convention. An Implementation Guide', United Nations, New York and Geneva

United Nations Environment Programme/The Prince of Wales Business Leaders Forum/Tufts University, Boston (1994) 'Partnerships For Sustainable Development. The Role of Business and Industry', PWBLF, London

United Nations Environment Programme/Task Force on Environment and Human Settlements (1998) United Nations, Nairobi

United Nations Environment Programme (1975/1995) 'Mediterranean Action Plan', adopted in 1975, revised in 1995, www.unepmap.org

United Nations Environment Programme (2001) Mediterranean Action Plan, ongoing work at www.unepmap.org

United Nations Environment Programme (2001) Draft Decision on International Environmental Governance Presented By the President of the Governing Council, Agenda Item 4(d), UNEP Governing Council

United Nations General Assembly (2000) The Millennium Declaration, UN, New York

United Nations Research Institute for Social Development (2000) 'What Choices Do Democracies Have in Globalizing Economies? Technocratic Policy Making and Democratization', report of the UNRISD International Conference, 27–28 April, Geneva

United Nations Secretary General Report (14 July 1997) 'Renewing the United Nations: A Programme for Reform', UN General Assembly Fifty-first session,

Agenda item 168, United Nations Reform: Measures and Proposals, United Nations Reform

United Nations Secretary-General Report (1999) Views of Member States, Members of the Specialized Agencies, Observers, Intergovernmental and Non-Governmental Organizations From All Regions On the Report of the Secretary-General on Arrangements and Practices For the Interaction of Non-Governmental Organizations in All Activities of the United Nations System. General Assembly Fifty-fourth session, Agenda item 59, Strengthening of the United Nations System

United Nations Secretary General Report (24 February 2000) 'Development of Guidelines on the Role and Social Responsibilities of the Private Sector', report to the Preparatory Committee for the Special Session of the General Assembly Entitled 'World Summit for Social Development and Beyond: Achieving Social Development for All in a Globalizing World', 2nd Session, A/AC.253/21

United Nations Secretary-General (2000) Guidelines on Cooperation between the United Nations and the Business Community, A/AC.253/21, www.un.org/partners/business/guide.htm

United Nations Secretary-General Report (14 March 2001) Major Groups. Report to the Commission on Sustainable Development Acting as the Preparatory Committee for the World Summit on Sustainable Development, organizational session, 30 April–2 May, E/CN.17/2001/PC/4

United Nations (1999) 'The UN Global Compact', www.unglobalcompact.org

United Nations (1992) Report of the United Nations Conference on Environment and Development: Agenda 21/Rio Declaration, 3–14 June, Rio de Janeiro

United States Federal Environment Protection Agency (1998) EPA Stakeholder Involvement Action Plan

Vaeyrynen, Raimo (ed) (1991) *New Directions in Conflict Theory. Conflict Resolution and Conflict Transformation*, Sage, London

Vary, Anna, Vecsenyi, Janos and Paprika, Zita, 'Argumatics: Representations and Facilitation of Decision-Making Negotiations', unpublished manuscript

Wagner, Ulrich (1994) *Eine sozialpsychologische Analyse von Intergruppenbeziehungen (A Social Psychological Analysis of Inter-Group Relations)*, Hogrefe, Göttingen

Wagner, Ulrich (2000) Intergruppenverhalten in Organisationen: Ein vernachlaessigter Aspekt bei der Zusammenarbeit in Projektgruppen (Inter-group Behaviour in Organizations: A Neglected Aspect of Cooperation in Project Groups), in R Fisch, Rudolf, D Beck and B Englich (eds) *Gruppen in Organisationen: Zusammenarbeit in Projektgruppen*, Verlag fuer Angewandte Psychologie, Göttingen

Watzlawick, Paul, Beavin, J H and Jackson, D (1967) *Pragmatics Of Human Communication*, Norton, New York

Webler, Thomas and Renn, Ortwin (1995) 'A Brief Primer on Participation: Philosophy and Practice' in O Renn, T Webler and P Wiedemann (eds) *Fairness and Competence in Citizen Participation. Evaluating Models for Environmental Discourse*, Kluwer, Dordrecht, Boston, London, pp17–33

Webler, Thomas (1995) 'Right' Discourse in Citizen Participation: An Evaluative Yardstick, in O Renn, T Webler and P Wiedemann (eds) *Fairness and Competence in Citizen Participation. Evaluating Models for Environmental Discourse*, Kluwer, Dordrecht, Boston, London, pp35–77

Wennberg, Ulrika (Global Responsibility Scandinavia) (2000) 'Global Responsibility. Bridging the Gap and Making New Links', presentation at the WBCSD 2000 Conference 'Euro Environment 2000, Conference on Industry & Environmental Performance', Aalborg, Denmark, October

Werksman, Jacob (1996) *Greening International Institutions*, Earthscan, London

Wetherall, Margaret S (1987) 'Social Identity and Group Polarization' in J Turner (ed) *Rediscovering the Social Group: A Self-Categorization Theory*, Blackwell, London

Wheelan, Susan A (1994) *Group Processes. A Developmental Perspective*, Allyn & Bacon, Boston, MA

Whiffen, Paul (2000) 'Techniques for Capturing Learning in Tearfund', draft, Tearfund, London

White, Sam E, Dittrich, John E and Lang, James R (1980) 'The Effects of Group Decision-Making Process and Problem-Situation Complexity on Implementation Attempts', *Administrative Science Quarterly*, no 25, pp428–440

Wiener, Daniel (2001) Urbane Visionen (Urban Visions), unpublished manuscript, ecos.ch ag, Basel

Wiener, Daniel and Rihm, Isabelle (2000) '30 Erfolgsfaktoren einer Lokalen Agenda 21 und aehnlichen partizipativen Prozessen' (30 Success Factors of Local Agenda 21 and Similar Participatory Processes), unpublished manuscript, ecos.ch ag, Basel

Willetts, Peter (1999) 'The Rules of the Game: The United Nations and Civil Society', in *Whose World is it Anyway*, United Nations Association of Canada, Ottawa, Canada

Wintermantel, Margaret (1993) Schoene Aussichten: Frauen an der Universitaet (Good Prospects: Women at University) in E Labouvie (ed) *Frauenleben – Frauen leben. Zur Geschichte und Gegenwart weiblicher Lebenswelten im Saarraum*, Roehrig, St Ingbert

Wissler, Dieter (2000) 'Public-Private Partnerships', statement at the World Bank Forum, Berlin, Germany, 27 November

Witte, Jan Martin and Benner, Thorsten (2001) 'Innovation in Governance. The Role of Global Public Policy Networks', paper presented at the UNED Forum Workshop 'Examples, Principles, Strategies', New York, April, www.earth summit2002.org/msp/workshop.htm

Women's Environment and Development Organization (WEDO) (2000) 'Engendering Local Agenda 21', Workshop Report, July, WEDO, New York

WomenWatch/United Nations Gateway for the Advancement of Women (2000) Beijing+5 Global Forum. Online Discussions on the 12 Critical Areas of Concern of the Beijing Platform for Action, archive, www.womenwatch.org/forum

World Business Council for Sustainable Development (WBCSD) (2000) 'The Global Mining Initiative', www.globalmining.com/index.asp

World Business Council for Sustainable Development (2000) 'Designing Better Governance. An Issue in Dialogue', Geneva, Switzerland

World Humanity Action Trust (2000) 'Governance for a Sustainable Future', reports of the Commissions of the World Humanity Action Trust, London, UK

World Resources Institute/Environmental Management and Law Association/PARTICIPA/Thailand Environment Institute (2001) 'The Access Initiative. An

Initiative to Promote Public Access to Environmental Decision-Making',
www.wri.org/governance/accessinit.html

World Resources Institute/Lawyers' Environmental Action Team/Lokayan (2001)
'An Independent Assessment of the World Commission on Dams', preliminary
findings, www.wcdassessment.org

Young, S and Church, C (2000) 'LA21 – The Future of Local Agenda 21 after
the Local Government Act', University of Manchester EPRU Paper 1/100

Notes

CHAPTER 1

1 *The Environment Council, UK:* 'Stakeholder – in the wider sense of the word 'stakeholder' refers to people who have an interest in a particular decision, either as individuals or representatives of a group'.

The United Nations on companies' stakeholders: 'Stakeholders [of the private sector] can be identified as those individuals of groups that have an interest, or take an interest, in the behaviour of a company both within and without the normal mode of operation. They therefore establish what the social responsibility of the company entails, or, at least, how they perceive it to be' (UN Secretary General, 2000).

The World Business Council on Sustainable Development: 'The broadest definition of 'stakeholder' brings in anyone who affects or is affected by a company's operations. The key new perception is that companies need to expand the range of interests considered in any new development from customers, shareholders, management and employees to such people as suppliers, local communities and pressure groups' (www.wbcsd.ch/aboutdfn.htm).

2 Agenda 21/Section III. Strengthening the Role of Major Groups/Chapter 23, Preamble:

'23.1. Critical to the effective implementation of the objectives, policies and mechanisms agreed to by Governments in all programme areas of Agenda 21 will be the commitment and genuine involvement of all social groups.

23.2. One of the fundamental prerequisites for the achievement of sustainable development is broad public participation in decision-making. Furthermore, in the more specific context of environment and development, the need for new forms of participation has emerged. This includes the need of individuals, groups and organizations to participate in environmental impact assessment procedures and to know about and participate in decisions, particularly those which potentially affect the communities in which they live and work. Individuals, groups and organizations should have access to information relevant to environment and development held by national authorities, including information on products and activities that have or are likely to have a significant impact on the environment, and information on environmental protection measures.'

3 A second worldwide survey is under way as a joint project of ICLEI, Capacity 21/UNDP and the UN Department of Social and Economic Affairs. The results should be available by December 2001.

4   Concluding her observations, she says: 'It is sometimes difficult to tell whether these trends are the start of something genuinely new or the last gasps of something very old. Are they, as the engineering professor and peace activist Ursula Franklin asked me, simply "wind blocks", creating temporary shelter from the corporate storm, or are they the foundation stones of some as yet unimagined, free-standing edifice? When I started this book, I honestly didn't know whether I was covering marginal atomized scenes of resistance or the birth of a potentially broad-based movement. But as time went on, what I clearly saw was a movement forming before my eyes' (p443). Klein describes the movement's agenda as 'one that embraces globalization but seeks to wrest it from the grasp of the multi-nationals' (p445), 'demanding a citizen-centred alternative to the international rule of the brands' (p446).

5   See Tannen (1998), Chapters 7 (pp215–243) and 9 (pp263–298).

6   Bahá'í International Community (2001). 'Sustainable Development the Spiritual Dimension', a statement by the Bahá'í International Community to the first session of the Preparatory Committee of the World Summit on Sustainable Development, 30 April–2 May New York.

7   Webler (1995, p38) distinguishes between ethical-normative and functional-analytic approaches. We call the first 'value-based' and the latter 'pragmatic'.

8   Reinicke et al exemplify this when they say: 'Effectiveness and efficiency cannot be the only yardsticks in designing new governance mechanisms; legitimacy and inclusion are equally important, not only in terms of a *Weltanschauung*, but also from a strategic and political perspective' (Reinicke et al, 2000, p23).

C<small>HAPTER</small> 2

1   Note that the definition refers to *perceived* incompatibility. One outcome of an MSP can be discovering that people's perceptions of one another and of each other's interests are inaccurate. Dietz (2001) outlines the following factors that make environmental problems especially contentious: a muddling of facts and values; facts that are uncertain; values that are unformed; changes that are concrete and permanent; harm to innocents and inequities; confusion of boundaries between the public and the private; a confusion of competences.

2   www.socialwatch.org

3   For a critical discussion of the trisectoral approach, see Chapter 3.

C<small>HAPTER</small> 3

1   Non-governmental organizations here mean all stakeholder groups that the United Nations recognizes as NGOs: trade unions, local authorities, not-for-profit organizations, women, youth, academics and other stakeholders.

2   This point was made clearly in a recent article by a leading French official, Laurence Tubiana (2001).

3 'Civil society' can be 'defined as the realm of social activity and organisations falling outside the spheres of government and business; (o)r defined as all sectors and activities falling outside the public sector, and thus embracing the work of business, voluntary and community organisations, trade unions, faiths, professional bodies and consumer organisations' (World Humanity Action Trust, 2000, p35).

CHAPTER 4

1 Such structuring is simplistic; we use it primarily for the purposes of presentation. Different structuring has been suggested, for example, by Webler (1995, p38) who asserts that normative-ethical and functional-analytic arguments fall under the meta-criteria of fairness and competence.

2 Governance is 'the strategic guidance of a particular organisation, set of organisational relationships or network of governmental and other institutions; governance is thus distant from the work of governments; it is a process of strategic oversight of organisations and of the implementation of their goals; governance of resource management systems refers to the legal and other institutional arrangements for setting the broad policies which regulate the use of resources' (World Humanity Action Trust, 2000, p36).

'There is a shift taking place in our understanding and practice of governance. Governance used to be principally about what governments do. Today, the concept is increasingly about balancing the roles, responsibilities, accountabilities and capabilities of: different levels of governments – local, national, regional and global; and different actors or sectors in society – public, private and civil society organisations and individual citizens. Governance can be defined as the framework through which political, economic, social and administrative authority is exercised at local, national and international levels. In today's world this framework consists of a wide variety of mechanisms, processes, institutions and relationships (including partnerships) through which individual citizens, groups and organisations can express their interests, exercise their rights and responsibilities, and mediate their difference' (The Prince of Wales Business Leaders Forum, 1996).

3 'We need to understand that there is much more to democracy than simply which candidate or party has majority support. . . . Yes, democracy implies majority rule. But that does not mean that minorities should be excluded from any say in decisions. Minority views should never be silenced. The minority must always be free to state its case, so that people can hear both sides before deciding who is right' (Annan, 2000).

'In a democracy, all power flows from the people who are the sovereign. Democracy can therefore be truly defined as how the common people would like to be governed, not how some people, including elected representatives, think they should be governed' (People First, 'Earth Charter Initiative', 2001).

4 People First go on to say that multi-stakeholder councils should become part of the mainstream governance as the constitutional upper house at all

levels, local, state and national. They 'can play a major role in promoting sustainability' (People First, via www.devalt.org).

5   The authors then say that it 'is certainly true that people have some interests and values in common, thus they organise themselves into labour unions, interest groups, corporations, and communities. At the same time, there is a great deal of conflict among people as they compete for scarce resources and power. Both of these elements are present in society and public participation is one of the realms where they occur' (ibid, p7). For a comprehensive introduction on participation in theory and practice (on environmental matters), see Webler and Renn (1995). Also see the principles of good practice in participation as worked out by the NGOs in the Aarhus process (see Chapter 7).

6   In other words, aiming at multi-subjectivity rather than objectivity. Cognitive psychology firmly asserts that all absorbing, processing and memorizing of information of the human cognitive system is essentially subjective. The physicist Heinz von Foerster has expressed this beautifully: 'Objectivity is a subject's delusion that observing can be done without him.' Subjectivity is due to perception being influenced by a multitude of factors which are specific to individuals and social groups, such as: memory (previous perception and learning), motivation (objectives, interests), attitudes, values and emotions.

7   'In its governmental relations, justice is the giving to every person exactly what he deserves, not necessarily involving any consideration of what any other may deserve; equity (the quality of being equal) is giving every one as much advantage, privilege, or consideration as is given to any other; it is that which is equally right or just to all concerned; equity is a close synonym for fairness and impartiality, but it has a legal precision that those words have not. In legal proceedings, the system of equity, devised to supply the insufficiencies of law, deals with cases to which the law by reason of its universality cannot apply. Integrity, rectitude, right, righteousness, and virtue denote conformity of personal conduct to the moral law, and thus necessarily include justice, which is giving others that which is their due. Lawfulness is an ambiguous word, meaning in its narrower sense mere legality, which may be far from justice, but in its higher sense signifying accordance with the supreme law or right, and thus including perfect justice. Justness refers rather to logical relations than to practical matters; as, we speak of the justness of a statement or of a criticism' (*Webster's Dictionary*, 1992, p532).

8   The preparedness of people to develop such a new aspect of their identity (eg as a 'member of a certain MSP') will vary depending on the strength of their previous set of social identities – the stronger the commitments to the groups they represent, the less likely they will develop an additional common identity with the new group. The strength of previous social identities largely depends on the degree by which the respective groups differs from the majority and on its size. Members of relatively small social groups which are very different from the majority tend to have a stronger social identity as a member of that group, meaning they will not be as prepared as majority members to develop a new identity. This is one reason why minority members are sometimes seen as 'keeping apart from the group'.

9   See, for example: Environics International, 1997, 1998, 1999; Environics International and The Prince of Wales Business Leaders Forum, 1999; Edelman News, 2000.

10 We are arguing within the present economic framework; discussions about alternatives to the currently dominant liberal market system are certainly necessary but not part of our considerations here. Rather, more spaces should be created for deliberations of such fundamental questions as the ways in which we want our societies and the global society to develop, including their economic systems – preferably in a participatory, multi-stakeholder fashion. In view of the extreme controversies that abound around this question, carefully starting to build such spaces and the necessary basis for dialogue seems a very timely task.

11 See also McGee and Norton, 2000; and Eden and Ackermann, 1998.

12 Learning also includes overcoming stereotypes and prejudice; this is helped by contact and collaboration – a desirable effect of MSPs.

13 See Neuberger (1996) for a (very entertaining!) – account of Human Resource Management consultants as jesters and comedians at the 'court' of corporate executive boards.

14 These are among the conditions of promoting trust listed by Renn et al, 1996, pp360–361.

15 Allowing for participation in individual capacities can be appropriate in online discussions with large numbers of participants, for example for the purpose of scoping those aspects which people feel are relevant to a particular issue (eg World Bank Development Report Online Discussion; Beijing+5 Global Forum). It can also be appropriate where issues are extremely contentious and the objective is not to reach an agreement between stakeholder groups but, for example, an independent report (eg The World Commission on Dams).

16 'Ethnic minorities: Social groups with a social and cultural identity distinct from dominant society. They have been historically disadvantaged; come from non-dominant sectors of society; have low social, economic and political status; and are determined to preserve, develop and transmit to future generations their ethnic identity as the basis of their continued existence as people' (WCD, 2000, p345; Glossary).

17 We use the term 'minorities' to refer to minorities in power and/or number. A single person can represent the most powerful stakeholder or be the best prepared participant and thus dominate a group; and a large number of representatives of a powerless stakeholder group can have no influence on a process.

18 For example: The WCD chose the format of a small and exclusive Commission, accompanied by a large and inclusive Forum which served as a 'sounding board'. At the Bergen Ministerial Dialogues, women contributed to the preparatory papers of the NGO group as the number of groups allowed to prepare papers was limited.

19 Edwards goes on to say: 'but there are different ways to validate these things: through representation (which usually confers to the right to participate in decision-making), and through effectiveness (which only confers to the right to be heard). Legitimacy in membership bodies is claimed through the normal democratic processes of elections and formal

sanctions that ensure that an agency is representative of, and accountable to, its constituents . . . By contrast, non-membership NGOs define their legitimacy according to legal compliance, effective oversight by their trustees, and recognition by other legitimate bodies that they have valuable knowledge and skills to bring to the table' (Edwards, 2000, p20).

20   This would include the group answering satisfactorily such questions as: Who controls the resources? Who determines the criteria? Whose institutional capacities are developed? Who will own the history of the experience? (Patel, 2000)

21   Important psychological aspects have been brought into the discussion, for example, by Watzlawick et al (1967) who put forward a number of 'axioms of communication' (excerpt):

- You cannot not communicate: meaning that even when we do not want to communicate, the mere fact that we are not communicating does transmit a message.
- Every communication has a content and a relationship aspect – ie one referring to the content of the message and one referring to the relationship between the persons communicating. In a way, the latter determines the former and thus constitutes some kind of meta-communication. More importantly, the two are not always in accordance – for example, people can convey an unfriendly message in a friendly tone. To clarify these levels and establish accordance, explicit meta-communication – communication about communication – is an important tool.

22   For example, the CSD in 1999 brought together stakeholders from a wide range of backgrounds to discuss sustainable tourism for the first time at a global level. This posed a challenge to all involved and was successful at least in the sense that it created a dialogue where people started to listen to each other's viewpoints.

23   The term 'minorities' can refer to smaller groups ('minority in numbers') or groups of less status and power ('power minorities').

24   This has been pointed out in many publications and by many interviewees whom we consulted. For example, the UK Coalition Against Poverty (UKCAP) talks about 'how genuine participation demands a huge change in attitudes and behaviour by policy makers and professionals'.

25   Renn et al (1995) have based their evaluation of models of environmental discourse on Habermas' work. They provide one of the very few practical approaches to analysing public participation mechanisms firmly rooted in state-of-the-art theory of communication and dialogue. The book is an excellent source for the purposes of developing design concepts for MSPs. Other authors have also employed the Habermas approach of the ideal speech situation to develop criteria that measure the performance of public participation discourse (see Renn et al, 1995). Note, however, that the approach has also been analysed as culturally specific.

26   Habermas refers to communicating as 'communicative action' to stress that he is concerned with what people *do* in discourse.

27   Habermas asserts that every speech act makes a 'validity claim', saying that as part of the underlying normative agreement that makes speech possible, a speaker who makes an assertion implicitly presupposes that

the validity claim can be verified to the satisfaction of all participants (see Webler, 1995, pp43–44).

28 Dietz adds a fifth criterion: making 'the most efficient possible use of resources', a 'standard criteria of welfare economics and utilitarian ethics' .

29 We have chosen to use the term 'consensus-building' instead of 'consultation'.

30 Note that this deals with 'investigating the truth', not finding it, holding it or naming it. The Bahá'í concept recognizes the subjectivity of interpretation (eg of holy texts) and hence no one is permitted to claim having found the 'true' interpretation of a holy text. Only the text itself has 'truth' (to the believer); upon reading it, all people necessarily develop a subjective reflection of the text.

31 Bahá'ís also strongly support consultative mechanisms of participation around governments and intergovernmental bodies: 'Institutions and those in positions of authority would do well to create conditions amenable to the meaningful investigation of truth, while fostering the understanding that human happiness and the establishment of peace, justice and unity are the ultimate goals of this investigation' (Bahá'í International Community: Consultation).

CHAPTER 5

1 Thanks and acknowledgments go to Dr Dieter Beck, Forschungsinstitut fuer oeffentliche Verwaltung, Speyer, Germany; Prof Dr Klaus Jonas, Technical University Chemnitz, Germany; Prof Dr Oswald Neuberger, University of Augsburg, Germany; Dr. Kai Sassenberg, Friedrich Schiller University Jena, Germany; Prof Dr Erich Witte, University of Hamburg, Germany. I also thank Minu Hemmati, Chris Church and Nader Farahwaschy for their critical comments on a draft version of this chapter.

2 'Social psychology: The scientific study of the effects of social and cognitive processes on the way individuals perceive, influence, and relate to others' (Smith and Mackie, 2000, Glossary). Organizational psychology can be defined as a specialized and applied field of social psychology, focusing on the specific social context of organizations such as private sector companies, public administration bodies and voluntary sector organizations.

3 Based on the review of research undertaken since Sherif and Sherif's (1953) summer camp experiments, Smith and Mackie (2000) summarize the conditions for successful cooperation between groups:

- a valued common goal, which eliminates competition for material and social resources;
- repeated opportunities to expose and disconfirm out-group stereotypes;
- successful results;
- equal partners, at least for the task at hand; and
- shared social norms.

4 Social Identity Theory (Turner et al, 1987; Tajfel and Turner 1979): Social Identity Theory (SIT) is one of the few social psychological theories dealing

with individual (psychological) reactions to social/societal realities. SIT describes society as composed of social groups or social categories rather than as individuals. SIT asserts that individuals partly perceive themselves as members of social groups or categories and are perceived as members of social groups by others. Different social groups differ with regard to their resources or status. Individuals are aware of their group membership and its social consequences. Low social status can lead to a threat of a positive social identity which individuals desire. Therefore, low status groups (minorities in power or number) strive for increased social identity. SIT describes various ways for individuals and for groups to achieve positive social identity – for example, through discriminating against groups of higher status. In other words, group membership will dominate the individual perception of oneself and others and be the main source of identity. Attention will be focused on the conditions that sustain or modify the boundaries between groups (the status and power of different groups, the legitimacy of these variables, the boundaries between groups). Social context is of the utmost importance (groups are in dynamic states of alliance or conflict). The context determines whether, at a given moment, people consider themselves as members of a specific group. For example, a certain social categorization such as ethnicity can be more or less salient (ie obvious) and therefore more or less important for perception and behaviour in different social situations (Hemmati et al, 1999).

5   A bias can be defined as a predisposition, an inclination or prepossession towards an object or view.

6   This recommendation is rooted in symbolic interactionism (Blumer, 1969; Charon, 1998) and social constructionist approaches (Gergen and Gergen, 1988) which assume that perspectives on reality are being negotiated, thus representing a result of social interaction.

7   Group dynamics as an area of research was born in the late 1930s – it endorsed beliefs in the collective strength of people and the value of cooperative interaction (Phillips and Wood, 1984).

Chapter 6

1   All the people who have contributed to obtaining that information are listed in Appendix VII, along with other people who commented on drafts, gave guidance on various chapters, etc.

Chapter 7

1   Also see Reinicke, 2000, who identifies four key challenges raised by non-state actor involvement in public policy networks: the 'selection challenge'; the 'inclusion challenge'; the 'asymmetric power challenge'; and the 'legitimacy challenge'.

2   Also see the AA1000 Standard developed by the Institute of Social and Ethical Accountability which requires that a management system documents the ways in which stakeholders were identified (see Bendell, 2000b, p2).

3   Such political decisions also relate to institutional changes for participation, on which there is yet little research. Some is under way, eg at the Institute for Development Studies in Sussex, UK (The Participation Group, eg Estrella, 2000), and should be considered. It will be important to know more about what has the institutionalization of participatory practice. There is also a need for open spaces for reflection and analysis within organizations seeking to set up participatory mechanisms (such as the United Nations and its agencies, government departments, etc).

4   This is, in fact, very much in tune with the recommendations coming out of family and marriage therapy – the most important phase is the first one, when people are asked to develop their definition(s) of a problem. It forces people to listen carefully and to role-take. Experiences have shown that investing time and effort in this phase is a crucial success factor.

5   Standard social 'high impact categories' are gender, ethnic group membership, age. For MSPs in the area of sustainable development, high impact categories are all Major Groups as of Agenda 21. However, depending on the issue, some Major Groups need to be differentiated into several high impact categories such as development and environment NGOs, or developing versus developed country NGOs, and others.

6   Reinicke et al (2000) discuss the 'operational and participatory gaps in governance' that Global Public Policy Networks (in many ways similar to MSPs) can fill.

7   UNED Forum is an example, operating domestically within the UK (as the UNED-UK Committee) and internationally. It has a UK-based multi-stakeholder Executive Committee, with members being elected or appointed within their sector and term limits, and an International Advisory Board with representatives of the key organizations from all sectors, aiming at regional and sectoral balance, and with newly introduced gender balance requirements.

8   Eden and Ackermann (1998), for example, have been developing the technique and suitable software for mapping procedures and work on the basis of 20 years of research and practical experiences. The authors use mapping procedures for organizational strategy development. For example, they conduct interviews with all executive members before a strategic board meeting. These are then translated into individual maps (and checked back) and meta-maps. Both become the basis of the strategy discussions among the board. It is interesting to see how many differences in board members' views of the overall purpose of a company and suitable strategies to pursue them can be uncovered through this technique for the benefit of well-informed discussions in the group.

9   See Markowitz (2000) for a detailed description and examples of creating community visions in Local Environmental Action Programmes in Central and Eastern Europe; see Reinicke et al (2000, pp65) for examples at the global level (WCD; Global Water Partnership).

10 See, for example, Knowledge Transform (2001), Whiffen (2000).

11 Powerful people tend to speak more and more assertively, criticize more, interrupt others more often and generally exert more influence (see Chapter 6). Often, powerful participants will also seek to marginalize the message of the minority if it threatens their self-interest. They may also

attempt to marginalize the messenger and undermine the status and credibility of minority representatives. In such cases, 'dialogue' is not what it should be but 'becomes a temporary anti-depressant or sedative, buying time for the powerful to act with impunity' (Franklin, 1999).

12   See Markowitz (2000, p155) for a brief and practical analysis of various decision-making rules and their implications for high- and low-stake decisions.

13   If marketing and PR specialists are able to 'sell' consumers (us!) the second car or refrigerator and many other items we don't actually need, they should also be able to 'sell' issues of sustainability and governance.

14   See Markowitz' (2000) guide to public outreach campaigns as part of his 'Guide to Implementing Local Environmental Action Programs in Central and Eastern Europe', a detailed and practical resource for stakeholder participation processes at the local level. A training manual for facilitators will be available in late 2001.

Index